Solr Cookbook
Third Edition

Solve real-time problems related to Apache Solr 4.x and 5.0 effectively with the help of over 100 easy-to-follow recipes

Rafał Kuć

BIRMINGHAM - MUMBAI

Solr Cookbook
Third Edition

First published: July 2011

Second edition: January 2013

Third edition: January 2015

Production reference: 1200115

Published by Packt Publishing Ltd.
Livery Place
35 Livery Street
Birmingham B3 2PB, UK.

ISBN 978-1-78355-315-0

www.packtpub.com

Credits

Author
Rafał Kuć

Reviewers
Sunil Gulabani
Charles Lee
Stefan Matheis
Marcelo Ochoa
Walt Stoneburner
Ning Sun

Commissioning Editor
Ashwin Nair

Acquisition Editor
Richard Brookes-Bland

Content Development Editor
Prachi Bisht

Technical Editors
Mrunal M. Chavan
Dennis John

Copy Editors
Sayanee Mukherjee
Rashmi Sawant

Project Coordinator
Sageer Parkar

Proofreaders
Simran Bhogal
Samuel Redman Birch
Maria Gould
Ameesha Green
Paul Hindle

Indexer
Tejal Soni

Graphics
Sheetal Aute

Production Coordinator
Nitesh Thakur

Cover Work
Nitesh Thakur

About the Author

Rafał Kuć is a born team leader and software developer. He currently works as a consultant and software engineer at Sematext Group, Inc., where he concentrates on open source technologies such as Apache Lucene and Solr, Elasticsearch, and Hadoop stack. He has more than 14 years of experience in various software branches—from banking software to e-commerce products. He focuses mainly on Java but is open to every tool and programming language that will make the achievement of his goal easier and faster. Rafał is also one of the founders of the `solr.pl` site, where he tries to share his knowledge and help people with the problems they face with Solr and Lucene. He is also a speaker at various conferences around the world, such as Lucene Eurocon, Berlin Buzzwords, ApacheCon, Lucene Revolution, and DevOps Days.

Rafał began his journey with Lucene in 2002, and it wasn't love at first sight. When he came back to Lucene in late 2003, he revised his thoughts about the framework and saw the potential in search technologies. Then, Solr came along and that was it. He started working with Elasticsearch in the middle of 2010. Currently, Lucene, Solr, Elasticsearch, and information retrieval are his main points of interest.

Rafał is also the author of *Apache Solr 3.1 Cookbook*, and the update to it, *Apache Solr 4.0 Cookbook*, both published by Packt Publishing. He also authored Elasticsearch-related books, *ElasticSearch Server* and its second edition, and the first and second editions of *Mastering ElasticSearch*, all published by Packt Publishing.

This book is a second update to the first book I ever wrote— *Apache Solr 3.1 Cookbook, Packt Publishing*. Again, similar to *Apache Solr Cookbook 4.0, Packt Publishing*, what meant to be an update turned out to be almost a complete rewrite because of the pending release of Solr 5.0 and the changes to Solr itself. Between Solr 4.0 and 5.0, there were a lot of changes and additions to Solr, and I know I didn't manage to gather them all in the recipes that are present in the book you are holding. However, I hope that if you are either using Solr 4.x or Solr 5.0, this book will help you overcome some common problems and will push your knowledge about Solr a bit further.

Acknowledgments

Although I would go the same way if I could go back in time, the time during the writing of this book was not easy for my family. The ones that suffered from this the most were my wife, Agnes, and my two great kids—son Philip and daughter Susanna. Without their patience and understanding, writing this book wouldn't have been possible. I would also like to thank my and Agnes' parents for their support and help.

I would like to thank all the people involved in creating, developing, and maintaining Lucene and Solr projects for their work and passion. Without them, this book wouldn't have been written.

Once again, thank you.

About the Reviewers

Sunil Gulabani is a technical geek in software development based in Ahmedabad, Gujarat, India. He graduated in commerce from S. M. Patel Institute of Commerce (SMPIC) and has a master's degree in computer applications from Ahmedabad Education Society Institute of Computer Studies (AESICS). He had been a top ranker while pursuing his master's degree.

He has also presented a paper *Effective Label Matching For Automated Evaluation of Use -- Case Diagrams* on Technology For Education (T4E)—IIIT Hyderabad, an IEEE conference, along with senior lecturers, Vinay Vachharajani and Dr. Jyoti Pareek.

Since 2011, he has been working as a software engineer and is cloud technology savvy. He has experience in developing enterprise solutions using Java (EE), Apache Solr, RESTful Web Services, GWT, Smart GWT, Amazon Web Services (AWS), Redis, Memcache, MongoDB, and others. He has a keen interest in system architecture and integration, data modeling, relational databases, and mapping with NoSQL for high throughput.

He is the author of *Developing RESTful Web Services with Jersey 2.0, Packt Publishing,* that looks at JAX-RS 2.0, which is an enhanced framework based on the RESTful architecture. He also reviewed the book *RESTful Web Services with Dropwizard, Packt Publishing*.

He also takes interest in writing tech blogs and is actively involved in knowledge-sharing communities such as JUG-Ahmedabad, GDG Ahmedabad, and Ahmedabad University.

You can visit him online at `http://www.sunilgulabani.com` and follow him on Twitter at `@sunil_gulabani`. He can be reached directly at `sunil_gulabani@yahoo.com`.

Stefan Matheis is a freelance backend engineer, currently living in Zurich, Switzerland. He likes to work on projects around API development, natural language processing, graph databases, and infrastructure management. Lately, he got involved in payment and logistics projects. Stefan is an Apache Lucene/Solr committer since 2012 as well as a member of the project management committee. His main contribution was the new Admin UI, which is shipped with all Solr releases since 4.0.

Marcelo Ochoa works at the System Laboratory of Facultad de Ciencias Exactas of the Universidad Nacional del Centro de la Provincia de Buenos Aires and is the CTO at `Scotas.com`, a company specialized in near real-time search solutions using Apache Solr and Oracle. He divides his time between university jobs and external projects related to Oracle and Big Data technologies. He has worked on several Oracle-related projects such as translation of Oracle manuals and multimedia CBTs. His background is in database, network, Web, and Java technologies. In the XML world, he is known as the developer of the DB Generator for the Apache Cocoon project, the open source projects DBPrism and DBPrism CMS, the Lucene-Oracle integration using Oracle JVM Directory implementation, and in the `Restlet.org` project, the Oracle XDB Restlet Adapter (an alternative to writing native REST web services inside the database-resident JVM).

Since 2006, he has been part of the Oracle ACE program; Oracle ACEs are known for their strong credentials as Oracle community enthusiasts and advocates, with candidates nominated by ACEs in the Oracle Technology and Applications communities.

He is the author of *Chapter 17, 360-Degree Programming the Oracle Database*, of the book, *Oracle Database Programming using Java and Web Services, Kuassi Mensah, Elsevier Digital Press*, and *Chapter 21, DB Prism: A Framework to Generate Dynamic XML from a Database*, of the book, *Professional XML Databases, Kevin Williams, Wrox Press*.

Walt Stoneburner is a software architect with over 25 years of commercial application development and consulting experience. Fringe passions involve quality assurance, configuration management, and security. If cornered, he might actually admit to liking statistics and authoring documentation as well.

He is easily amused by programming language design, collaborative applications, Big Data, knowledge management, data visualization, and ASCII art. Self-described as a closet geek, Walt also evaluates software products and consumer electronics, draws comics, runs a freelance photography studio specializing in portraits and art (`CharismaticMoments.com`), writes humor pieces, performs sleights of hand, enjoys game design, and can occasionally be found on ham radio.

Walt can be reached directly via email at `wls@wwco.com` or `Walt.Stoneburner@gmail.com`. He publishes a tech and humor blog called the Walt-O-Matic at `http://www.wwco.com/~wls/blog/`.

His other book reviews and contributions include:

- *AntiPatterns and Patterns in Software Configuration Management, John Wiley & Sons* (ISBN 978-0-471-32929-9, p. xi)
- *Exploiting Software: How to Break Code, Addison-Wesley Professional* (ISBN 978-0-201-78695-8, p. xxxiii)
- *Ruby on Rails Web Mashup Projects, Packt Publishing* (ISBN 978-1-847193-93-3)
- *Building Dynamic Web 2.0 Websites with Ruby on Rails, Packt Publishing* (ISBN 978-1-847193-41-4)
- *Instant Sinatra Starter, Packt Publishing* (ISBN 978-1782168218)
- *C++ Multithreading Cookbook, Packt Publishing* (978-1-78328-979-0)
- *Learning Selenium Testing Tools with Python, Packt Publishing* (978-1-78398-350-6)
- *Whittier* (ASIN B00GTD1RBS)
- Cooter Brown's *South Mouth Book of Hillbilly Wisdom, CreateSpace Independent Publishing Platform* (ISBN 978-1-482340-99-0)

Ning Sun is a software engineer currently working for a China-based start-up, LeanCloud, providing one-stop Backend as a Service (BaaS) for mobile apps. Being a startup engineer, he solves various kinds of problems and plays different kinds of roles. However, he has always been an enthusiast for open source technology. He contributes to several open source projects and has also learned a lot from them.

Ning worked on `Delicious.com` in 2013, which is known as one of the most important websites in early Web 2.0 EAR. The search for Delicious is fully powered by a Solr cluster, and it might be one of the largest deployments for Solr.

You can always find Ning on `Github.com/sunng87` and `Twitter.com/Sunng`.

www.PacktPub.com

Support files, eBooks, discount offers, and more

For support files and downloads related to your book, please visit `www.PacktPub.com`.

Did you know that Packt offers eBook versions of every book published, with PDF and ePub files available? You can upgrade to the eBook version at `www.PacktPub.com` and as a print book customer, you are entitled to a discount on the eBook copy. Get in touch with us at `service@packtpub.com` for more details.

At `www.PacktPub.com`, you can also read a collection of free technical articles, sign up for a range of free newsletters and receive exclusive discounts and offers on Packt books and eBooks.

`https://www2.packtpub.com/books/subscription/packtlib`

Do you need instant solutions to your IT questions? PacktLib is Packt's online digital book library. Here, you can search, access, and read Packt's entire library of books.

Why subscribe?

- Fully searchable across every book published by Packt
- Copy and paste, print, and bookmark content
- On demand and accessible via a web browser

Free access for Packt account holders

If you have an account with Packt at `www.PacktPub.com`, you can use this to access PacktLib today and view 9 entirely free books. Simply use your login credentials for immediate access.

Table of Contents

Preface

Welcome to *Solr Cookbook, Third Edition*. You will be taken on a tour of the most common problems that a user might face while dealing with Apache Solr. You will also explore some of the features that were recently introduced in Solr. You will learn how to deal with the problems when configuring and setting up Solr, handle common queries, fine-tune Solr instances, set up and use SolrCloud, use faceting and grouping, fighting common problems, and many more things. Each and every recipe is based on real-life problems and provides solutions along with detailed descriptions of the configuration and code that was used.

What this book covers

Chapter 1, Apache Solr Configuration, covers Solr configuration recipes, along with setting up ZooKeeper, migrating from master to slave, and configuring Solr for different use cases.

Chapter 2, Indexing Your Data, as the name suggests, explains data indexing, such as binary files indexing, using Data Import Handler, language detection, updating a single field of document, and much more.

Chapter 3, Analyzing Your Text Data, concentrates on common problems when analyzing your data, such as stemming, geographical location indexing, or using synonyms.

Chapter 4, Querying Solr, describes querying Apache Solr, such as nesting queries, affecting the scoring of documents, phrase searching, or using the parent-child relationship.

Chapter 5, Faceting, is dedicated to the faceting mechanism in which you can find the information needed to overcome some problems that you might encounter while working with Solr and faceting.

Chapter 6, Improving Solr Performance, focuses on improving your Apache Solr cluster performance with information such as cache configuration, indexing speed up, and much more.

Chapter 7, In the Cloud, covers the cloud side of Solr—SolrCloud, setting up collections, replicas configuration, distributed indexing and searching, as well as aliasing and shard manipulation.

Chapter 8, Using Additional Functionalities, explains how we can highlight long text fields, sort results on the basis of function value, check user spelling mistakes, and use the grouping functionality.

Chapter 9, Dealing with Problems, is a small chapter dedicated to the most common situations such as memory problems, tuning segment merges, and others.

Chapter 10, Real-life Situations, describes how to handle real-life situations such as implementing different autocomplete functionalities, using near real-time search, or improving query relevance.

What you need for this book

In order to run most of the examples in this book, you will need Java Runtime Environment 1.7 or the newer version and of course, the 4.10 or the newer version of Apache Solr search server. To run examples found in this book, you might need a web browser or a command-line tool that is able to run HTTP requests such as curl.

The recipes in this book (unless stated otherwise) are tested in a Linux environment with the latest available Version of Solr 5.0. For Windows-based hosts, the single quotes should be replaced with double quotes in the commands. Remember that during the writing of this book, the final Version of Solr 5.0 was not released and there might have been changes between the version used during testing and the released Version of Solr 5.0.

A few chapters in this book require additional software such as Apache ZooKeeper 3.4.3 or Jetty.

Who this book is for

This book is for intermediate Solr Developers who are willing to learn and implement pro-level practices, techniques, and solutions. This edition will specifically appeal to developers who wish to quickly get to grips with the changes and new features of Apache Solr 5.

Sections

In this book, you will find several headings that appear frequently (Getting ready, How to do it, How it works, There's more, and See also).

To give clear instructions on how to complete a recipe, we use these sections as follows:

Getting ready

This section tells you what to expect in the recipe, and describes how to set up any software or any preliminary settings required for the recipe.

How to do it...

This section contains the steps required to follow the recipe.

How it works...

This section usually consists of a detailed explanation of what happened in the previous section.

There's more...

This section consists of additional information about the recipe in order to make the reader more knowledgeable about the recipe.

See also

This section provides helpful links to other useful information for the recipe.

Conventions

In this book, you will find a number of text styles that distinguishes between different kinds of information. Here are some examples of these styles, and an explanation of their meaning.

Code words in text, database table names, folder names, filenames, file extensions, pathnames, dummy URLs, user input, and Twitter handles are shown as follows: "The `lib` entry in the `solrconfig.xml` file tells Solr to look for all the JAR files from the `../../langid` directory."

A block of code is set as follows:

```
<field name="id" type="string" indexed="true" stored="true"
required="true" multiValued="false" />
<field name="name" type="text_general" indexed="true" stored="true"/>
<field name="description" type="text_general" indexed="true"
stored="true" />
<field name="langId" type="string" indexed="true" stored="true" />
```

When we wish to draw your attention to a particular part of a code block, the relevant lines or items are set in bold:

```
<field name="id" type="string" indexed="true" stored="true"
required="true" multiValued="false" />
<field name="name" type="text_general" indexed="true" stored="true"/>
<field name="description" type="text_general" indexed="true"
stored="true" />
<field name="langId" type="string" indexed="true" stored="true" />
```

Any command-line input or output is written as follows:

```
curl 'localhost:8983/solr/update?commit=true' -H 'Content-
type:application/json' -d '[{"id":"1","file":{"set":"New file name"}}]'
```

New terms and important words are shown in bold. Words that you see on the screen, for example, in menus or dialog boxes, appear in the text like this: "The **Overview** page for a collection gives you basic statistics about the core of the collection such as number of documents, heap memory usage, version of the index, number of segments, and so on."

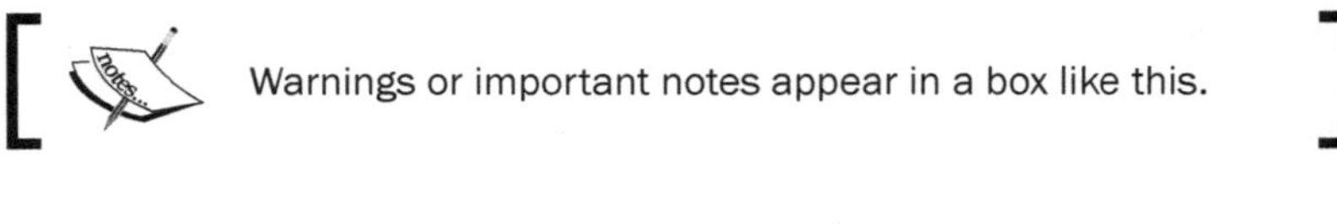

Warnings or important notes appear in a box like this.

Tips and tricks appear like this.

Reader feedback

Feedback from our readers is always welcome. Let us know what you think about this book—what you liked or may have disliked. Reader feedback is important for us to develop titles that you really get the most out of.

To send us general feedback, simply send an e-mail to `feedback@packtpub.com`, and mention the book title via the subject of your message.

If there is a topic that you have expertise in and you are interested in either writing or contributing to a book, see our author guide on `www.packtpub.com/authors`.

Customer support

Now that you are the proud owner of a Packt book, we have a number of things to help you to get the most from your purchase.

Downloading the example code

You can download the example code files for all Packt books you have purchased from your account at `http://www.packtpub.com`. If you purchased this book elsewhere, you can visit `http://www.packtpub.com/support` and register to have the files e-mailed directly to you.

Errata

Although we have taken every care to ensure the accuracy of our content, mistakes do happen. If you find a mistake in one of our books—maybe a mistake in the text or the code—we would be grateful if you would report this to us. By doing so, you can save other readers from frustration and help us improve subsequent versions of this book. If you find any errata, please report them by visiting `http://www.packtpub.com/submit-errata`, selecting your book, clicking on the **errata submission form** link, and entering the details of your errata. Once your errata are verified, your submission will be accepted and the errata will be uploaded on our website, or added to any list of existing errata, under the Errata section of that title. Any existing errata can be viewed by selecting your title from `http://www.packtpub.com/support`.

Piracy

Piracy of copyright material on the Internet is an ongoing problem across all media. At Packt, we take the protection of our copyright and licenses very seriously. If you come across any illegal copies of our works, in any form, on the Internet, please provide us with the location address or website name immediately so that we can pursue a remedy.

Please contact us at `copyright@packtpub.com` with a link to the suspected pirated material.

We appreciate your help in protecting our authors, and our ability to bring you valuable content.

Questions

You can contact us at `questions@packtpub.com` if you are having a problem with any aspect of the book, and we will do our best to address it.

1
Apache Solr Configuration

In this chapter, we will cover the following recipes:

- Running Solr on a standalone Jetty
- Installing ZooKeeper for SolrCloud
- Migrating configuration from master-slave to SolrCloud
- Choosing the proper directory configuration
- Configuring the Solr spellchecker
- Using Solr in a schemaless mode
- Limiting I/O usage
- Using core discovery
- Configuring SolrCloud for NRT use cases
- Configuring SolrCloud for high-indexing use cases
- Configuring SolrCloud for high-querying use cases
- Configuring the Solr heartbeat mechanism
- Changing similarity

Introduction

Setting up an example for a Solr instance is not a hard task. We have all that is provided with the Solr distribution package, which we need for the example deployment. In fact, this is the simplest way to run Solr. It is very convenient for local development because you don't need any additional software, apart from Java, which is already installed and you can control when to run Solr and easily change its configuration. However, the example instance of Solr will probably not be the optimized way in terms of your deployment. For example, the default cache configurations are most likely not good for your deployment; there are only sample warming queries that don't reflect your production queries, there are field types you don't need, and so on. This is why I will show a few configuration-related recipes in this chapter.

If you don't have any experience with Apache Solr, refer to the Apache Solr tutorial, which can be found at `http://lucene.apache.org/solr/tutorial.html`, before reading this book. You can also check articles regarding Solr on `http://solr.pl` and `http://blog.sematext.com`.

This chapter focuses on Solr configuration. It starts with showing you how to set up Solr, install ZooKeeper for SolrCloud, migrate your old master-slave configuration to a SolrCloud deployment, and also covers some more advanced topics such as near real-time indexing and searching. We will also go through tuning Solr for specific use cases and the configurations of some more advanced functionality, such as the scoring algorithm.

One more thing before we go on—remember that while writing the book, the main version of Solr used was 4.10. All the recipes were also tested on Solr 5.0 in the newest version available, but the Solr 5.0 itself has not been released.

Running Solr on a standalone Jetty

The simplest way to run Apache Solr on the Jetty servlet container is to run the provided example configuration based on an embedded Jetty. This is very simple if you use the provided example deployment. However, it is not suited for production deployment, where you will have the standalone Jetty installed. In this recipe, I will show you how to configure and run Solr on a standalone Jetty container.

Getting ready

First, you need to download the Jetty servlet container for your platform. You can get your download package from an automatic installer, such as `apt-get`, or you can download it from `http://download.eclipse.org/jetty/`. In addition to this, read the *Using core discovery* recipe of this chapter for more information.

While writing this recipe, I used Solr Version 4.10 and Jetty Version 8.1.10. Solr 5.0 will stop providing the WAR file for deployment on the external web application container and will be ready for installation as it is.

How to do it...

The first step is to install the Jetty servlet container, which is beyond the scope of this book, so we will assume that you have Jetty installed in the `/usr/share/jetty` directory.

1. Let's start with copying the `solr.war` file to the `webapps` directory of the installed Jetty (so that the whole path is `/usr/share/jetty/webapps`). In addition to this, we need to create a temporary directory in the installed Jetty, so let's create the `tmp` directory in the Jetty installation directory.
2. Next, we need to copy and adjust the `solr-jetty-context.xml` file from the `contexts` directory of the Solr example distribution to the `contexts` directory of the installed Jetty. The final file contents should look like this:

```
<?xml version="1.0"?>
<!DOCTYPE Configure PUBLIC "-//Jetty//Configure//EN" "http://www.
eclipse.org/jetty/configure.dtd">
<Configure class="org.eclipse.jetty.webapp.WebAppContext">
 <Set name="contextPath"><SystemProperty name="hostContext"
default="/solr"/></Set>
 <Set name="war"><SystemProperty name="jetty.home"/>/webapps/solr.
war</Set>
 <Set name="defaultsDescriptor"><SystemProperty name="jetty.
home"/>/etc/webdefault.xml</Set>
 <Set name="tempDirectory"><Property name="jetty.home"
default="."/>/tmp</Set>
</Configure>
```

3. Now, we need to copy the `jetty.xml` and `webdefault.xml` files from the `etc` directory of the Solr distribution to the configuration directory of Jetty; in our case, to the `/usr/share/jetty/etc` directory.
4. The next step is to copy the Solr core (`https://wiki.apache.org/solr/SolrTerminology`) configuration files to the appropriate directory. I'm talking about files such as `schema.xml`, `solrconfig.xml`, and so forth—the files that can be found in the `solr/collection1/conf` directory of the example Solr distribution. These files should be put in the `core_name/conf` directory inside a folder specified by the `solr.solr.home` system variable (in my case, this is the `/usr/share/solr` directory). For example, if we want our core to be named `example_data`, we should put the mentioned configuration files in the `/usr/share/solr/example_data/conf` directory.

5. In addition to this, we need to put the `core.properties` file in the `/usr/share/solr/example_data` directory. The file should be very simple and contain the single property, `name`, with the value of the name of the core, which in our case should look like the following:

```
name=example_data
```

6. The next step is optional and is only needed for SolrCloud deployments. For such deployments, we need to create the `zoo.cfg` file in the `/usr/share/solr/` directory with the following contents:

```
tickTime=2000
initLimit=10
syncLimit=5
```

7. The final configuration file we need to create is the `solr.xml` file, which should be put in the `/usr/share/solr/` directory. The contents of the file should look like this:

```
<?xml version="1.0" encoding="UTF-8" ?>
<solr>
 <solrcloud>
  <str name="host">${host:}</str>
  <int name="hostPort">${jetty.port:8983}</int>
  <str name="hostContext">${hostContext:solr}</str>
  <int name="zkClientTimeout">${zkClientTimeout:30000}</int>
  <bool name="genericCoreNodeNames">
            ${genericCoreNodeNames:true}</bool>
 </solrcloud>
 <shardHandlerFactory name="shardHandlerFactory"
            class="HttpShardHandlerFactory">
  <int name="socketTimeout">${socketTimeout:0}</int>
  <int name="connTimeout">${connTimeout:0}</int>
 </shardHandlerFactory>
</solr>
```

8. The final step is to include the `solr.solr.home` property in the Jetty startup file. If you have installed Jetty using software such as `apt-get`, then you need to update the `/etc/default/jetty` file and add the `-Dsolr.solr.home=/usr/share/solr` parameter to the `JAVA_OPTIONS` variable of the file. The whole line with this variable will look like this:

```
JAVA_OPTIONS="-Xmx256m -Djava.awt.headless=true -Dsolr.solr.home=/
usr/share/solr/"
```

> If you didn't install Jetty with `apt-get` or a similar software, you might not have the `/etc/default/jetty` file. In this case, add the `-Dsolr.solr.home=/usr/share/solr` parameter to the Jetty startup file.

We can now run Jetty to see if everything is okay. To start Jetty, which was already installed, use the `apt-get` command, as shown:

```
/etc/init.d/jetty start
```

If there are no exceptions during startup, we have a running Jetty with Solr deployed and configured. To check whether Solr is running, visit `http://localhost:8983/solr/`.

Congratulations, you have just successfully installed, configured, and run the Jetty servlet container with Solr deployed.

How it works...

For the purpose of this recipe, I assumed that we needed a single core installation with only the `schema.xml` and `solrconfig.xml` configuration files. Multicore installation is very similar; it differs only in terms of the Solr configuration files—one needs more than a single core defined.

The first thing we did was copied the `solr.war` file and created the `tmp` directory. The WAR file is the actual Solr web application. The `tmp` directory will be used by Jetty to unpack the WAR file.

The `solr-jetty-context.xml` file that we place in the `context` directory allows Jetty to define the context for a Solr web application. As you can see in its contents, we have set the context to be `/solr`, so our Solr application will be available under `http://localhost:8983/solr/`. We also need to specify where Jetty should look for the WAR file (the `war` property), where the web application descriptor file (the `defaultsDescriptor` property) is, and finally, where the temporary directory will be located (the `tempDirectory` property).

Copying the `jetty.xml` and `webdefault.xml` files is important. The standard Solr distribution comes with Jetty configuration files prepared for high load; for example, we can avoid the distributed deadlock.

The next step is to provide configuration files for the Solr core. These files should be put in the `core_name/conf` directory, which is created in a folder specified by the system's `solr.solr.home` variable. Since our core is named `example_data`, and the `solr.solr.home` property points to `/usr/share/solr`, we place our configuration files in the `/usr/share/solr/example_data/conf` directory. Note that I decided to use the `/usr/share/solr` directory as the base directory for all Solr configuration files. This ensures the ability to update Jetty without the need to override or delete the Solr configuration files.

The `core.properties` file allows Solr to identify the core that it will try to load. By providing the `name` property, we tell Solr what name the core should have. In our case, its name will be `example_data`.

The `zoo.cfg` file is optional, is only needed when setting up SolrCloud, and is used by Solr to specify ZooKeeper client properties. The `tickTime` property specifies the number of milliseconds of each **tick**. The tick is the unit of time in ZooKeeper client connections. The `initLimit` property specifies the number of ticks the initial synchronization phase can take, and the `syncLimit` property specifies the number of ticks that can pass between sending a request and getting an acknowledgement. For example, because the `syncLimit` property is set to `5` and `tickTime` is `2000`, the maximum time between sending the request and getting the acknowledgement is 10,000 milliseconds (`syncLimit` multiplied by `tickTime`).

The `solr.xml` file is described in the *Using core discovery* recipe in this chapter.

If you installed Jetty with the `apt-get` command or a similar software, then you need to update the `/etc/default/jetty` file to include the `solr.solr.home` variable for Solr to be able to see its configuration directory.

After all these steps, we will be ready to launch Jetty. If you installed Jetty with `apt-get` or similar software, you can run Jetty with the first command shown in the example. Otherwise, you can run Jetty with the `java -jar start` command from the Jetty installation directory.

After running the example query in your web browser, you should see the Solr front page as a single core. Congratulations, you have successfully configured and run the Jetty servlet container with Solr deployed.

There's more...

There are a few more tasks that you can perform to counter some problems while running Solr within the Jetty servlet container. The most common tasks that I encountered during my work are described in the ensuing sections.

I want Jetty to run on a different port

Sometimes, it's necessary to run Jetty on a port other than the default one. We have two ways to achieve this:

- Add an additional start up parameter, `jetty.port`. The startup command looks like this:

  ```
  java -Djetty.port=9999 -jar start.jar
  ```

- Change the `jetty.xml` file to do what you need to change the following line:

```
<Set name="port"><SystemProperty name="jetty.port"
default="8983"/></Set>
```

  The line should be changed to a port that we want Jetty to listen to requests from:

```
<Set name="port"><SystemProperty name="jetty.port"
default="9999"/></Set>
```

Buffer size is too small

Buffer overflow is a common problem when our queries get too long and too complex, for example, when using many logical operators or long phrases. When the standard HEAD buffer is not enough, you can resize it to meet your needs. To do this, add the following line to the Jetty connector in the `jetty.xml` file, which will specify the size of the buffer in bytes. Of course, the value shown in the example can be changed to the one that you need:

```
<Set name="requestHeaderSize">32768</Set>
```

After adding the value, the connector definition should look more or less like this:

```
<Call name="addConnector">
 <Arg>
  <New class="org.mortbay.jetty.bio.SocketConnector">
   <Set name="port"><SystemProperty name="jetty.port"
      default="8080"/></Set>
   <Set name="maxIdleTime">50000</Set>
   <Set name="lowResourceMaxIdleTime">1500</Set>
   <Set name="requestHeaderSize">32768</Set>
  </New>
 </Arg>
</Call>
```

Installing ZooKeeper for SolrCloud

You might know that in order to run SolrCloud, the distributed Solr deployment, you need to have Apache ZooKeeper installed. Zookeeper is a centralized service for maintaining configurations, naming, and provisioning service synchronizations. SolrCloud uses ZooKeeper to synchronize configurations and cluster states to help with leader election and so on. This is why it is crucial to have a highly available and fault-tolerant ZooKeeper installation. If you have a single ZooKeeper instance, and it fails, then your SolrCloud cluster will crash too. So, this recipe will show you how to install ZooKeeper so that it's not a single point of failure in your cluster configuration.

Getting ready

The installation instructions in this recipe contain information about installing ZooKeeper Version 3.4.6, but it should be useable for any minor release changes of Apache ZooKeeper. To download ZooKeeper, visit `http://zookeeper.apache.org/releases.html`. This recipe will show you how to install ZooKeeper in a Linux-based environment. For ZooKeeper to work, Java needs to be installed.

How to do it...

Let's assume that we have decided to install ZooKeeper in the `/usr/share/zookeeper` directory of our server, and we want to have three servers (with IPs `192.168.1.1`, `192.168.1.2`, and `192.168.1.3`) hosting a distributed ZooKeeper installation. This can be done by performing the following steps:

1. After downloading the ZooKeeper installation, we create the necessary directory:

   ```
   sudo mkdir /usr/share/zookeeper
   ```

2. Then, we unpack the downloaded archive to the newly created directory. We do this on three servers.
3. Next, we need to change our ZooKeeper configuration file and specify the servers that will form a ZooKeeper quorum. So, we edit the `/usr/share/zookeeper/conf/zoo.cfg` file and add the following entries:

   ```
   clientPort=2181
   dataDir=/usr/share/zookeeper/data
   tickTime=2000
   initLimit=10
   syncLimit=5
   server.1=192.168.1.1:2888:3888
   server.2=192.168.1.2:2888:3888
   server.3=192.168.1.3:2888:3888
   ```

4. Now, the next thing we need to do is create a file called `myid` in the `/usr/share/zookeeper/data` directory. The file should contain a single number that corresponds to the server number. For example, if ZooKeeper is located on `192.168.1.1`, it will be `1`, and if ZooKeeper is located on `192.168.1.3`, it will be `3`, and so on.
5. Now, we can start the ZooKeeper servers with the following command:

   ```
   /usr/share/zookeeper/bin/zkServer.sh start
   ```

6. If everything goes well, you should see something like:

```
JMX enabled by default
Using config: /usr/share/zookeeper/bin/../conf/zoo.cfg
Starting zookeeper ... STARTED
```

That's all. Of course, you can also add the ZooKeeper service to start automatically as your operating system starts up, but this is beyond the scope of the recipe and book.

How it works...

I talked about the ZooKeeper quorum and started this using three ZooKeeper nodes. ZooKeeper operates in a quorum, which means that at least 50 percent plus one server needs to be available and connected. We can start with a single ZooKeeper server, but such deployment won't be highly available and resistant to failures. So, to be able to handle at least a single ZooKeeper node failure, we need at least three ZooKeeper nodes running.

Let's skip the first part because creating the directory and unpacking the ZooKeeper server is quite simple. What I would like to concentrate on are the configuration values of the ZooKeeper server. The `clientPort` property specifies the port on which our SolrCloud servers should connect to ZooKeeper. The `dataDir` property specifies the directory where ZooKeeper will hold its data. Note that ZooKeeper needs read and write permissions to the directory. So far so good, right? So, now, the more advanced properties, such as `tickTime`, specified in milliseconds is the basic time unit for ZooKeeper. The `initLimit` property specifies how many ticks the initial synchronization phase can take. Finally, `syncLimit` specifies how many ticks can pass between sending the request and receiving an acknowledgement.

There are also three additional properties present, `server.1`, `server.2`, and `server.3`. These three properties define the addresses of the ZooKeeper instances that will form the quorum. The values for each of these properties are separated by a colon character. The first part is the IP address of the ZooKeeper server, and the second and third parts are the ports used by ZooKeeper instances to communicate with each other.

The last thing is the `myid` file located in the `/usr/share/zookeeper/data` directory. The contents of the file is used by ZooKeeper to identify itself. This is why we need to properly configure it so that ZooKeeper is not confused. So, for the ZooKeeper server specified as `server.1`, we need to write `1` to the `myid` file.

Downloading the example code

You can download the example code files for all Packt books you have purchased from your account at `http://www.packtpub.com`. If you purchased this book elsewhere, you can visit `http://www.packtpub.com/support` and register to have the files e-mailed directly to you.

Migrating configuration from master-slave to SolrCloud

After the release of Apache Solr 4.0, many users wanted to leverage SolrCloud-distributed indexing and querying capabilities. SolrCloud is also very useful when it comes to handling collections as you can create them on-the-fly, add replicas, and split already created shards, and this is only an example of the possibilities given by SolrCloud. Now, for releases after Solr 4.0, people are going for SolrCloud even more frequently. It's not hard to upgrade your current master-slave configuration to work on SolrCloud, but there are some things you need to take care of. With the help of the following recipe, you will be able to easily upgrade your cluster.

Getting ready

Before continuing further, it is advised to read the *Installing Zookeeper for SolrCloud* and *Running Solr on a standalone Jetty* recipes of this chapter. They will show you how to set up a Zookeeper cluster to be ready for production use and how to configure Jetty and Solr to work with each other.

How to do it...

1. We will start with altering the `schema.xml` file. In order to use your old index structure with SolrCloud, you need to add the following fields to the already defined index structure (add the following fragment to the `schema.xml` file in its `fields` section):

   ```
   <field name="_version_" type="long" indexed="true"
     stored="true" multiValued="false"/>
   ```

2. Now, let's switch to the `solrconfig.xml` file, starting with the replication handlers. First, you need to ensure that you have a replication handler set up. Remember that you shouldn't add master- or slave-specific configurations to it. So, the replication handler configuration should look like this:

   ```
   <requestHandler name="/replication" class="solr.
   ReplicationHandler" />
   ```

3. In addition to this, you need to have the administration panel handlers present, so the following configuration entry should be present in your `solrconfig.xml` file:

   ```
   <requestHandler name="/admin/" class="solr.admin.AdminHandlers" />
   ```

4. The last request handler that should be present is the real-time `get` handler, which should be defined as follows (the following should also be added to the `solrconfig.xml` file):

```
<requestHandler name="/get" class="solr.RealTimeGetHandler">
 <lst name="defaults">
  <str name="omitHeader">true</str>
  <str name="wt">json</str>
 </lst>
</requestHandler>
```

5. The next thing SolrCloud needs in order to properly operate is the transaction log configuration. The following fragment should be added to the `solrconfig.xml` file:

```
<updateLog>
 <str name="dir">${solr.data.dir:}</str>
</updateLog>
```

6. The last thing is the `solr.xml` file. The example `solr.xml` file should look like this:

```
<solr>
 <solrcloud>
  <str name="host">${host:}</str>
  <int name="hostPort">${jetty.port:8983}</int>
  <str name="hostContext">${hostContext:solr}</str>
  <int name="zkClientTimeout">${zkClientTimeout:30000}</int>
  <bool   name="genericCoreNodeNames">${genericCoreNodeNames:tr
ue}</bool>
 </solrcloud>
 <shardHandlerFactory name="shardHandlerFactory"   class="HttpShar
dHandlerFactory">
  <int name="socketTimeout">${socketTimeout:0}</int>
  <int name="connTimeout">${connTimeout:0}</int>
 </shardHandlerFactory>
</solr>
```

That's all. Your Solr instance configuration files are now ready to be used with SolrCloud.

How it works...

Now, let's see why all these changes are needed in order to use our old configuration files with SolrCloud.

The `_version_` field is used by Solr to enable document versioning and optimistic locking, which ensures that you won't have the newest version of your document overwritten by mistake. As a result of this, SolrCloud requires the `_version_` field to be present in the index structure. Adding this field is simple—you just need to place another field definition that is stored, indexed, and based on a long type, that's all.

As for the replication handler, you should remember not to add slave- or master-specific configurations, but only a simple request handler definition, as shown in the previous example. The same applies to the administration panel handlers; they need to be available under the default URL address.

The real-time `get` handler is responsible for getting the updated documents right away. In general, the documents are not available to search if the Lucene index searcher is not open, which happens after a hard or soft commit command (we will talk more about commit and soft commit in the *Configuring SolrCloud for NRT use cases* recipe of this chapter). This handler allows Solr (and also you) to retrieve the latest version of the document without the need to reopen the searcher, and thus, even if the document is not yet visible during a usual search operation. This is done by using the transaction log if the document is not yet indexed. The configuration is very similar to usual request handler configurations; you need to add a new handler with the `name` property set to `/get` and the `class` property set to `solr.RealTimeGetHandler`. In addition to this, we want the handler to omit response headers (the `omitHeader` property set to `true`) and return a response in JSON (with the `wt` property set to `json`). We omit the headers so that we have responses that are easier to parse.

One of the last things that is needed by SolrCloud is the transaction log, which enables real-time get operations to be functional. The transaction log keeps track of all the uncommitted changes and enables real-time `get` handlers to retrieve them. In order to turn on transaction log usage, one should add the `updateLog` tag to the `solrconfig.xml` file and specify the directory where the transaction log directory should be created (by adding the `dir` property, as shown in the example). In the previous configuration, we tell Solr that we want to use the Solr data directory as the place to store transaction log directories.

Finally, Solr needs you to keep the default address for the core administrative interface, so you should remember to have the `adminPath` property set to the value shown in the example (in the `solr.xml` file). This is needed in order for Solr to be able to manipulate cores.

We already talked about the `solr.xml` file contents in the *Running Solr on a standalone Jetty* recipe in this chapter, so refer to that recipe if you are not familiar with the contents.

Choosing the proper directory configuration

One of the most crucial properties of Apache Lucene and Solr is the Lucene Directory implementation. The directory interface provides an abstraction layer for all I/O operations for the Lucene library. Although it seems simple, choosing the right directory implementation can affect the performance of your Solr setup in a drastic way. This recipe will show you how to choose the right directory implementation.

How to do it...

In order to use the desired directory, all you need to do is choose the right directory factory implementation and inform Solr about it. Let's assume that you want to use `NRTCachingDirectory` as your directory implementation. In order to do this, you need to place (or replace if it is already present) the following fragment in your `solrconfig.xml` file:

```
<directoryFactory name="DirectoryFactory" class="solr.
NRTCachingDirectoryFactory" />
```

That's all. The setup is quite simple, but I think that the question that will arise is what directory factories are available to use. When this book was written, the following directory factories were available:

- `solr.StandardDirectoryFactory`
- `solr.SimpleFSDirectoryFactory`
- `solr.NIOFSDirectoryFactory`
- `solr.MMapDirectoryFactory`
- `solr.NRTCachingDirectoryFactory`
- `solr.HdfsDirectoryFactory`
- `solr.RAMDirectoryFactory`

Now, let's see what each of these factories provides.

How it works...

Before we get into the details of each of the presented directory factories, I would like to comment on the directory factory configuration parameter. All you need to remember is that the `name` attribute of the `directoryFactory` tag should be set to `DirectoryFactory`, and the `class` attribute should be set to the directory factory implementation of your choice. Also, some of the directory implementations can take additional parameters that define their behavior. We will talk about some of them in other recipes in the book (for example, in the *Limiting I/O usage* recipe in this chapter).

If you want Solr to make decisions for you, you should use the `solr.StandardDirectoryFactory` directory factory. It is filesystem-based and tries to choose the best implementation based on your current operating system and Java virtual machine used. If you implement a small application that won't use many threads, you can use the `solr.SimpleFSDirectoryFactory` directory factory that stores the index file on your local filesystem, but it doesn't scale well with a high number of threads. The `solr.NIOFSDirectoryFactory` directory factory scales well with many threads, but remember that it doesn't work well on Microsoft Windows platforms (it's much slower) because of a JVM bug (`http://bugs.java.com/bugdatabase/view_bug.do?bug_id=6265734`).

The `solr.MMapDirectoryFactory` directory factory has been the default directory factory for Solr for 64-bit Linux systems since Solr 3.1. This directory implementation uses virtual memory and the kernel feature called `mmap` to access index files stored on disk. This allows Lucene (and thus Solr) to directly access the I/O cache. This is desirable, and you should stick to this directory if near real-time searching is not needed.

If you need near real-time indexing and searching, you should use `solr.NRTCachingDirectoryFactory`. It is designed to store some parts of the index in memory (small chunks), and thus speeds up some near real-time operations greatly. By saying near real-time, we mean that the documents are available within milliseconds from indexing.

If you want to know more about near real-time search and indexing, refer to a great explanation on the phrase on Solr wiki, available at `https://wiki.apache.org/lucene-java/NearRealtimeSearch`.

The `solr.HdfsDirectoryFactory` is used when Solr runs on HDFS filesystems, so inside a Hadoop cluster. If you are using Solr inside a Hadoop cluster, then it is almost certain that you'll want to use the directory implementation.

The last directory factory, `solr.RAMDirectoryFactory`, is the only one that is not persistent. The whole index is stored in the RAM memory, and thus, you'll lose your index after a restart or server crash. Also, you should remember that replication won't work when using `solr.RAMDirectoryFactory`. One might ask why I should use this factory? Imagine a volatile index autocomplete functionality or for unit tests of your query's relevance, or just anything you can think of when you don't need to have persistent and replicated data. However, remember that this directory is not designed to hold large amounts of data.

Configuring the Solr spellchecker

If you are used to the way the spellchecker worked in the previous Solr versions, then you might remember that it required its own index to give you spelling corrections. This approach had some disadvantages, such as the need to rebuild the index on each Solr node or replicate the spellchecker index between the nodes. With Solr 4.0, a new spellchecker implementation was introduced, `solr.DirectSolrSpellchecker`. It allows you to use your main index to provide spelling suggestions and doesn't need to be rebuilt after every commit. Now, let's see how to use this new spellchecker implementation in Solr.

How to do it...

First, let's assume we have a field in the index called `title` in which we hold the titles of our documents. What's more, we don't want the spellchecker to have its own index, and we would like to use this `title` field to provide spelling suggestions. In addition, we would like to decide when we want spelling suggestions. In order to do this, we need to do two things:

1. First, we need to edit our `solrconfig.xml` file and add the spellchecking component, the definition of which can look like this:

   ```
   <searchComponent name="spellcheck" class="solr.
   SpellCheckComponent">
    <str name="queryAnalyzerFieldType">text_general</str>
    <lst name="spellchecker">
     <str name="name">direct</str>
     <str name="field">title</str>
     <str name="classname">solr.DirectSolrSpellChecker</str>
     <str name="distanceMeasure">internal</str>
     <float name="accuracy">0.8</float>
     <int name="maxEdits">1</int>
     <int name="minPrefix">1</int>
     <int name="maxInspections">5</int>
     <int name="minQueryLength">3</int>
     <float name="maxQueryFrequency">0.01</float>
    </lst>
   </searchComponent>
   ```

2. Now, we need to add a proper request handler configuration that will use the preceding search component. To do this, we need to add the following section to the `solrconfig.xml` file:

   ```
   <requestHandler name="/spell" class="solr.SearchHandler"
   startup="lazy">
    <lst name="defaults">
     <str name="df">title</str>
     <str name="spellcheck.dictionary">direct</str>
     <str name="spellcheck">on</str>
     <str name="spellcheck.extendedResults">true</str>
     <str name="spellcheck.count">5</str>
     <str name="spellcheck.collate">true</str>
     <str name="spellcheck.collateExtendedResults">true</str>
    </lst>
    <arr name="last-components">
     <str>spellcheck</str>
    </arr>
   </requestHandler>
   ```

3. That's all. In order to get spelling suggestions, we need to run the following query:

   ```
   /spell?q=disa
   ```

4. In response, we will get something like this:

   ```
   <?xml version="1.0" encoding="UTF-8"?>
   <response>
    <lst name="responseHeader">
     <int name="status">0</int>
     <int name="QTime">5</int>
    </lst>
   <result name="response" numFound="0" start="0">
   </result>
   <lst name="spellcheck">
    <lst name="suggestions">
     <lst name="disa">
      <int name="numFound">1</int>
      <int name="startOffset">0</int>
      <int name="endOffset">4</int>
      <int name="origFreq">0</int>
      <arr name="suggestion">
       <lst>
        <str name="word">data</str>
        <int name="freq">1</int>
       </lst>
      </arr>
     </lst>
     <bool name="correctlySpelled">false</bool>
     <lst name="collation">
      <str name="collationQuery">data</str>
      <int name="hits">1</int>
      <lst name="misspellingsAndCorrections">
       <str name="disa">data</str>
      </lst>
     </lst>
    </lst>
   </lst>
   </response>
   ```

If you check your `data` folder, you will see that there is no directory responsible for holding the spellchecker index. Now, let's see how this works.

How it works...

Now, let's get into some specifics about how the configuration shown in the preceding example works. We will start from the search component configuration. The `queryAnalyzerFieldType` property tells Solr which field configuration should be used to analyze the query passed to the spellchecker. The `name` property sets the name of the spellchecker, which is used in the handler configuration later. The `field` property specifies which field should be used as the source for the data used to build spelling suggestions. As you probably figured out, the `classname` property specifies the implementation class, which in our case is `solr.DirectSolrSpellChecker`, enabling us to omit having a separate spellchecker index; spellchecker will just use the main index. The next parameters visible in the previous configuration specify how the Solr spellchecker should behave; however, this is beyond the scope of this recipe (if you want to read more about the parameters, visit the `http://wiki.apache.org/solr/SpellCheckComponent` URL).

The last thing is the request handler configuration. Let's concentrate on all the properties that start with the `spellcheck` prefix. First, we have `spellcheck.dictionary`, which, in our case, specifies the name of the spellchecking component we want to use (note that the value of the property matches the value of the `name` property in the search component configuration). We tell Solr that we want spellchecking results to be present (the `spellcheck` property with the `on` value), and we also tell Solr that we want to see the extended result format, which allows us to see more with regard to the results (`spellcheck.extendedResults` set to `true`). In addition to the previous configuration properties, we also said that we want to have a maximum of five suggestions (the `spellcheck.count` property), and we want to see the collation and its extended results (`spellcheck.collate` and `spellcheck.collateExtendedResults` both set to `true`).

There's more...

Let's see one more thing—the ability to have more than one spellchecker defined in a request handler.

More than one spellchecker

If you want to have more than one spellchecker handling spelling suggestions, you can configure your handler to use multiple search components. For example, if you want to use search components (spellchecking ones) named `word` and `better` (you have to have them configured), you can add multiple `spellcheck.dictionary` parameters to your request handler. This is what your request handler configuration will look like:

```
<requestHandler name="/spell" class="solr.SearchHandler"
startup="lazy">
<requestHandler name="/spell" class="solr.SearchHandler"
startup="lazy">
 <lst name="defaults">
```

```
    <str name="df">title</str>
    <str name="spellcheck.dictionary">direct</str>
    <str name="spellcheck.dictionary">word</str>
    <str name="spellcheck.dictionary">better</str>
    <str name="spellcheck">on</str>
    <str name="spellcheck.extendedResults">true</str>
    <str name="spellcheck.count">5</str>
    <str name="spellcheck.collate">true</str>
    <str name="spellcheck.collateExtendedResults">true</str>
  </lst>
  <arr name="last-components">
    <str>spellcheck</str>
  </arr>
</requestHandler>
```

Using Solr in a schemaless mode

Many use cases allow us to define our index structure upfront. We can look at the data, see which parts are important, which we want to search, how we want to do it, and finally, we can create the `schema.xml` file that we will use. However, this is not always possible. Sometimes, you don't know the data structure before you go into production, or you know very little about it. Of course, we can use dynamic fields, but such an approach is limited. This is why the newest versions of Solr allow us to use the so-called schemaless mode in which Solr is able to guess the type of data and create a field for it.

How to do it...

Let's assume that we don't know anything about the data and we want to fully rely on Solr when it comes to it.

1. To do this, we start with the `schema.xml` file—the `fields` section of it. We need to include two fields, so our `schema.xml` file looks as follows:

   ```
   <field name="id" type="string" indexed="true" stored="true"
   required="true" multiValued="false" />
   <field name="_version_" type="long" indexed="true" stored="true"/>
   ```

2. In addition to this, we need to specify the unique identifier. We do this by including the following section in the `schema.xml` file:

   ```
   <uniqueKey>id</uniqueKey>
   ```

3. In addition, we need to have the field types defined. To do this we add a section that looks as follows:

```
<fieldType name="string" class="solr.StrField"
sortMissingLast="true" />
<fieldType name="long" class="solr.TrieLongField"
precisionStep="0" positionIncrementGap="0"/>
<fieldType name="booleans" class="solr.BoolField"
sortMissingLast="true" multiValued="true"/>
<fieldType name="tlongs" class="solr.TrieLongField"
precisionStep="8" positionIncrementGap="0" multiValued="true"/>
<fieldType name="tdoubles" class="solr.TrieDoubleField"
precisionStep="8" positionIncrementGap="0" multiValued="true"/>
<fieldType name="tdates" class="solr.TrieDateField"
precisionStep="6" positionIncrementGap="0" multiValued="true"/>

<fieldType name="text" class="solr.TextField"
positionIncrementGap="100" multiValued="true">
 <analyzer type="index">
  <tokenizer class="solr.StandardTokenizerFactory"/>
  <filter class="solr.LowerCaseFilterFactory"/>
 </analyzer>
 <analyzer type="query">
  <tokenizer class="solr.StandardTokenizerFactory"/>
  <filter class="solr.LowerCaseFilterFactory"/>
 </analyzer>
</fieldType>
```

4. Now, we can switch to the `solrconfig.xml` file to add the so-called managed index schema. We do this by adding the following configuration snippet to the root section of the `solrconfig.xml` file:

```
<schemaFactory class="ManagedIndexSchemaFactory">
 <bool name="mutable">true</bool>
 <str name="managedSchemaResourceName">managed-schema</str>
</schemaFactory>
```

5. We alter our `update` request handler to include additional update chains (we can just alter the same section in the `solrconfig.xml` file we already have):

```
<requestHandler name="/update" class="solr.UpdateRequestHandler">
 <lst name="defaults">
  <str name="update.chain">add-unknown-fields</str>
 </lst>
</requestHandler>
```

6. Finally, we define the used update request processor chain by adding the following section to the `solrconfig.xml` file:

```
<updateRequestProcessorChain name="add-unknown-fields">
 <processor class="solr.RemoveBlankFieldUpdateProcessorFactory"/>
 <processor class="solr.ParseBooleanFieldUpdateProcessorFactory"/>
 <processor  class="solr.ParseLongFieldUpdateProcessorFactory"/>
 <processor class="solr.ParseDoubleFieldUpdateProcessorFactory"/>
 <processor class="solr.ParseDateFieldUpdateProcessorFactory">
  <arr name="format">
   <str>yyyy-MM-dd</str>
  </arr>
 </processor>
 <processor class="solr.AddSchemaFieldsUpdateProcessorFactory">
  <str name="defaultFieldType">text</str>
  <lst name="typeMapping">
   <str name="valueClass">java.lang.Boolean</str>
   <str name="fieldType">booleans</str>
  </lst>
  <lst name="typeMapping">
   <str name="valueClass">java.util.Date</str>
   <str name="fieldType">tdates</str>
  </lst>
  <lst name="typeMapping">
   <str name="valueClass">java.lang.Long</str>
   <str name="valueClass">java.lang.Integer</str>
   <str name="fieldType">tlongs</str>
  </lst>
  <lst name="typeMapping">
   <str name="valueClass">java.lang.Number</str>
   <str name="fieldType">tdoubles</str>
  </lst>
 </processor>
 <processor class="solr.LogUpdateProcessorFactory"/>
 <processor class="solr.RunUpdateProcessorFactory"/>
</updateRequestProcessorChain>
```

Now, if we index a document, it looks like this:

```
<add>
 <doc>
  <field name="id">1</field>
  <field name="title">Test document</field>
  <field name="published">2014-04-21</field>
  <field name="likes">12</field>
 </doc>
</add>
```

Solr will index it without any problem, creating fields such as `titles`, `likes`, or `published`, with a proper format. We can check them by running a `q=*:*` query, which will result in the following response:

```
<?xml version="1.0" encoding="UTF-8"?>
<response>
 <lst name="responseHeader">
  <int name="status">0</int>
  <int name="QTime">1</int>
  <lst name="params">
   <str name="q">*:*</str>
  </lst>
 </lst>
<result name="response" numFound="1" start="0">
 <doc>
  <str name="id">1</str>
  <arr name="title">
   <str>Test document</str>
  </arr>
  <arr name="published">
   <date>2014-04-21T00:00:00Z</date>
  </arr>
  <arr name="likes">
   <long>12</long>
  </arr>
  <long name="_version_">1466477993631154176</long></doc>
 </result>
</response>
```

How it works...

We start with our index having two fields, `id` and `_version_`. The `id` field is used as the unique identifier; we informed Solr about this by adding the `unqiueKey` section in `schema.xml`. We will need it for functionalities such as document updates, deletes by identifiers, and so forth. The `_version_` field is used by Solr internally, and is required by some Solr functionalities (such as optimistic locking); this is why we include it. The rest of the fields will be added automatically.

We also need to define the field types that we will use. Apart from the `string` type used by the `id` field, and the `long` type used by the `_version_` field, it contains types our documents will use. We will also define these types in our custom processor chain in the `solrconfig.xml` file.

The next thing is very important; the managed schema factory that we defined in `solrconfig.xml`, which is a `ManagedIndexSchemaFactory` type (the `class` property set to this value). By adding this section, we say that we want Solr to manage our `schema.xml` file. This means that Solr will load the `schema.xml` file during startup, change its name to `schema.xml.bak`, and will then create a file called `managed-schema` (the value of the `managedSchemaResourceName` property). From this point, we shouldn't modify our index structure manually—we should either let Solr do it during indexation or add and alter fields using the schema API (we will talk about this in the *Altering the index structure on a live collection* recipe in *Chapter 8, Using Additional Functionalities*). Since I assume that we will use the schema API, I've set the `mutable` property to `true`. If we want to disallow using the schema API, we should set the `mutable` property to `false`.

Note that you need to have a single `schemaFactory` defined, and it needs to be set to the `ManagedIndexSchemaFactory` type. If it is not set to this type, field discovery will not work and the indexation will result in an error.

We also need to include an update request processor chain. Since we want all index requests to use our custom request chain, we add the `update.chain` property and set it to `add-unknown-fields` in the `defaults` section of our `update` request handler configuration.

Finally, the second most important thing in this recipe is our update request processor chain called `add-unknown-fields` (the same as we used in the update processor configuration). It defines several update processors that allow us to get the functionality of fields and their types' discoveries. The `solr.RemoveBlankFieldUpdateProcessorFactory` processor factory removes empty fields from the documents we send to indexation. The `solr.ParseBooleanFieldUpdateProcessorFactory` processor factory is responsible for parsing Boolean fields; `solr.ParseLongFieldUpdateProcessorFactory` parses fields that have data that uses the long type; `solr.ParseDoubleFieldUpdateProcessorFactory` parses fields with data of double type; and `solr.ParseDateFieldUpdateProcessorFactory` parses the date-based fields. We specify the format we want Solr to recognize (we will discuss this in more detail in the *Using parsing update processors to parse data* recipe in *Chapter 2, Indexing Your Data*).

Finally, we include the `solr.AddSchemaFieldsUpdateProcessorFactory` processor factory that adds the actual fields to our managed schema. We specify the default field type to `text` by adding the `defaultFieldType` property. This type will be used when no other type will match the field. After the default field type definition, we see four lists called `typeMapping`. These sections define the field type mappings Solr will use. Each list contains at least one `valueClass` property and one `fieldType` property. The `valueClass` property defines the type of data Solr will assign to the field type defined by the `fieldType` property.

In our case, if Solr finds a date (`<str name="valueClass">java.util.Date</str>`) value in a field, it will create a new field using the `tdates` field type (`<str name="fieldType">tdates</str>`). If Solr finds a long or an integer value, it creates a new field using the `tlongs` field type. Of course, a field won't be created if it already exists in our managed schema. The name of the field created in our managed schema will be the same as the name of the field in the indexed document.

Finally, the `solr.LogUpdateProcessorFactory` processor factory tells Solr to write information about the update to log, and the `solr.RunUpdateProcessorFactory` processor factory tells Solr to run the update itself.

As we can see, our data includes fields that we didn't specify in the `schema.xml` file, and the document was indexed properly, which allows us to assume that the functionality works. If you want to check how our index structure looks like after indexation, use the schema API; you can do it yourself after reading the *Retrieving information about the index structure* recipe in *Chapter 8, Using Additional Functionalities*.

One thing to remember is that by default, Solr is able to automatically detect field types such as Boolean, integer, float, long, double, and date.

Take a look at `https://cwiki.apache.org/confluence/display/solr/Schemaless+Mode` for further information regarding the Solr schemaless mode.

Limiting I/O usage

As you might know, the Lucene index is divided into smaller pieces called segments, and each segment is stored on disk. Depending on the indexing and merge policy settings, Lucene, from time to time, merges two or more segments into a new one. This operation requires reading the old segments and writing a new one with the information from the old segments. The merges can happen at the same time when Solr indexes data and queries are run. The same goes for writing the segments; it can be pretty expensive when it comes to I/O usage.
It is because of this that Solr allows us to configure the limits for I/O usage. This recipe will show you how to do this.

Getting ready

Before continuing further with this recipe, read the *Choosing the proper directory configuration* recipe of this chapter to see what directories are available and how to configure them.

How to do it...

Let's assume that we want to limit the I/O usage for our use case that uses `solr.MMapDirectoryFactory`. So, in the `solrconfig.xml` file, we will have the following configuration present:

```
<directoryFactory name="DirectoryFactory" class="solr.
MMapDirectoryFactory">
</directoryFactory>
```

Now, let's introduce the following limits:

- We allow Solr to write a maximum of 20 MB per second during segment writes
- We allow Solr to write a maximum of 10 MB per second during segment merges
- We allow Solr to read a maximum of 50 MB per second

To do this, we change our previous configuration to the following:

```
<directoryFactory name="DirectoryFactory" class="solr.
MMapDirectoryFactory">
 <double name="maxWriteMBPerSecFlush">20</double>
 <double name="maxWriteMBPerSecMerge">10</double>
 <double name="maxWriteMBPerSecRead">50</double>
</directoryFactory>
```

After altering the configuration, all we need to do is restart Solr and the limits will be taken into consideration.

How it works...

The logic behind setting the limits is very simple. All directories that extend the Solr `CachingDirectoryFactory` class allow us to set the `maxWriteMBPerSecFlush`, `maxWriteMBPerSecMerge` and `maxWriteMBPerSecRead` properties. The mentioned directory implementations are all the directory implementations that were mentioned in the *Choosing the proper directory configuration* recipe of this chapter.

The `maxWriteMBPerSecFlush` property allows us to tell Solr how many megabytes per second can be written by Solr during segment flush (so, during the write operation that is not triggered by segment merging). The `maxWriteMBPerSecMerge` property allows us to specify how many megabytes per second can be written by Solr during segment merge. Finally, the `maxWriteMBPerSecRead` property specifies the amount of megabytes allowed to be read per second. One thing to remember is that the values are approximated, not exact.

Limiting I/O usage can be very handy, especially in deployments where I/O usage is at its maximum. During query peak hours, when we want to solve server queries as fast as we can, we need to minimize the indexing and merging impact. With proper configuration that is adjusted to our needs, we can just limit the I/O usage and still serve queries with the latency we want.

Using core discovery

Until Solr 4.4, `solr.xml` needed to include mandatory information, such as the cores definition. This was needed because Solr used this information to get and load the defined cores and their properties, basically information that was required for Solr to operate properly. Starting from Solr 4.4, a new structure of the `solr.xml` file was introduced, and in addition to this, a process called core discovery was implemented. Due to these changes, we are not forced to describe the core in the `solr.xml` file, but instead, we can use simple text files, and Solr will automatically load the appropriate cores. This recipe will show you how to use the core discovery process.

How to do it...

Using the new core discovery process is very simple.

1. We start with creating the `solr.xml` file, which should be put in the home directory of Solr. The contents of the file should look like the following:

```
<?xml version="1.0" encoding="UTF-8" ?>
<solr>
 <solrcloud>
  <str name="host">${host:}</str>
  <int name="hostPort">${jetty.port:8983}</int>
  <str name="hostContext">${hostContext:solr}</str>
  <int name="zkClientTimeout">${zkClientTimeout:30000}</int>
  <bool name="genericCoreNodeNames">
            ${genericCoreNodeNames:true}</bool>
 </solrcloud>
 <shardHandlerFactory name="shardHandlerFactory"
            class="HttpShardHandlerFactory">
  <int name="socketTimeout">${socketTimeout:0}</int>
  <int name="connTimeout">${connTimeout:0}</int>
 </shardHandlerFactory>
</solr>
```

2. After this, we are ready to use the core discovery. For each core, apart from the standard configuration stored in the `conf` directory, we need to create the `core.properties` file, which should be placed in the same directory as the `conf` directory. For example, if we have a core named `sample_core`, our very simple `core.properties` file will look like this:

```
name=sample_core
```

That's all; during startup, Solr will load our core.

How it works...

The `solr.xml` file is the same one that is provided with the Solr example deployment, and it contains the default values related to Solr configuration. The `host` property specifies the hostname, and the `hostPort` property specifies the port on which Solr will run (it will be taken from the `jetty.port` property, and is by default `8983`). The `hostContext` property specifies the web application context under which Solr will be available (by default, it is `solr`). In addition to this, we can specify the ZooKeeper client session timeout by using the `zkClientTimeout` property (used only in the SolrCloud mode, defaulting to 30,000 milliseconds). By default, we also say that we want Solr to use generic core names for SolrCloud, and we can change this by specifying `false` in the `genericCoreNodeNames` property.

There are two additional properties that relate to **shard handling**. The `socketTimeout` property specifies the timeout of socket connection, and the `connTimeout` property specifies the timeout of connection. Both the properties are used to create clients used by Solr to communicate between shards. The connection timeout specifies the timeout when Solr connects to another shard, and it takes a long time; the socket timeout is about the time to wait for the response to be back.

The simplest `core.properties` file is an empty file, in which case, Solr will try to choose the core name for us. However, in our case, we wanted to give the core a name we've chosen, and because of this, we included a single `name` entry that defines the name Solr will assign to the core. You should remember that Solr will try to load all the cores that have the `core.properties` file present, and the core name doesn't have to live in the directory of the same name.

Of course, the `name` property is not the only property available for usage. There are other properties, but in most cases, you'll use the `name` property only:

- `name`: This is the name of the core.
- `config`: This is the configuration filename, which defaults to `solrconfig.xml`.
- `dataDir`: This is the directory where data is stored. By default, Solr will use a directory called `data` that is created on the same level as the `conf` directory.

- `ulogDir`: This is the directory where the transaction log entries are stored. For performance reasons, it might be good to store transaction logfiles on a disks other than the index files.
- `schema`: This is the name of the file describing the index structure, which defaults to `schema.xml`.
- `shard`: This is the identifier of the shard.
- `collection`: This is the name of the collection the core belongs to.
- `roles`: This is the core role definition.
- `loadOnStartup`: This can take a value of `true` or `false`. It defaults to `true`, which means Solr will load the core during startup.
- `transient`: This can take a value of `true` or `false`. It defaults to `false`, which means that the core can't be automatically unloaded by Solr.
- `coreNodeName`: This is the name of the core used by SolrCloud.

Finally, it is worth saying that the old `solr.xml` format will not be supported in Solr 5.0, so it is good to get familiar with the new format now.

There's more...

If you want to see all the properties and sections exposed by the new `solr.xml` format, refer to the official Apache Solr documentation located at `https://cwiki.apache.org/confluence/display/solr/Format+of+solr.xml`.

Configuring SolrCloud for NRT use cases

Nowadays, we are used to getting information as soon as we can. We want our data to be indexed fast, efficiently, and be available for searching as soon as possible; in perfect cases, right after they were sent for indexation. This is what near real time in Solr is all about– the ability to search the documents right after they are sent for indexation or with a very short latency. This recipe will show you how to configure Solr, especially SolrCloud for such use cases.

How to do it...

I assume that you already have SolrCloud set up and ready to go (if you don't, refer to the *Creating a new SolrCloud cluster* recipe in *Chapter 7, In the Cloud*); you will now know how to update your collection configuration and be interested in near real-time search.

Let's assume that we want our data to be available about one second after it's indexed. To do this, we need to change the `solrconfig.xml` file so that its update handler section looks as shown:

```
<updateHandler class="solr.DirectUpdateHandler2">
 <updateLog>
  <str name="dir">${solr.ulog.dir:}</str>
 </updateLog>

 <autoSoftCommit>
  <maxTime>1000</maxTime>
 </autoSoftCommit>

 <autoCommit>
  <maxTime>300000</maxTime>
  <openSearcher>false</openSearcher>
 </autoCommit>
</updateHandler>
```

That's all; after a restart or configuration reload, documents should be available to search after about one second.

How it works...

By changing the configuration of the update handler, we introduced three things. First, using the `<updateLog>` section, we told Solr to use the update log functionality. The transaction log (another name for this functionality) is a file where Solr writes raw documents so that they can be used in a recovery process. In SolrCloud, each instance of Solr needs to have its own transaction log configured. When a document is sent for indexation, it gets forwarded to the shard leader and the leader sends the document to all its replicas. After all the replicas respond to the leader, the leader itself responds to the node that sent the original request, and this node reports the indexing status to the client. At this point in time, the document is written into a transaction log, not yet indexed, but safely written; so, if a failure occurs (for example, the server shuts down), the document is not lost. During a startup process, the transaction log is replayed and the documents stored in it are indexed, so even if they were not indexed, they will be if a failure happens. After the process of storing the data in transaction logs, Solr can easily index the data located there.

The second thing is the `autoSoftCommit` section. This is a new autocommit option introduced in Solr 4.0. It basically allows us to reopen the index searcher without closing and opening a new one. For us, this means that our documents that were sent for indexation will start to be visible and available to search. We do this once every `1000` milliseconds as configured using the `maxTime` tag. The soft commit was introduced because reopening is easier to do and is less resource intensive than closing and opening a new index searcher. In addition to this, it doesn't persist the data to disk by creating a new segment.

However, one has to remember that even though the soft commit is less resource intensive, it is still not free. Some Solr caches will have to be reloaded, such as the filter, document, or query result caches. We will get into more configuration details in the *Configuring SolrCloud for high-indexing use cases* and *Configuring SolrCloud for high-querying use cases* recipes in this chapter.

The last thing is the autocommit defined in the `autoCommit` section, which is called the hard autocommit. It is responsible for flushing data and closing the index segment used for it (because of this segment, merge might start in the background). In addition to this, the hard autocommit also closes the transaction log and opens a new one. We've configured this operation to happen every 5 minutes (`300000` milliseconds). What we also included is the `<openSearcher>false</openSearcher>` section. This means that Solr won't open a new index searcher during a hard auto commit operation. We do this on purpose; we define index searcher opening periods in the soft autocommit section. If we set the `openSearcher` section to `true`, Solr will close the old index searcher, open a new one, and automatically warm caches. Before Solr 4.0, this was the only way to have documents visible for searching when using autocommit.

One additional thing to remember is that with soft autocommit set to reopen the searcher very often, all the top level caches, such as the filter, document, and query result caches, will be invalidated. It is worth thinking and doing performance tests if the cache (all or some of them) are actually worth being used at all. I would like to give a clear advice here, but this is highly dependent on the use case. You can read more about cache configuration in the *Configuring the document cache*, *Configuring the query result cache*, and *Configuring the filter cache* recipes in *Chapter 6*, *Improving Solr Performance*.

Configuring SolrCloud for high-indexing use cases

Solr is designed to work under high load, both when it comes to querying and indexing. However, the default configuration provided with the example Solr deployment is not sufficient when it comes to these use cases. This recipe will show you how to prepare your SolrCloud collection configuration for use cases when the indexing rate is very high.

Getting ready

Before continuing reading the recipe, read the *Running Solr on a standalone Jetty* and *Configuring SolrCloud for NRT use cases* recipes in this chapter.

How to do it...

In very high indexing use cases, there are chances that you'll use bulk indexing to index your data. In addition to this, because we are talking about SolrCloud, we'll use autocommit so that we can leave the data durability and visibility management to Solr. Let's discuss how to prepare configuration for a use case where indexing is high, but the querying is quite low; for example, when using Solr for log centralization solutions.

Let's assume that we are indexing more than 1,000 documents per second and that we have four nodes, each of 12 cores and 64 GB of RAM. Note that this specification is not something we need to index the number of documents, but they are here for reference.

1. First, we'll start with the autocommit configuration, which will look as follows (we add this to the `solrconfig.xml` file):

```
<updateHandler class="solr.DirectUpdateHandler2">
 <updateLog>
  <str name="dir">${solr.ulog.dir:}</str>
 </updateLog>

 <autoSoftCommit>
  <maxTime>600000</maxTime>
 </autoSoftCommit>

 <autoCommit>
  <maxTime>15000</maxTime>
  <openSearcher>false</openSearcher>
 </autoCommit>
</updateHandler>
```

2. The second step is to adjust the number of indexing threads. To do this, we add the following information to the `indexConfig` section of `solrconfig.xml`:

```
<maxIndexingThreads>10</maxIndexingThreads>
```

3. The third step is to adjust the memory buffer size for each indexing thread. To do this, we add the following information to the `indexConfig` section of `solrconfig.xml`:

```
<ramBufferSizeMB>128</ramBufferSizeMB>
```

Now, let's discuss what each of these changes mean.

How it works...

We started with tuning the autocommit setting, which you should be aware of after reading this recipe. Since we are not worried about documents being visible as soon as they are indexed, we set the soft autocommit's `maxTime` property to `600000`. This means that we will reopen the searcher every 10 minutes, so our documents will be visible maximum 10 minutes after they are sent to indexation.

The one thing to look at is the short time for hard commit, which is every 15 seconds (the `maxTime` property of the `autoCommit` section set to `15000`). We did this because we don't want transaction logs to contain a high number of entries because this can cause problems during the recovery process.

We also increased the default number of threads an index writer can use from the default `8` to `10` by setting the `maxIndexingThreads` property. Since we have 12 cores on each machine, and we are not querying much, we can allow more threads using the index writer. If the index writer uses the number of threads that's equal to the `maxIndexingThreads` property, the next thread will wait for one of the currently running to end. Remember that the `maxIndexingThreads` property sets the maximum allowed indexing threads, which doesn't mean they will be used every time.

We also increased the default RAM buffer size from `100` to `128` using the `ramBufferSizeMB` property. We did this to allow Lucene to buffer as many documents as needed in memory. If the size of the documents in the buffer is larger than the given value of the `ramBufferSizeMB` property, Lucene will flush the data to the directory, which will decide what else to do. We have to remember though that we are also using autocommit, so the data will be flushed every 15 seconds because of hard autocommit settings.

Remember that we didn't take into consideration the size of the cluster because we had the maximum number of nodes. You should remember that if I/O is the bottleneck when indexing, spreading the collection among more nodes should help with the indexing load.

In addition to this, you might want to look at the merging policy and segment merge processes as this can become a major bottleneck. If you are interested, refer to the *Tuning segment merging* recipe in *Chapter 9, Dealing with Problems*.

Configuring SolrCloud for high-querying use cases

One of the things that Solr is really great for is high-querying use cases. Whether they are distributed queries using SolrCloud or single node queries running in master-slave environments, Solr does very well when it comes to handling queries and scaling. In this recipe, we will concentrate on use cases where we index quite a small amount of documents per second, but we want to have them at low latency.

Getting ready

Before continuing to read this recipe, read the *Running Solr on a standalone Jetty*, *Configuring SolrCloud for NRT use cases*, and *Configuring SolrCloud for high-indexing use cases* recipes of this chapter.

How to do it...

Giving general advice for high-querying use cases is pretty hard because it very much depends on the data, cluster structure, query structure, and target latency. In this recipe, we will look at three things—configuration, scaling, and overall general advices. Let's assume that we have four nodes, each having 128 GB of RAM and large disks, and we have 100 million documents we want to search across.

We should start with sizing our cluster. In general, this means choosing the right number of nodes, the right number of shards and replicas for your collections, and the memory. The general advice is to index some portion of your data and see how much space is used. For example, assuming you've indexed 1,000 documents and they are taking 1 MB of disk space, we can now calculate the disk space needed by 100 million documents; this will give us about 100 GB of total disk space used. With a replication factor of 2, we will need 200 GB, which means our four nodes should be enough to have the data cached by the operating system. In addition to this, we will need memory for Solr to operate (we can help ourselves calculate how much we will need using `http://svn.apache.org/repos/asf/lucene/dev/trunk/dev-tools/size-estimator-lucene-solr.xls`).

Given these facts, we can end up with a minimum of four shards and a replication factor of 2, which will give us a leader shard and its replica for each of the four initial shards we created the collection with. However, going for more initial shards might be better for scaling in the later stage of your application life cycle.

After we know some information, we can prepare the autocommit settings. To do this, we alter our `solrconfig.xml` configuration file and include the following update handler configuration:

```
<updateHandler class="solr.DirectUpdateHandler2">

 <updateLog>
  <str name="dir">${solr.ulog.dir:}</str>
 </updateLog>

 <autoSoftCommit>
  <maxTime>30000</maxTime>
 </autoSoftCommit>

 <autoCommit>
  <maxTime>600000</maxTime>
  <openSearcher>false</openSearcher>
 </autoCommit>
</updateHandler>
```

In addition to this, we should adjust caching, which is covered in the *Configuring the document cache*, *Configuring the query result cache*, and *Configuring the filter cache* recipes in *Chapter 6, Improving Solr Performance*.

In addition to all this, you might want to look at the merging policy and segment merge processes as this can become a major bottleneck. If you are interested, refer to the *Tuning segment merging* recipe in *Chapter 9, Dealing with Problems*.

How it works...

We started with sizing questions and estimations. Remember that the numbers you will extrapolate from the small portion of data are not exact numbers, they are estimations. What's more, we now know that in order to have our index fully cached by the operating system, we will need at least 200 GB of RAM memory that can be used for the system cache because we will have at least one shard and its physical copy. Of course, the four nodes with 128 GB of RAM are more or less a perfect case when we will be able to have our indices cached. This is because we will have a total of 512 GB of RAM across all nodes. Given the fact that we will end up with four leader shards, one on each machine, four replicas, again one on each machine, and that our index will be evenly divided, it will give us 50 GB of data on each node (25 GB for leader and the same for replica because it is an exact copy).

A few words about having more shards—sometimes, if you expect your data to grow, it is good to create a collection with more shards initially and place multiple ones on a single node. This gives more flexibility when you add new nodes; you can migrate some shards without the need to split them, or you can create a new collection with new shards and reindex your data.

Next, we adjust the autocommit section. Since we don't need near real-time searching, we decide not to stress Solr too much and set the soft autocommit to `60000` milliseconds, which means that the data will be visible after 1 minute from indexing. In general, if you will, the more often you reopen the searcher, the more pressure is put on Solr, and thus, the queries will be slower. So, if you query heavily, you should set the soft autocommit to the maximum time allowed by your use case.

Of course, we also included the hard autocommit and set it to be executed every 10 minutes. We decided to go for this because we don't index much data, so the index shouldn't be changed too often, and the transaction log shouldn't be too large.

Configuring the Solr heartbeat mechanism

Solr is designed to be scalable, fault tolerant, and have a high up time so that we can have our search service always ready. Many of the deployments, whether they are still master-slave setups or SolrCloud ones, still use some kind of load-balancing and health-checking mechanism. Solr comes with a request handler that is designed to handle health-checking requests, and this recipe will show you how to set it up.

How to do it...

Setting up the heartbeat mechanism in Solr is very easy. One just needs to add the following section to the `solrconfig.xml` file:

```
<requestHandler name="/admin/ping" class="solr.PingRequestHandler">
 <lst name="invariants">
  <str name="q">solrpingquery</str>
 </lst>
</requestHandler>
```

This is all. Of course, if we need all our cores and collections to respond to the health requests, we should include the previous section in the `solrconfig.xml` files for all of them. After this, run a query to the admin/ping handler of our Solr instance, for example:

```
curl 'localhost:8983/solr/heartbeat_core/admin/ping'
```

Solr will respond with a status response, for example:

```
<?xml version="1.0" encoding="UTF-8"?>
<response>
<lst name="responseHeader"><int name="status">0</int><int
name="QTime">6</int><lst name="params"/></lst><str name="status">OK</str>
</response>
```

How it works...

The configuration is really simple; we defined a new request handler that will be available under the `/admin/ping` address (of course, we have to prefix it with the host address and core name). The class implementing the handle is the one dedicated to handle the heartbeat mechanism request, `solr.PingRequestHandler`. We also defined that the `q` parameter for all the ping requests will be `solrpingquery` and the request won't be able to overwrite this parameter (because we included it in the `invariants` section). The ping query should be as simple as it can get so that it runs blazingly fast; what's more, it is usually good for it not to return any search results.

As you can see, the response contains the `status` section, which in our case has the value of `OK`. In the case of an error, the `status` section will contain the error code.

There's more...

The `solr.PingRequestHandler` handler allows us to enable and disable the heartbeat mechanism without shutting down the whole Solr instance.

Enabling and disabling the heartbeat mechanism

If we want to disable and enable the heartbeat mechanism without taking down the whole Solr instance, we need to introduce a property called `healthcheckFile` to our request handler configuration, for example:

```
<requestHandler name="/admin/ping" class="solr.PingRequestHandler">
 <lst name="invariants">
  <str name="q">solrpingquery</str>
 </lst>
 <str name="healthcheckFile">server-enabled.txt</str>
</requestHandler>
```

Now, to enable the heartbeat mechanism, one should run the following command:

```
curl 'localhost:8983/solr/heartbeat_core/admin/ping?action=enable'
```

By running this, Solr will create a file named `server-enabled.txt` in the directory the data directory is located at. This file will contain information about when the heartbeat mechanism is enabled.

To disable the heartbeat mechanism, one should run the following command:

```
curl 'localhost:8983/solr/heartbeat_core/admin/ping?action=disable'
```

This command will delete the previously created file.

We can also check the heartbeat status by running the following command:

```
curl 'localhost:8983/solr/heartbeat_core/admin/ping?action=status'
```

Changing similarity

Most times, the default way to calculate the score of your documents is what you need. However, sometimes you need more from Solr than just the standard behavior. For example, you might want shorter documents to be more valuable compared to longer ones. Let's assume that you want to change the default behavior and use different score calculation algorithms for the `description` field of your index. This recipe will show you how to leverage this functionality.

Getting ready

Before choosing one of the score calculation algorithms available in Solr, it's good to read a bit about them. The detailed description of all the algorithms is beyond the scope of this recipe and the book (although a simple description is mentioned later in the recipe), but I suggest visiting the Solr wiki page (or Javadocs) and reading basic information about the available implementations.

How to do it...

For the purpose of this recipe, let's assume we have the following index structure (just add the following entries to your `schema.xml` file):

```
<field name="id" type="string" indexed="true" stored="true"
required="true" />
<field name="name" type="text_general" indexed="true" stored="true"/>
<field name="description" type="text_general_dfr" indexed="true"
stored="true" />
```

The `string` and `text_general` types are available in the default `schema.xml` file provided with the example Solr distribution. However, we want `DFRSimilarity` to be used to calculate the score for the `description` field. In order to do this, we introduce a new type, which is defined as follows (just add the following entries to your `schema.xml` file):

```
<fieldType name="text_general_dfr" class="solr.TextField"
positionIncrementGap="100">
 <analyzer type="index">
  <tokenizer class="solr.StandardTokenizerFactory"/>
  <filter class="solr.StopFilterFactory" ignoreCase="true"
words="stopwords.txt" enablePositionIncrements="true" />
  <filter class="solr.LowerCaseFilterFactory"/>
 </analyzer>
 <analyzer type="query">
  <tokenizer class="solr.StandardTokenizerFactory"/>
  <filter class="solr.StopFilterFactory" ignoreCase="true"
words="stopwords.txt" enablePositionIncrements="true" />
  <filter class="solr.SynonymFilterFactory" synonyms="synonyms.txt"
ignoreCase="true" expand="true"/>
  <filter class="solr.LowerCaseFilterFactory"/>
 </analyzer>
 <similarity class="solr.DFRSimilarityFactory">
  <str name="basicModel">P</str>
  <str name="afterEffect">L</str>
  <str name="normalization">H2</str>
  <float name="c">7</float>
 </similarity>
</fieldType>
```

Also, to use the per-field similarity, we have to add the following entry to your `schema.xml` file:

```
<similarity class="solr.SchemaSimilarityFactory"/>
```

That's all. Now, let's have a look and see how this works.

How it works...

The index structure previously presented is pretty simple as there are only three fields. The one thing we are interested in is that the `description` field uses our own custom field type called `text_generanl_dfr`.

The thing we are most interested in is the new field type definition called `text_general_dfr`. As you can see, apart from the index and query analyzer, there is an additional section called `similarity`. It is responsible for specifying which similarity implementation to use to calculate the score for a given field. You are probably used to defining field types, filters, and other things in Solr, so you probably know that the `class` attribute is responsible for specifying the class that implements the desired similarity implementation, in our case, `solr.DFRSimilarityFactory`. Also, if there is a need, you can specify additional parameters that configure the behavior of your chosen similarity class. In the previous example, we specified the four additional parameters of `basicModel`, `afterEffect`, `normalization`, and `c`, all of which define the `DFRSimilarity` behavior.

The `solr.SchemaSimilarityFactory` class is required to specify the similarity for each field.

Although the recipe is not about all the similarities available, I wanted to list the available ones. Note that each similarity might require and use different configuration parameters (all of them are described in the provided Javadocs). The list of currently available similarity factories are:

- `solr.DefaultSimilarityFactory`: This is the default Lucene similarity implementing the default scoring algorithm (the Javadoc is available at `http://lucene.apache.org/solr/4_10_0/solr-core/org/apache/solr/search/similarities/DefaultSimilarityFactory.html`).
- `solr.SweetSpotSimilarityFactory`: This is the extension to the default similarity factory, providing additional parameters to tune scoring behaviors (the Javadoc is available at `http://lucene.apache.org/solr/4_10_0/solr-core/org/apache/solr/search/similarities/SweetSpotSimilarityFactory.html`).
- `solr.BM25SimilarityFactory`: This is the similarity model that bases the score calculation on the probabilistic model, estimating the probability of finding a document for a given query. It is said that this similarity performs best on short texts (the Javadoc is available at `http://lucene.apache.org/solr/4_10_0/solr-core/org/apache/solr/search/similarities/BM25SimilarityFactory.html`).
- `solr.DFRSimilarityFactory`: This similarity is based on the divergence from the randomness probability model (the Javadoc is available at `http://lucene.apache.org/solr/4_10_0/solr-core/org/apache/solr/search/similarities/DFRSimilarityFactory.html`).
- `solr.IBSimilarityFactory`: This similarity is based on the information-based probability model, which is similar to the one used for divergence from the randomness model (the Javadoc is available at `http://lucene.apache.org/solr/4_10_0/solr-core/org/apache/solr/search/similarities/IBSimilarityFactory.html`).

- `solr.LMDirichletSimilarityFactory`: This similarity is based on Bayesian smoothing using Dirichlet priors (the Javadoc is available at `http://lucene.apache.org/solr/4_10_0/solr-core/org/apache/solr/search/similarities/LMDirichletSimilarityFactory.html`).
- `solr.LMJelinekMercerSimilarityFactory`: This similarity is based on the Jelinek-Mercer smoothing method (the Javadoc is available at `http://lucene.apache.org/solr/4_10_0/solr-core/org/apache/solr/search/similarities/LMJelinekMercerSimilarityFactory.html`).

Note that after the similarity model changes, full document reindexing should be performed.

There's more...

In addition to per-field similarity definition, you can also configure the global similarity.

Changing the global similarity

Apart from specifying the similarity class on a per-field basis, you can choose fields other than the default one in a global way. For example, if you want to use `BM25Similarity` as the default field, you should add the following entry to your `schema.xml` file:

```
<similarity class="solr.BM25SimilarityFactory"/>
```

As with the per-field similarity, you need to provide the name of the factory class that is responsible for creating the appropriate similarity class.

2
Indexing Your Data

In this chapter, we will cover the following topics:

- Indexing PDF files
- Counting the number of fields
- Using parsing update processors to parse data
- Using scripting update processors to modify documents
- Indexing data from a database using Data Import Handler
- Incremental imports with DIH
- Transforming data when using DIH
- Indexing multiple geographical points
- Updating document fields
- Detecting the document language during indexation
- Optimizing the primary key indexation
- Handling multiple currencies

Introduction

Indexing data is one of the most crucial things in Lucene and Solr deployment. When your data is not indexed properly, your search results will be poor. When the search results are poor, it's almost certain the users will not be satisfied with the application that uses Solr. This is why we need our data to be prepared and indexed as timely and correctly as possible.

On the other hand, preparing data is not an easy task. Nowadays, we have more and more data floating around. We need to index multiple formats of data from multiple sources. Do we need to parse the data manually and prepare the data in XML format? The answer is no; we can let Solr do this for us. This chapter will concentrate on the indexing process and data preparation, starting with how to index data that is a binary PDF file to how to use Data Import Handler to fetch data from database and index it with Apache Solr and describing how we can detect the document language during indexation. We will also learn how to modify the data during indexation so that we don't have to prepare everything upfront.

Indexing PDF files

The library on the corner, we used to go to, wants to expand its collection and become available for the wider public through the World Wide Web. It asked its book suppliers to provide sample chapters of all the books in PDF format so that they can share it with online users. With all the samples provided by the supplier comes a problem—how to extract data for the search box from more than 900,000 PDF files. Solr can do it with the use of Apache Tika (`http://tika.apache.org/`). This recipe will show you how to handle such a task.

How to do it...

To index PDF files, we will need to set up Solr to use extracting request handlers. To do this, we will take the following steps:

1. First, let's edit our Solr instance, `solrconfig.xml`, and add the following configuration:

```
<requestHandler name="/update/extract" class="solr.extraction.
ExtractingRequestHandler">
 <lst name="defaults">
  <str name="fmap.content">text</str>
  <str name="lowernames">true</str>
  <str name="uprefix">attr_</str>
  <str name="captureAttr">true</str>
 </lst>
</requestHandler>
```

2. Next, create the `extract` folder anywhere on your system (I created the folder in the directory where Solr is installed, on the same level as the `lib` directory of Solr) and place the `solr-cell-4.10.0.jar` file from the `dist` directory (you can find it in the Solr distribution archive). After this, you have to copy all the libraries from the `contrib/extraction/lib/` directory to the `extract` directory you created before.

3. In addition to this, we need the following entries added to the `solrconfig.xml` file (adjust the path to the one matching your system):

   ```
   <lib dir="../../extract" regex=".*\.jar" />
   ```

   This is actually all that you need to do in terms of configuration.

4. The next step is the index structure. To simplify the example, I decided to choose the following index structure (place it in your `schema.xml` file):

   ```
   <field name="id" type="string" indexed="true" stored="true"
   required="true" multiValued="false" />
   <field name="text" type="text_general" indexed="true"
   stored="true"/>"/>
   <dynamicField name="attr_*" type="text_general" indexed="true"
   stored="true" multiValued="true""/>"/>
   ```

5. To test the indexing process, I created a PDF file, `book.pdf`, using Bullzip PDF Printer (`www.bullzip.com`), which contains the text `This is an updated version of Solr cookbook` only. To index this file, I used the following command:

   ```
   curl "http://localhost:8983/solr/cookbook/update/extract?literal.
   id=1&commit=true" -F "myfile=@book.pdf"
   ```

   You should see the following response:

   ```
   <?xml version="1.0" encoding="UTF-8"?>
   <response>
   <lst name="responseHeader"><int name="status">0</int><int
   name="QTime">1383</int></lst>
   </response>
   ```

6. To see what was indexed, I ran the following within a web browser:

   ```
   http://localhost:8983/solr/cookbook/select/?q=text:solr&fl=attr_
   creator,attr_modified
   ```

   In return, I got the following response:

   ```
   <?xml version="1.0" encoding="UTF-8"?>
   <response>
    <lst name="responseHeader">
     <int name="status">0</int>
     <int name="QTime">1</int>
     <lst name="params">
      <str name="q">text:solr</str>
      <str name="fl">attr_creator,attr_modified</str>
     </lst>
   ```

```
    </lst>
    <result name="response" numFound="1" start="0">
     <doc>
      <arr name="attr_creator">
       <str>Rafał Kuć</str>
      </arr>
      <arr name="attr_modified">
       <str>2014-05-07T11:30:09Z</str>
      </arr>
     </doc>
    </result>
   </response>
```

How it works...

A binary file parsing is implemented in Solr using the Apache Tika framework. Tika is a toolkit used to detect and extract metadata and structured text from various types of documents, not only binary files but also HTML and XML files.

Solr has a dedicated handler that uses Apache Tika. To be able to use it, we need to add a handler based on the `solr.extraction.ExtractingRequestHandler` class to our `solrconfig.xml` file, as shown in the preceding example.

In addition to the handler definition, we need to specify where Solr should look for the additional libraries we placed in the `extract` directory we created. The `dir` attribute of the `lib` tag should be pointing to the path to the created directory. The `regex` attribute is the regular expression telling Solr which files to load. The base directory is the Solr home directory, so if you use relative paths, you should remember this.

Now, let's discuss the default configuration parameters. The `fmap.content` parameter tells Solr to what field content the parsed document should be put. In our case, the parsed content will go to the field named `text`. The next parameter, `lowernames`, set to `true`, tells Solr to lower all names that come from Tika and make them lowercased. The next parameter, `uprefix`, is very important. It tells Solr how to handle fields that are not defined in the `schema.xml` file. The name of the field returned from Tika will be added to the value of the parameter and sent to Solr. For example, if Tika returns a field named `creator`, and we don't have such a field in our index, then Solr will try to index it under a field named `attr_creator`, which is a dynamic field. The last parameter tells Solr to index Tika XHTML elements into separate fields named after these elements. Remember that Tika can return multiple attributes of the same name; this is why we defined the dynamic field as a multivalued one.

Next, we have a command that sends a PDF file to Solr. We send a file to the `/update/extract` handler with two parameters. First, we define a unique identifier. It's useful to be able to do this during document sending because most of the binary documents won't have an identifier in its contents. To pass the identifier, we use the `literal.id` parameter. The second parameter we send to Solr is information to perform a commit immediately after document processing.

The test file I created for the purpose of the recipe contained the simple sentence `This is an updated version of Solr cookbook`. Of course, Tika will extract way more information from the PDF, such as creation time, creator, and many more attributes. We queried Solr with a simple query, and to keep the response simple, we limited the returned fields to only `attr_creator` and `attr_modified`. In response, I got one document that matched the given query. As you can see, Solr was able to extract both the creator and the file modification date. If you want to see all the information extracted by Solr, just remove the `fl` parameter.

Counting the number of fields

Imagine a situation where we have a simple document to be indexed to Solr with titles and tags. What we will want to do is separate the premium documents that have more tag values because they are better in terms of our business. Of course, we can count the number of tags ourselves, but why not let Solr do this? This recipe will show you how to do this with Solr.

How to do it...

Let's look at the steps we need to take to count the number of field values.

1. We start with the index structure. What we need to do is put the following section in the `schema.xml` file:

```
<field name="id" type="string" indexed="true" stored="true"
required="true" />
<field name="title" type="text_general" indexed="true"
stored="true"/>
<field name="tags" type="string" indexed="true" stored="true"
multiValued="true"/>
<field name="tags_count" type="int" indexed="true" stored="true"/>
```

2. The next thing is our test data, which looks as follows:

```
<add>
 <doc>
  <field name="id">1</field>
  <field name="title">Solr Cookbook 4</field>
  <field name="tags">solr</field>
```

```
 </doc>
 <doc>
  <field name="id">2</field>
  <field name="title">Solr Cookbook 4 second edition</field>
  <field name="tags">search</field>
  <field name="tags">solr</field>
  <field name="tags">cookbook</field>
 </doc>
</add>
```

3. In addition to this, we need to alter our `solrconfig.xml` file. First, we add the proper update request processor to the file:

```
<updateRequestProcessorChain name="count">
 <processor class="solr.CloneFieldUpdateProcessorFactory">
  <str name="source">tags</str>
  <str name="dest">tags_count</str>
 </processor>
 <processor class="solr.CountFieldValuesUpdateProcessorFactory">
  <str name="fieldName">tags_count</str>
 </processor>
 <processor class="solr.DefaultValueUpdateProcessorFactory">
  <str name="fieldName">tags_count</str>
  <int name="value">0</int>
 </processor>
 <processor class="solr.LogUpdateProcessorFactory" />
 <processor class="solr.RunUpdateProcessorFactory" />
</updateRequestProcessorChain>
```

4. We would also like to have our update processor be used with every indexing request, so we change our `/update` handler in the `solrconfig.xml` file so that it looks like this:

```
<requestHandler name="/update" class="solr.UpdateRequestHandler">
 <lst name="defaults">
  <str name="update.chain">count</str>
 </lst>
</requestHandler>
```

5. Now, if we want to use the count information Solr automatically added, we will send the following query:

```
http://localhost:8983/solr/cookbook/select?q=title:cookbook&bf=fie
ld(tags_count)&defType=edismax
```

6. Solr will position the document with more tags at the top of the result list:

```
<?xml version="1.0" encoding="UTF-8"?>
<response>
 <lst name="responseHeader">
  <int name="status">0</int>
  <int name="QTime">1</int>
  <lst name="params">
   <str name="q">title:cookbook</str>
   <str name="defType">edismax</str>
   <str name="bf">field(tags_count)</str>
  </lst>
 </lst>
 <result name="response" numFound="2" start="0">
  <doc>
   <str name="id">2</str>
   <str name="title">Solr Cookbook 4 second edition</str>
   <arr name="tags">
    <str>search</str>
    <str>solr</str>
    <str>cookbook</str>
   </arr>
   <int name="tags_count">3</int>
   <long name="_version_">1467535763434373120</long></doc>
  <doc>
   <str name="id">1</str>
   <str name="title">Solr Cookbook 4</str>
   <arr name="tags">
    <str>solr</str>
   </arr>
   <int name="tags_count">1</int>
   <long name="_version_">1467535763382992896</long></doc>
  </result>
</response>
```

Now, let's see how it works.

How it works...

The index structure is quite simple. It contains a unique identifier field, a title, a field holding tags, and a field holding the count of tags. As you can see, in the example data, we provide the identifier of the document, its title, and the tags. What we don't provide is the number of tags that we calculate during indexation.

We also defined a new update request processor chain called `count`. It contains five update processors.

The first update processor, `solr.CloneFieldUpdateProcessorFactory`, is responsible for copying the value of the field defined by the `source` property to a field defined by the `dest` property. The second update processor, `solr.CountFieldValuesUpdateProcessorFactory`, replaces the actual value of the field defined by the `fieldName` property with the count of values. This is why we need the `solr.CloneFieldUpdateProcessorFactory` update processor before `solr.CountFieldValuesUpdateProcessorFactory`. The third update processor, `solr.DefaultValueUpdateProcessorFactory`, sets the default value (defined by the `value` property) for the field defined by the `fieldName` property. The other request processors are responsible for logging the request information and running the update. By defining this chain, we tell Solr that we want the `tags` field to be cloned into `tags_count` first, then we want the counts to be calculated and placed in the `tags_count` field; if we don't have a value in the `tags_count` field, we set it to `0`.

We also define the `solr.UpdateRequestHandler` configuration and then alter the default configuration by adding the `defaults` section and including the `update.chain` property to `count` (our update request processor chain name). This means that our defined update request processor chain will be used with every indexing request.

Our query searches for every document that includes the `cookbook` term in the `title` field. We will also use the `edismax` query parser (`defType=edismax`). We also include a simple boosting function that boosts documents by the value of their `tags_count` field (`bf=field(tags_count)`). As you can see in the results, we get what we wanted to achieve.

Using parsing update processors to parse data

Let's assume that we are running a bookstore, we want to sort our books by the publication date, and run faceting on the number of likes each book gets. However, we get all our data in XML, and we don't have data in the proper format, and so on. The good thing is that we can tell Solr to parse our data property so that we don't have to change what we already have. This recipe will show you how to do this.

Getting ready

Before continuing with this recipe, I suggest reading the *Counting the number of fields* recipe of this chapter to get used to updating the request processor configuration.

How to do it...

Let's look at the steps we need to take to make data parsing work.

1. First, we need to prepare our index structure, so we add the following section to the `schema.xml` file:

```
<field name="id" type="string" indexed="true" stored="true"
required="true" />
<field name="title" type="text_general" indexed="true"
stored="true" />
<field name="published" type="date" indexed="true" stored="true"
/>
<field name="likes" type="long" indexed="true" stored="true" />
```

2. In addition to this, we need a custom update request processor chain defined. To do this, we add the following section to the `solrconfig.xml` file:

```
<updateRequestProcessorChain name="parse">
 <processor class="solr.ParseLongFieldUpdateProcessorFactory">
  <str name="fieldName">likes</str>
 </processor>
 <processor class="solr.ParseDateFieldUpdateProcessorFactory">
  <str name="fieldName">published</str>
  <arr name="format">
   <str>yyyy-MM-dd</str>
  </arr>
 </processor>
 <processor class="solr.LogUpdateProcessorFactory" />
 <processor class="solr.RunUpdateProcessorFactory" />
</updateRequestProcessorChain>
```

3. The third step is to alter the `/update` request handler configuration by adding the following section to our `solrconfig.xml` file:

```
<requestHandler name="/update" class="solr.UpdateRequestHandler">
 <lst name="defaults">
  <str name="update.chain">parse</str>
 </lst>
</requestHandler>
```

4. Now, we can index our data, which looks like this:

```
<add>
 <doc>
  <field name="id">1</field>
```

```
    <field name="title">Solr Cookbook 4</field>
    <field name="published">2013-01-10</field>
    <field name="likes">10</field>
  </doc>
</add>
```

5. After we send our data, we can check a simple query like this:

```
http://localhost:8983/solr/cookbook/select?q=*:*&sort=published+de
sc&facet=true&facet.field=likes
```

The response from Solr looks as follows:

```
<?xml version="1.0" encoding="UTF-8"?>
 <response>
  <lst name="responseHeader">
   <int name="status">0</int>
   <int name="QTime">106</int>
   <lst name="params">
    <str name="q">*:*</str>
    <str name="facet.field">likes</str>
    <str name="sort">published desc</str>
    <str name="facet">true</str>
   </lst>
  </lst>
  <result name="response" numFound="1" start="0">
   <doc>
    <str name="id">1</str>
    <str name="title">Solr Cookbook 4</str>
    <date name="published">2013-01-10T00:00:00Z</date>
    <long name="likes">10</long>
    <long name="_version_">1468068127952601088</long></doc>
  </result>
 <lst name="facet_counts">
  <lst name="facet_queries"/>
  <lst name="facet_fields">
  <lst name="likes">
   <int name="10">1</int>
  </lst>
 </lst>
 <lst name="facet_dates"/>
 <lst name="facet_ranges"/>
 </lst>
</response>
```

As you can see, the data was properly parsed, the sorting works, and faceting also works, so let's see how it was possible.

How it works...

Our data is very simple. Each book is described with its identifier (the `id` field), the title (the `title` field), the publication day (the `published` field), and the number of likes (the `likes` field). The `published` field is of the `date` type for proper date-based sorting, and the `likes` field is of the `long` type.

Our defined update request processor chain consists of two new processors that we are not familiar with. The first processor, `solr.ParseLongFieldUpdateProcessorFactory`, is responsible for parsing the data to a `long` type. It takes the field defined in the `fieldName` property from the document sent to indexation and parses it. The second processor is `solr.ParseDateFieldUpdateProcessorFactory`, which we already talked about in the *Using Solr in a schemaless mode* recipe in *Chapter 1, Apache Solr Configuration*, but let's a recap. It takes the field defined in the `fieldName` property from the document sent to indexation and tries to parse its value using the date formats defined using the `format` array. We only defined a single format, but you can put multiple formats if this is what you need.

For a description of the possible formats, refer to `http://joda-time.sourceforge.net/apidocs/org/joda/time/format/DateTimeFormat.html`.

We also defined the `solr.UpdateRequestHandler` configuration, and then altered the default configuration by adding the `defaults` section and including the `update.chain` property to `script` (our update request processor chain name). This means that our defined update request processor chain will be used with every indexing request.

After indexing our data and running a query, we will see that our data has proper field types. We will also see that sorting works on the `published` field, which was parsed into data, although our `published` field content was not in a format understandable by Solr.

See also

- If you want to see all the possibilities of parsing different field types, refer to the Javadoc of `solr.FieldMutatingUpdateProcessorFactory` available at `http://lucene.apache.org/solr/4_10_0/solr-core/org/apache/solr/update/processor/FieldMutatingUpdateProcessorFactory.html`. The classes extending this class provide a nice description of the additional possibilities.

Using scripting update processors to modify documents

Sometimes, we need to modify documents during indexing, and we don't want to do this on the indexing application side. For example, we have documents describing the Internet sites. What we want to be able to do is filter the sites on the basis of the protocol used, for example, `http` or `https`. We don't have this information; we only have the whole URL address. Let's see how we can achieve this with Solr.

Getting ready

Before continuing with the following recipe, I suggest reading the *Counting the number of fields* recipe of this chapter to get used to updating request processor configuration.

How to do it...

The following steps will take you through the process of achieving our goal:

1. First, we start with the index structure, putting the following section in the `schema.xml` file:

```
<field name="id" type="string" indexed="true" stored="true"
required="true" />
<field name="url" type="text_general" indexed="true"
stored="true"/>
<field name="protocol" type="string" indexed="true" stored="true"
/>
```

2. The next step is configuring Solr by adding a new update request processor chain called `script`. We do this by adding the following section to our `solrconfig.xml` file:

```
<updateRequestProcessorChain name="script">
 <processor class="solr.StatelessScriptUpdateProcessorFactory">
  <str name="script">script.js</str>
 </processor>
 <processor class="solr.LogUpdateProcessorFactory" />
 <processor class="solr.RunUpdateProcessorFactory" />
</updateRequestProcessorChain>
```

3. The third step is to alter the `/update` request handler configuration by adding the following section to our `solrconfig.xml` file:

```
<requestHandler name="/update" class="solr.UpdateRequestHandler">
 <lst name="defaults">
```

```
    <str name="update.chain">script</str>
  </lst>
</requestHandler>
```

4. Finally, we need the script mentioned in the update request processor chain configuration, which we called `script.js` and stored in the `conf` directory (the same directory where the `schema.xml` file is placed). The content of the `script.js` file looks as follows:

```
functionfunction processAdd(cmd) {
  doc = cmd.solrDoc;
  url = doc.getFieldValue("url");
  if (url != null) {
  parts = url.split(":");
  if (parts != null && parts.length > 0) {
     doc.setField("protocol", parts[0]);
    }
  }
}

function processDelete(cmd) {
}

function processMergeIndexes(cmd) {
}

function processCommit(cmd) {
}

function processRollback(cmd) {
}

function finish() {
}
```

Our example data looks as follows:

```
<add>
 <doc>
  <field name="id">1</field>
  <field name="url">http://solr.pl/</field>
 </doc>
 <doc>
  <field name="id">2</field>
  <field name="url">https://drive.google.com/</field>
 </doc>
</add>
```

5. After indexing our data, we can try our script out by running the following query:

 `http://localhost:8983/solr/cookbook/select?q=*:*&fq=protocol:http`

 The response from Solr should be similar to the following:

```
<?xml version="1.0" encoding="UTF-8"?>
 <response>
 <lst name="responseHeader">
  <int name="status">0</int>
  <int name="QTime">1</int>
  <lst name="params">
   <str name="q">*:*</str>
   <str name="fq">protocol:http</str>
  </lst>
 </lst>
 <result name="response" numFound="1" start="0">
  <doc>
   <str name="id">1</str>
   <strname="url">http://solr.pl/</str>
   <strname="protocol">http</str>
   <long name="_version_">1468022030035058688</long></doc>
 </result>
</response>
```

As you can see, everything works as it should, so now let's see how it worked.

How it works...

Our data is very simple. Each document is described with its identifier (the `id` field), the URL (the `url` field), and the field holding the protocol (the `protocol` field). The first two fields will be passed in the data; the `protocol` field will be filled automatically by our update request processor chain.

The next thing is to configure our update request processor chain. We already described most of the configuration details in the *Counting the number of fields* recipe of this chapter. The new thing is the `solr.StatelessScriptUpdateProcessorFactory` processor. It allows us to define a script (using the `script` property) that will be used to process our documents. In our case, this script is called `script.js`. Solr will load this script and use it for each document passed through the update request processor chain.

We also defined the `solr.UpdateRequestHandler` configuration, and then altered the default configuration by adding the `defaults` section and including the `update.chain` property to `script` (our update request processor chain name). This means that our defined update request processor chain will be used with every indexing request.

Finally, we come to the juicy part of the recipe, the `script.js` script. The `solr.StatelessScriptUpdateProcessorFactory` processor allows us to alter Solr behavior using the following script functions:

- `processAdd`: This function is executed when a document is added to the index. In our case, we will put our code in this function.
- `processDelete`: This function is executed when a delete operation is sent to Solr.
- `processMergeIndexes`: This function is executed when the `index merge` command is sent to Solr.
- `processCommit`: This function is executed when the `commit` command is sent to Solr.
- `processRollback`: This function is executed when the `rollback` command is sent to Solr.
- `finish`: Any code that should be run after the script that finished executing is put in this method.

Apart from the `finish` function, all the other functions have a single argument that represents the command sent to Solr.

As already mentioned, we only need to provide logic in the `processAdd` function. We start by retrieving the Solr document from the command (the `cmd` object) and then store the document in the `doc` variable (`doc = cmd.solrDoc;`). Next, we get the `url` field of the document (`url = doc.getFieldValue("url");`). We check whether the field is defined (`if (url != null)`); if it is, we split the URL using the `:` character. This means that for the `http://solr.pl` URL, we should get an array containing the two parts `http` and `//solr.pl`. We are interested in the first value. We check if the `parts` variable, which was returned by the `split` function, is defined and if it has elements (`if (parts != null &&parts.length> 0)`). If the condition is true, we just set a new field using the first element in the `parts` array, which will contain the protocol.

After indexing our data and running a query that filters the documents to only those that has the `http` protocol, we see that we did the job right.

See also

- If you want to read more about `solr.StatelessScriptUpdateProcessorFactory`, refer to the Solr Javadoc available at `http://lucene.apache.org/solr/4_10_0/solr-core/org/apache/solr/update/processor/StatelessScriptUpdateProcessorFactory.html`

Indexing data from a database using Data Import Handler

One of our clients has a problem. His database of users grows to such a size that even a simple SQL select takes too much time, and he seeks how to improve the search times. Of course, he has heard about Solr, but he doesn't want to generate XML or any other data format and push it to Solr; he would like the data to be fetched. What can we do about it? Well, there is one thing—we can use one of the contribute modules of Solr, which is the Data Import Handler. This task will show you how to configure the basic setup of the Data Import Handler and how to use it.

How to do it...

Let's assume that we have a database table. To select users from our table, we use the following SQL query:

```
SELECT user_id, user_name FROM users
```

The response might look like this:

```
| user_id | user_name      |
| 1       | John Kowalski |
| 2       | Amanda Looks   |
```

We also have a second table called `users_description`, where we store the descriptions of users. The SQL query to get data about a particular user looks like this:

```
SELECT desc FROM users_description WHERE user_id = 1
```

The response will look as follows:

```
| desc      |
| superuser|
```

Now, let's look at the steps we need to take to set up a Data Import Handler and let Solr connect to the database and start indexing the preceding data:

1. First, we need to copy the appropriate libraries that are required to use the Data Import Handler. So, let's create the `dih` folder anywhere on the system (I created the folder in the directory where Solr is installed, on the same level as the `lib` directory of Solr) and place the `solr-dataimporthandler-4.10.0.jar` and `solr-dataimporthandler-extras-4.10.0.jar` files from the Solr distribution `dist` directory. In addition to this, we need the following entry to be added to the `solrconfig.xml` file:

   ```
   <lib dir="../../dih" regex=".*\.jar" />
   ```

2. Next, we need to modify the `solrconfig.xml` file. You should add an entry like this:

```
<requestHandler name="/dataimport" class="solr.DataImportHandler">
 <lst name="defaults">
  <str name="config">db-data-config.xml</str>
 </lst>
</requestHandler>
```

3. Now, we will create the `db-data-config.xml` file that is responsible for the Data Import Handler configuration. It should have contents like the following example:

```
<dataConfig>
 <dataSource driver="org.postgresql.Driver"
url="jdbc:postgresql://localhost:5432/users" user="users"
password="secret" />
 <document>
  <entity name="user" query="SELECT user_id, user_name FROM
users">
   <field column="user_id" name="id" />
   <field column="user_name" name="name" />
   <entity name="user_desc" query="SELECT desc FROM users_
description WHERE user_id=${user.user_id}">
    <field column="desc" name="description" />
   </entity>
  </entity>
 </document>
</dataConfig>
```

If you want to use other database engines, change the `driver`, `url`, `user`, and `password` fields.

4. Now, let's create a sample index structure. We just add the following section to our `schema.xml` file:

```
<field name="id" type="string" indexed="true" stored="true"
required="true"/>
<field name="name" type="text" indexed="true" stored="true" />
<field name="description" type="text" indexed="true"
stored="true"/>
```

5. One more thing before the indexation—you should copy an appropriate JDBC driver to the `lib` directory of your Solr installation or the `dih` directory we created before. You can get the driver library for PostgreSQL at `http://jdbc.postgresql.org/download.html`.

6. Now, we can start indexing. We run the following query to Solr:

```
http://localhost:8983/solr/cookbook/dataimport?command=full-import
```

7. As you might know, the HTTP protocol is asynchronous, and thus, you won't be updated on how the process of indexing is going. To check the status of the indexing process, you can run the `status` command, which looks like this:

```
http://localhost:8983/solr/cookbook/dataimport?command=status
```

This is how we configure the Data Import Handler.

How it works...

First, we have a `solrconfig.xml` part that actually defines a new request handler, the Data Import Handler, to be used by Solr. We specify the `class` attribute, telling Solr which handler to use, which is `solr.DataImportHandler`, in our case. We also said it will be available under the `/dataimport` address by using the `name` property. The `<str name="config">` XML tag specifies the name of the Data Import Handler configuration file.

The second listing is the actual configuration of the Data Import Handler. I used the JDBC source connection sample to illustrate how to configure the Data Import Handler. The contents of this configuration file start with the root tag named `dataConfig`, which is followed by a second tag defining a data source named `dataSource`. In the example I used, the PostgreSQL (`http://www.postgresql.org/`) database, and thus, the JDBC driver, `org.postgresql.Driver`. We also define the database connection URL (the attribute named `url`) and the database credentials (the attributes `user` and `password`).

Next, we have a document definition, a document that will be constructed by the Data Import Handler and indexed to Solr. To define this, we use the tag named `document`. The document definition is made of database queries, which are the entities.

The entity is defined by a name (the `name` attribute) and SQL query (the `query` attribute). The entity name can be used to reference values in subqueries; you can see an example of such a behavior in the second entity named `user_desc`. As you might already have noticed, entities can be nested to handle subqueries. The SQL query is there to fetch the data from the database and use it to fill the entity variables that will be indexed.

After the entity comes the mapping definition. There is a single `field` tag for every column returned by a query, but this is not a must; the Data Import Handler can guess what the mapping is (for example, where the entity field name matches the column name), but I tend to use mappings because I find it easier to maintain. However, let's get back to fields. A field is defined by two attributes: `column`, which is the column name returned by a query and `name`, which is the field to which the data will be written.

Next, we have a Solr query to start the indexing process. There are actually five commands that can be run:

- `/dataimport?command=status`: This command will return the actual status.
- `/dataimport?command=full-import`: This command will start the full import process. Remember that the default behavior is to delete the index contents at the beginning.
- `/dataimport?command=delta-import`: This command will start the incremental indexing process (which is explained in the *Incremental imports with DIH* recipe later in this chapter).
- `/dataimport?command=reload-config`: This command will force the configuration reload.
- `/dataimport?command=abort`: This command will stop the indexing process.

There's more...

There is one more thing that I think you should know, which is explained in the following section.

How to change the default behavior of deleting index contents at the beginning of a full import

If you don't want to delete the index contents at the start of full indexing using the Data Import Handler, add the `clean=false` parameter to your query. An example query should look like this:

```
http://localhost:8983/solr/cookbook/data?command=full-
import&clean=false
```

Incremental imports with DIH

In most use cases, indexing the data from scratch during every indexation doesn't make sense. Why index your 1,00,000 documents when only 1,000 were modified or added? This is where the Solr Data Import Handler delta queries come in handy. Using them, we can index our data incrementally. This recipe will show you how to set up the Data Import Handler to use delta queries and index data in an incremental way.

Getting ready

Refer to the *Indexing data from a database using Data Import Handler* recipe in this chapter to get to know the basics of the Data Import Handler configuration. I assume that Solr is set up according to the description given in the mentioned recipe.

How to do it...

We will reuse parts of the configuration shown in the *Indexing data from a database using Data Import Handler* recipe in this chapter, and we will modify it. Execute the following steps:

1. The first thing you should do is add an additional column to the tables you use, a column that will specify the last modification date of the record. So, in our case, let's assume that we added a column named `last_modified` (which should be a timestamp-based column). Now, our `db-data-config.xml` will look like this:

```
<dataConfig>
 <dataSource driver="org.postgresql.Driver"
url="jdbc:postgresql://localhost:5432/users" user="users"
password="secret" />
 <document>
  <entity name="user" query="SELECT user_id, user_name FROM users"
deltaImportQuery="select user_id, user_name FROM users WHERE user_
id = '${dih.delta.user_id}'" deltaQuery="SELECT user_id FROM users
WHERE last_modified &gt; '${dih.last_index_time}'">
    <field column="user_id" name="id" />
    <field column="user_name" name="name" />
    <entity name="user_desc" query="select desc from users_
description where user_id=${user.user_id}">
     <field column="desc" name="description" />
    </entity>
  </entity>
 </document>
</dataConfig>
```

2. After this, we run a new kind of query to start the delta import:

```
http://localhost:8983/solr/cookbook/dataimport?command=delta-
import
```

How it works...

First, we modified our database table to include a column named `last_modified`. We need to ensure that the column will contain the last modified date of the record it corresponds to. Solr will not modify the database, so you have to ensure that your application will do this.

When running a delta import, the Data Import Handler will start by reading a file named `dataimport.properties` inside a Solr configuration directory. If it is not present, the Data Import Handler will assume that no indexing was ever made. Solr will use this file to store information about the last indexation time, and this file will be updated or created after indexation is finished. The last index time will be stored as a timestamp. As you can guess, the Data Import Handler uses this timestamp to distinguish whether the data was changed. It can be used in a query by using a special variable, `${dih.last_index_time}`.

You might already have noticed the two differences—two additional attributes defining entities named `user`, `deltaQuery`, and `deltaImportQuery`. The `deltaQuery` attribute is responsible for getting the information about users that were modified since the last index. Actually, it only gets the users' unique identifiers and uses the `last_modified` column we added to determine which users were modified since the last import. The `deltaImportQuery` attribute gets users with the appropriate unique identifier (which was returned by `deltaQuery`) to get all the needed information about the user. One thing worth noticing is the way that I used the user identifier in the `deltaImportQuery` attribute; we did this using `${dih.delta.user_id}`. We used the `dih.delta` variable with its `user_id` property (which is the same as the table column name) to refer to the user identifier.

You might notice that I left the `query` attribute in the entity definition. It's left on purpose; you might need to index the full data once again so that the configuration will be useful for full as well as partial imports.

Next, we have a query that shows how to run the delta import. You might notice that compared to the full import, we didn't use the `full-import` command; we sent the `delta-import` command instead.

The statuses that are returned by Solr are the same as those with the full import, so refer to the appropriate chapters to see what information they carry.

One more thing—the delta queries are only supported for the default `SqlEntityProcessor`. This means that you can only use these queries with JDBC data sources.

See also

- For information about the efficiency of a Data Import Handler, full and delta imports, refer to `http://wiki.apache.org/solr/DataImportHandlerDeltaQueryViaFullImport`

Transforming data when using DIH

Data that is stored in our data source is not always in a form we would like it to be indexed in our Solr cluster. For example, imagine that you want to split the first and second names into two fields during indexing because these two reside in a single column in the database and are separated by a whitespace character. Of course, we can modify our database, but in most cases this is not possible. Can we do this? Of course we can, we just need to add some more configuration details to the Data Import Handler configuration. This recipe will show you how to do this.

Getting ready

Refer to the *Indexing data from a database using Data Import Handler* recipe in this chapter.

How to do it...

We will reuse the data from the *Indexing data from a database using Data Import Handler* recipe in this chapter. So, to select users from our table, we use the following SQL query:

```
SELECT user_id, user_name FROM users
```

The response in the text client looks as follows:

```
| user_id | user_name      |
| 1       | John Kowalski  |
| 2       | Amanda Looks   |
```

Our task is to split the first and second names from the `user_name` column and place it in the two fields `firstname` and `secondname`. The steps we need to take are as follows:

1. First, we need to change the index structure so that our field definitions in the `schema.xml` file look as follows:

   ```
   <field name="id" type="string" indexed="true" stored="true"
   required="true"/>
   <field name="firstname" type="string" indexed="true"
   stored="true"/>
   <field name="secondname" type="string" indexed="true"
   stored="true"/>
   <field name="description" type="text" indexed="true"
   stored="true"/>
   ```

2. Now, we need to modify our `db-data-config.xml` file (the one we created earlier) so that it looks as follows:

```
<dataConfig>
 <dataSource driver="org.postgresql.Driver"
url="jdbc:postgresql://localhost:5432/users" user="users"
password="secret" />
<script><![CDATA[
  function splitName(row) {
   var nameTable = row.get('user_name').split(' ');
   row.put('firstname', nameTable[0]);
   row.put('secondname', nameTable[1]);
   row.remove('user_name');
   return row;
  }
 ]]></script>
 <document>
  <entity name="user" transformer="script:splitName" query="SELECT
user_id, user_name, description FROM users">
   <field column="user_id" name="id" />
   <field column="firstname" />
   <field column="secondname" />
   <entity name="user_desc" query="SELECT desc FROM users_
description WHERE user_id=${user.user_id}">
    <field column="desc" name="description" />
   </entity>
  </entity>
 </document>
</dataConfig>
```

3. Now, you can follow the normal indexing procedure that was discussed in the *Indexing data from a database using Data Import Handler* recipe in this chapter.

How it works...

The first two listings are the sample SQL query and result given by a database. Next, we have a field definition part of a `schema.xml` file that defines four fields. Look at the example database rows once again. See the difference? We have four fields in our index structure, while our database rows have only two columns. We must split the contents of the `user_name` column into the two index fields `firstname` and `secondname`. To do this, we will use the JavaScript language and script transformer functionality of the Data Import Handler.

The `solrconfig.xml` file is the same as the one discussed in the *Indexing data from a database using Data Import Handler* recipe in this chapter, so I'll skip this as well.

Next, we have the updated contents of the `db-data-config.xml` file, which we use to define the behavior of the Data Import Handler. The first and biggest difference is the `script` tag that holds our scripts and alters the data. The scripts should be held in the CDATA section. I defined a simple function called `splitName` that takes one parameter, the database row (remember that the functions that operate on the entity data should always take one parameter, which actually is an instance of the `Map<String, Object>` Java object). The first thing in the function is to get the contents of the `user_name` column, split it with the space character, and assign it into a JavaScript array. Then, we create two additional columns in the processed rows `firstname` and `secondname`. The contents of these rows come from the JavaScript table we created. Then, we remove the `user_name` column because we don't want it to be indexed. The last operation is the returning of the processed row.

To enable script processing, you must add one additional attribute to the entity definition; this is the `transformer` attribute with contents similar to that of `script:functionName`. In our example, it looks like `transformer="script:splitName"`. It tells the Data Import Handler to use the defined function name for every row returned by the query.

This is how it works. The rest is the usual indexing process described in the *Indexing data from a database using Data Import Handler* recipe in this chapter, so I'll skip this as well.

There's more...

There is one more thing I want to mention; check out the following section for more information.

Using scripts other than JavaScript

If you want to use a language other than JavaScript, then you have to specify it in the `language` attribute of the `<script>` tag. Just remember that the scripting language that you want to use must be supported by Java. The example definition will look like this:

```
<script language="ECMAScript">…</script>
```

Indexing multiple geographical points

Let's assume we have a website allowing you to search for companies not only using key words but also using a geographical location. In the real world, companies tend to have more than a single location. This is where we hit a limitation in the default spatial field used by Solr; we can only have a single location indexed using it. So, we have to create multiple documents for each company location and use group collapsing, or we can use a different field type that allows multivalued location fields. The recipe will show you how to do the latter.

How to do it...

The following steps will take you through the process of enabling the indexation of multivalued spatial fields.

1. First, we need to prepare our index structure by adding the following section to the `schema.xml` file:

   ```
   <field name="id" type="string" indexed="true" stored="true"
   required="true" />
   <field name="name" type="text_general" indexed="true"
   stored="true" />
   <field name="loc" type="location_recursive" indexed="true"
   stored="true" multiValued="true" />
   ```

2. We also need the `location_recursive` field type defined, so we add the following type to the same `schema.xml` file:

   ```
   <fieldType name="location_recursive" class="solr.
   SpatialRecursivePrefixTreeFieldType" distErrPct="0.025"
   maxDistErr="0.000009" units="degrees" />
   ```

3. Now, we can index our data, which looks as follows:

   ```
   <add>
    <doc>
     <field name="id">1</field>
     <field name="name">Burger Deluxe</field>
     <field name="loc">51.30,-0.12</field>
     <field name="loc">38.89,-77.03</field>
    </doc>
    <doc>
     <field name="id">2</field>
     <field name="name">Chips and fish D.C. exclusive</field>
     <field name="loc">38.89,-77.03</field>
    </doc>
   </add>
   ```

4. So, if we want to get all companies that are located within 50 kilometers from the centre of London, we will send the following query:

   ```
   http://localhost:8983/solr/cookbook/select?q=*:*&fq={!geofilt}&sfi
   eld=loc&pt=51.30,-0.12&d=50
   ```

The results returned by Solr will look as follows:

```
<?xml version="1.0" encoding="UTF-8"?>
<response>
 <lst name="responseHeader">
  <int name="status">0</int>
  <int name="QTime">1</int>
  <lst name="params">
   <str name="q">*:*</str>
   <str name="pt">51.30,-0.12</str>
   <str name="d">50</str>
   <str name="fq">{!geofilt}</str>
   <str name="sfield">loc</str>
  </lst>
 </lst>
 <result name="response" numFound="1" start="0">
  <doc>
   <str name="id">1</str>
   <str name="name">Burger Deluxe</str>
   <arr name="loc">
    <str>51.30,-0.12</str>
    <str>38.89,-77.03</str>
   </arr>
   <long name="_version_">1468077157967200256</long></doc>
 </result>
</response>
```

As we can see, everything works as it should, so let's learn how it was done.

How it works...

Each company is described with three fields: the company identifier (the `id` field), the company name (the `name` field), and multivalued company locations (the `loc` field).

To be able to index multiple locations, we use a new field type that we defined, `location_recursive`. It uses the `solr.SpatialRecursivePrefixTreeFieldType` class, which is new in Solr 4. It offers more features compared to the `solr.LatLonType` field type and is faster when it comes to filtering of spatial data. We configured it using three properties:

- `distErrPct`: This defines the default precision for the fields that store points. The value of the property can vary from `0.0` to `0.5`. The closer the value is to `0`, the more precise the field will be, but the indexing will be slower, and the index will be larger. If we set the value of the property closer to `0.5`, the queries against the field will be faster, but at the cost of less precision.

- `maxDistErr`: This defines the highest level of details required to index data. The default empty value means the detail level is of one meter, about `0.000009` degrees, which is exactly the value we used. The setting is required for the `solr.SpatialRecursivePrefixTreeFieldType` field type to internally calculate a spatial grid.
- `units`: This is the unit used by the type; right now, the only value possible is `degrees`.

As you can see, the first company in our example data has two locations. The first location is the centre of London, and the second location is the centre of Washington, D.C. The second document has a single location, only in Washington, D.C.

Our query asks for all documents (`q=*:*`) and uses the `geofilt` filter (`fq={!geofilt}`). The `geofilt` filter needs three additional parameters to be passed:

- `sfield`: This is the field used for spatial search, our `loc` field.
- `pt`: This is the latitude and longitude of the point from which the distance will be calculated. In our case, it is the centre of London city.
- `d`: This is the distance from the given point. In our case, it is `50`, which means 50 kilometers.

As you can see, only a single document is returned by the query; the first query has the location as London, which means that everything works as it should.

See also

- In addition to indexing multiple geographical points, `solr.SpatialRecursivePrefixTreeFieldType` is also capable of indexing shapes (although Solr needs additional libraries in such cases). If you are interested in such functionalities, refer to the official Solr documentation and the page dedicated to spatial search, which is available at `https://cwiki.apache.org/confluence/display/solr/Spatial+Search`.

Updating document fields

Imagine that you have a system where you store documents your users upload. In addition to this, your users can add other users to have access to the files they uploaded. Before Solr 4, you had to reindex the whole document to update it. With the release of Solr 4 and later versions, we are allowed to update a single field if we fulfill some basic requirements. This recipe will show you how to do this.

How to do it...

Let's look at the steps we need to take to update the document field:

1. For the purpose of the recipe, let's assume we have the following index structure (put the following entries into your `schema.xml` file):

   ```
   <field name="id" type="string" indexed="true" stored="true"
   required="true" />
   <field name="file" type="text_general" indexed="true"
   stored="true"/>
   <field name="count" type="int" indexed="true" stored="true"/>
   <field name="user" type="string" indexed="true" stored="true"
   multiValued="true" />
   ```

2. In addition to this, we need the `_version_` field:

   ```
   <field name="_version_" type="long" indexed="true" stored="true"/>
   ```

   That's all when it comes to the `schema.xml` file.

3. In addition to this, let's assume we have the following data indexed:

   ```
   <add>
    <doc>
     <field name="id">1</field>
     <field name="file">Sample file</field>
     <field name="count">2</field>
     <field name="user">gro</field>
     <field name="user">negativ</field>
    </doc>
   </add>
   ```

4. So, we have a sample file and two usernames specifying which users in our system can access the file. However, what if we want to add another user called `jack`? Is it possible? To add the value to a field that has multiple values, we should send the following command:

   ```
   curl 'localhost:8983/solr/cookbook/update?commit=true' -H
   'Content-type:application/json' -d '[{"id":"1","user":{"add":"ja
   ck"}}]'
   ```

   Let's see if it works by sending the following query:

   ```
   http://localhost:8983/solr/cookbook/select?q=*:*&indent=true
   ```

   The response sent by Solr is as follows:

   ```
   <?xml version="1.0" encoding="UTF-8"?>
   <response>
    <lst name="responseHeader">
     <int name="status">0</int>
     <int name="QTime">0</int>
   ```

```
  <lst name="params">
   <str name="q">*:*</str>
  </lst>
 </lst>
 <result name="response" numFound="1" start="0">
  <doc>
   <str name="id">1</str>
   <str name="file">Sample file</str>
   <int name="count">2</int>
   <arr name="user">
    <str>gro</str>
    <str>negativ</str>
    <str>jack</str>
   </arr>
   <long name="_version_">1467522939960164352</long></doc>
 </result>
</response>
```

As you can see, it works without any problems.

5. Now, imagine that one of the users changed the name of the document, and we want to update the `file` field of this document to match the change. In order to do so, we should send the following command:

   ```
   curl 'localhost:8983/solr/cookbook/update?commit=true' -H
   'Content-type:application/json' -d '[{"id":"1","file":{"set":"New
   file name"}}]'
   ```

6. Again, we send the same query as before to see if the command succeeds:

```
<?xml version="1.0" encoding="UTF-8"?>
<response>
 <lst name="responseHeader">
  <int name="status">0</int>
  <int name="QTime">1</int>
  <lst name="params">
   <str name="q">*:*</str>
  </lst>
 </lst>
 <result name="response" numFound="1" start="0">
  <doc>
   <str name="id">1</str>
   <str name="file">New file name</str>
   <int name="count">2</int>
   <arr name="user">
    <str>gro</str>
    <str>negativ</str>
    <str>jack</str>
   </arr>
   <long name="_version_">1467522994255429632</long></doc>
 </result>
</response>
```

7. Finally, let's increment the `count` field, which specifies how many times the file is accessed. To do this, we run the following command:

```
curl 'localhost:8983/solr/cookbook/update?commit=true' -H
'Content-type:application/json' -d '[{"id":"1","count":{"i
nc":1}}]'
```

8. Again, we send the same query as before to see if the command succeeds:

```
<?xml version="1.0" encoding="UTF-8"?>
<response>
 <lst name="responseHeader">
  <int name="status">0</int>
  <int name="QTime">1</int>
  <lst name="params">
   <str name="q">*:*</str>
  </lst>
 </lst>
 <result name="response" numFound="1" start="0">
  <doc>
   <str name="id">1</str>
   <str name="file">New file name</str>
   <int name="count">3</int>
   <arr name="user">
    <str>gro</str>
    <str>negativ</str>
    <str>jack</str>
   </arr>
   <long name="_version_">1467523747367878656</long></doc>
 </result>
</response>
```

Again, the command works well. So, let's see how Solr does this.

How it works...

As you can see, the index structure is pretty simple; we have the document identifier and its name and users that can access the file. As you can see, all the fields in the index are marked as `stored` (`stored="true"`). This is required for the partial update functionality to work. This is because, under the hood, Solr takes all the values from the fields and updates the one we tell it to update. So, it is just a typical document indexing, but instead of you having to provide all the information, it's Solr's responsibility to get it from the index.

Another thing that is required for the atomic update functionality to work is the `_version_` field. You don't have to set it during indexation; it is used internally by Solr. The example data we index is also very simple. It is a single document with two users defined.

The interesting stuff comes with the `update` command. As you can see, this command is run against a standard update handler you run indexation against. The `commit=true` parameter tells Solr to perform the commit operation right after update. The `-H 'Content-type:application/json'` part is responsible for setting the correct HTTP headers for the update request.

Next, we have the request contents. It is sent as a JSON object. We specify that we are interested in the document with identifier `1` (`"id":"1"`). We want to change the `user` field and add the `jack` value to this field (the `add` command). So, as you can see, the `add` command is used when we want to add a new value to a field that can hold multiple values.

The second command shows how to change the value of a single-valued field. It is very similar to what we had before, but instead of using the `add` command, we use the `set` command. Again, as you can see, it works perfectly.

The third command shown in the recipe illustrates how to increment a field. We can run this command against any numeric field. We need to use the `inc` command and specify a number that will be added to the value of the field in the index. In our case, we add `1`.

Note that apart from the `add`, `set`, and `inc` commands, we can also remove values (the `remove` command) using regex (the `removeregex` command). The number of commands can grow with time, so keep an eye on `https://cwiki.apache.org/confluence/display/solr/Updating+Parts+of+Documents`.

Detecting the document language during indexation

Imagine a situation when you have users from different countries and you would like to give them a choice to only see content you index that is written in their native language. However, there is one problem; your documents don't have their language identified, so we need to do this ourselves. Let's see how we can identify the language of the documents during indexing time and store this information along with the documents in the index for later use.

How to do it...

For language identification, we will use one of the Solr contribution modules, but let's start from the beginning:

1. For the purpose of the recipe, I assume that we will use the following index structure (we just need to add the following to the `schema.xml` file):

```
<field name="id" type="string" indexed="true" stored="true"
required="true" multiValued="false" />
<field name="name" type="text_general" indexed="true"
stored="true"/>
```

```
<field name="description" type="text_general" indexed="true"
stored="true" />
<field name="langId" type="string" indexed="true" stored="true" />
```

2. The next thing we need to do is create a `langid` directory somewhere on your filesystem (I'll assume that the directory is created in the same directory that Solr is installed and on the same level as the `lib` directory of Solr) and copy the following libraries to this directory:
   - `solr-langid-4.10.0.jar` (from the `dist` directory of the Apache Solr distribution)
   - `jsonic-1.2.7.jar` (from the `contrib/langid/lib` directory of the Apache Solr distribution)
   - `langdetect-1.1-20120112.jar` (from the `contrib/langid/lib` directory of the Apache Solr distribution)
3. The next step is to inform Solr that it should load the libraries we just copied. We do this by adding the following information to the `solrconfig.xml` file:

```
<lib dir="../../langid/" regex=".*\.jar" />
```

4. In addition to this, we configure a new update processor by adding the following to the `config` section of the `solrconfig.xml` file:

```
<updateRequestProcessorChain name="langid">
 <processor class="org.apache.solr.update.processor.
LangDetectLanguageIdentifierUpdateProcessorFactory">
  <str name="langid.fl">name,description</str>
  <str name="langid.langField">langId</str>
  <str name="langid.fallback">en</str>
 </processor>
 <processor class="solr.LogUpdateProcessorFactory" />
 <processor class="solr.RunUpdateProcessorFactory" />
</updateRequestProcessorChain>
```

5. Now, we need some data to be indexed. I decided to use the following test data that contains the same document in two languages, English and German (stored in the `data.xml` file):

```
<add>
 <doc>
  <field name="id">1</field>
  <field name="name">First</field>
```

```
  <field name="description">Water is a chemical substance with the
chemical formula H2O. A water molecule contains one oxygen and two
hydrogen atoms connected by covalent bonds. Water is a liquid at
ambient conditions, but it often co-exists on Earth with its solid
state, ice, and gaseous state (water vapor or steam). Water also
exists in a liquid crystal state near hydrophilic surfaces.[1]
[2] Under nomenclature used to name chemical compounds, Dihydrogen
monoxide is the scientific name for water, though it is almost
never used.</field>
 </doc>
 <doc>
  <field name="id">2</field>
  <field name="name">Zweite</field>
  <field name="description">Wasser (H2O) ist eine chemische
Verbindung aus den Elementen Sauerstoff (O) und Wasserstoff
(H). Wasser ist die einzige chemische Verbindung auf der Erde,
die in der Natur in allen drei Aggregatzuständen vorkommt.
Die Bezeichnung Wasser wird dabei besonders für den flüssigen
Aggregatzustand verwendet. Im festen (gefrorenen) Zustand spricht
man von Eis, im gasförmigen Zustand von Wasserdampf.</field>
 </doc>
</add>
```

6. Now, let's index the data. To index the preceding test file, use the following commands:

```
curl 'http://localhost:8983/solr/cookbook/update?update.
chain=langid' --data-binary @data.xml -H 'Content-
type:application/xml'
```

```
curl 'http://localhost:8983/solr/cookbook/update?update.
chain=langid' --data-binary '<commit/>' -H 'Content-
type:application/xml'
```

7. After sending the previous two queries, we can finally test if they work. We will just ask Solr to return all the documents by sending the `q=*:*` query. Solr returns the following results:

```
<?xml version="1.0" encoding="UTF-8"?>
<response>
 <lst name="responseHeader">
  <int name="status">0</int>
  <int name="QTime">0</int>
  <lst name="params">
   <str name="q">*:*</str>
   <str name="indent">true</str>
```

```
  </lst>
 </lst>
 <result name="response" numFound="2" start="0">
  <doc>
   <str name="id">1</str>
   <str name="name">First</str>
   <str name="description">&gt;Water is a chemical substance with
the chemical formula H2O. A water molecule contains one oxygen and
two hydrogen atoms connected by covalent bonds. Water is a liquid
at ambient conditions, but it often co-exists on Earth with its
solid state, ice, and gaseous state (water vapor or steam). Water
also exists in a liquid crystal state near hydrophilic surfaces.
[1][2] Under nomenclature used to name chemical compounds,
Dihydrogen monoxide is the scientific name for water, though it is
almost never used.</str>
   <str name="langId">en</str>
   <long name="_version_">1467520138652680192</long></doc>
  <doc>
   <str name="id">2</str>
   <str name="name">Zweite</str>
   <str name="description">Wasser (H2O) ist eine chemische
Verbindung aus den Elementen Sauerstoff (O) und Wasserstoff
(H). Wasser ist die einzige chemische Verbindung auf der Erde,
die in der Natur in allen drei Aggregatzuständen vorkommt.
Die Bezeichnung Wasser wird dabei besonders für den flüssigen
Aggregatzustand verwendet. Im festen (gefrorenen) Zustand spricht
man von Eis, im gasförmigen Zustand von Wasserdampf.</str>
   <str name="langId">de</str>
   <long name="_version_">1467520138716643328</long></doc>
 </result>
</response>
```

As you can see, the `langId` field is filled with the correct language.

How it works...

The index structure we use is quite simple; it contains four fields, and we are most interested in the `langId` field that won't be supplied with the data. However, instead of this, we want Solr to fill it.

Note that language detection doesn't do any language-specific analysis.

The mentioned libraries are needed in order for language identification to work. The `lib` entry in the `solrconfig.xml` file tells Solr to look for all the JAR files from the `langid` directory we created. Remember to change the `dir` property to reflect your setup.

Now, the update request processor chain definition comes. We need this definition to include our `org.apache.solr.update.processor.LangDetectLanguageIdentifierUpdateProcessorFactory` processor in order to detect the document language. The `langid.fl` property tells the defined processor which fields should be used to detect the language. The `langid.langField` property specifies to which field the detected language should be written. The last property, `langid.fallback`, tells the language detection library what language should be set if it fails to detect a language. The `solr.LogUpdateProcessorFactory` and `solr.RunUpdateProcessorFactory` processors log the updates and actually run them. Also, it is worth mentioning that we used the language detection library available at `https://code.google.com/p/language-detection/`, which detects 53 languages right now and is based on the naïve Bayesian filter.

As for data indexing, in order to use the defined update request processor chain, we need to tell Solr that we want it to be used. In order to do this, when sending data to Solr, we specify an additional parameter called `update.chain` with the name of the update chain we want to use, which in our case is `langid`. The `--data-binary` switch tells the `curl` command to send data in a binary format, and the `-H` switch tells `curl` which content type should be used. In the end, we send the `commit` command to write the data to the Lucene index. One thing to remember is that we can include our update chain name in the update handler configuration so that it can be used automatically.

There's more...

If you don't want to use the aforementioned processor to detect the document language, you can use the one that uses the Apache Tika library.

Language identification based on Apache Tika

If the `LangDetectLanguageIdentifierUpdateProcessorFactory` class is not good enough for you, you can try using language identification based on the Apache Tika library. In order to do this, you need to provide all the libraries from the `contrib/extraction` directory in the Apache Solr distribution package instead of the ones from `contrib/langid/lib`, and instead of using the `org.apache.solr.update.processor.LangDetectLanguageIdentifierUpdateProcessorFactory` processor, use `org.apache.solr.update.processor.TikaLanguageIdentifierUpdateProcessorFactory`. So, the final configuration should look like this:

```
<updateRequestProcessorChain name="langid">
 <processor class="org.apache.solr.update.processor.
TikaLanguageIdentifierUpdateProcessorFactory">
```

```
    <str name="langid.fl">name,description</str>
    <str name="langid.langField">langId</str>
    <str name="langid.fallback">en</str>
  </processor>
  <processor class="solr.LogUpdateProcessorFactory" />
  <processor class="solr.RunUpdateProcessorFactory" />
</updateRequestProcessorChain>
```

However, remember to still specify the `update.chain` parameter during indexing, or add the defined processor to your update handler configuration.

Optimizing the primary key indexation

Most of the data stored in Solr has some kind of primary key. Primary keys are different from most of the fields in your data as each document has a unique value stored because they are primary, and in most cases, unique. However, this search on the primary field is not always as fast as you would expect when you compare to other databases. So, is there anything we can do to make it faster? With Solr 4.0, we can, and this recipe will show you how to improve the execution time of queries run against unique fields in Solr.

Keep in mind that the method shown in this recipe is very case dependent, and you might not see a great performance increase with the mentioned change. What's more, if you are using the newest version of Solr/Lucene, the pulsing codec is already a part of the default Lucene posting format.

How to do it...

1. Let's assume we have the following field defined as the unique key for our Solr collection. So, in your `schema.xml` file, you will have the following:

   ```
   <field name="id" type="string" indexed="true" stored="true"
   required="true" />
   ```

2. Of course, we have the following entry in the `schema.xml` file:

   ```
   <uniqueKey>id</uniqueKey>
   ```

3. Now, we will want to use Lucene's flexible indexing and `PulsingCodec` to handle the `id` field. In order to do this, we introduce the following field type (just place it in the `types` section of your `schema.xml` file):

   ```
   <fieldType name="string_pulsing" class="solr.StrField"
   postingsFormat="Pulsing40"/>
   ```

4. In addition to this, we need to change the `id` field definition to use the new type. So, we should change the `type` attribute from `string` to `string_pulsing`:

```
<field name="id" type="string_pulsing" indexed="true"
stored="true" required="true" />
```

5. Also, we need to put the following entry in the `solrconfig.xml` file:

```
<codecFactory class="solr.SchemaCodecFactory"/>
```

That's all. Now, you can start indexing your data.

How it works...

The changes we made use the new feature introduced in Apache Lucene 4.0 and Solr; it's the so-called *flexible indexing*. It allows us to modify the way data is written into an inverted index, and thus, configure it to our own needs. In the previous example, we used the `PulsingCodec` (`postingsFormat="Pulsing40"`) in order to store the unique values in a special way. The idea behind this codec is that the data for low-frequency terms is written in a special way to save a single I/O seek operation when retrieving documents for those terms from the index. This is why, in some cases, when you do a noticeable amount of searches to your unique field (or any high cardinality field indexed with `PulsingCodec`), you can see a drastic performance increase for the fields.

The last change, the one we made to the `solrconfig.xml` file, is required; without it, Solr will not let us use specified codes and will throw an exception during startup. It just specifies which codec factory should be used to create codec instances.

See also

- For more information about pulsing codec, take a look at the Mike McCandless blog available at `http://blog.mikemccandless.com/2010/06/lucenes-pulsingcodec-on-primary-key.html`

Handling multiple currencies

Imagine a situation where you run an e-commerce site and sell your products all over the world. One day, you say that you want to calculate the currencies by yourself and have all the goodies that Solr gives you on all the currencies you support. You can, of course, add multiple fields, one for each currency. On the other hand, you can use the new functionality introduced in Solr 4 and create a field that will use the provided currency exchange rates. This recipe will show you how to configure and use multiple currencies using a single field in the index.

How to do it...

1. Let's start with creating a sample index structure by modifying the `schema.xml` file so that the field definition looks like this:

```
<field name="id" type="string" indexed="true" stored="true"
required="true" />
<field name="name" type="text_general" indexed="true"
stored="true" />
<field name="price" type="currencyField" indexed="true"
stored="true" />
```

2. In addition to this, we need to provide the definition for the type the `price` field is based on (again we add the following to the `schema.xml` file):

```
<fieldType class="solr.CurrencyField" name="currencyField"
defaultCurrency="USD" currencyConfig="currencyExchange.xml" />
```

3. Another file that we need to create is the `currencyExchange.xml` file, which should be placed in the `conf` directory of your collection and contain the following:

```
<?xml version="1.0" ?>
<currencyConfig version="1.0">
 <rates>
  <rate from="USD" to="EUR" rate="0.743676" comment="European
Euro" />
  <rate from="USD" to="HKD" rate="7.801922" comment="HONG KONG
Dollar" />
  <rate from="USD" to="GBP" rate="0.647910" comment="UNITED
KINGDOM Pound" />
 </rates>
</currencyConfig>
```

4. Now we can index some example data. For the usage of this recipe, I decided to index the following documents:

```
<add>
 <doc>
  <field name="id">1</field>
  <field name="name">Test document one</field>
  <field name="price">10.10,USD</field>
 </doc>
 <doc>
  <field name="id">2</field>
  <field name="name">Test document two</field>
  <field name="price">12.01,USD</field>
 </doc>
</add>
```

5. Now, let's check if this works. Our second document costs `12.01 USD`, and we define the exchange rate for the Euro to `0.743676`. This gives us about 7.5 EUR for the first document, and about 8.9 EUR for the second document. Let's check this by sending the following query to Solr:

```
http://localhost:8983/solr/cookbook/select?q=name:document&fq=pric
e:[8.00,EUR TO 9.00,EUR]
```

The result returned by Solr is the following:

```
<?xml version="1.0" encoding="UTF-8"?>
<response>
 <lst name="responseHeader">
  <int name="status">0</int>
  <int name="QTime">1</int>
  <lst name="params">
   <str name="fq">price:[8.00,EUR TO 9.00,EUR]</str>
   <str name="q">name:document</str>
  </lst>
 </lst>
 <result name="response" numFound="1" start="0">
  <doc>
   <str name="id">2</str>
   <str name="name">Test document two</str>
   <str name="price">12.01,USD</str>
   <long name="_version_">1467445704565719040</long>
  </doc>
 </result>
</response>
```

As you can see, we got the document we wanted.

How it works...

The idea behind the functionality is simple—we create a field based on a certain type and provide a file with the currency exchange rate, that's all. After this, we can query our Solr instance with the use of all the currencies we defined exchange rates for. Now, let's discuss all the preceding configuration changes in detail.

The index structure is very simple; it contains three fields of which one is responsible for holding the price of the document and is based on the `currencyField` type. The mentioned type is based on `solr.CurrencyField`. Its `defaultCurrency` attribute specifies the default currency for all the fields using this type. This is important because Solr will return prices in the defined default currency, no matter what currency is used during the query. The `currencyConfig` attribute specifies the name of the file with the exchange rate definition.

Our `currencyExchange.xml` file provides the exchange rates for three currencies:

- EUR
- HKD
- GBP

The file should be structured similar to the previous example. This means that each exchange rate should have the `from` attribute telling Solr from which currency the exchange will be done, the `to` attribute specifying to which currency the exchange will be done, and the `rate` attribute specifying the actual exchange rate. In addition to this, it can also have the `comment` attribute if we want to include some short comment.

During indexing, we need to specify the currency we want the data to be indexed with. In the previous example, we indexed data with USD. This is done by specifying the price, a comma character, and the currency code after it. So, the `10.10,USD` value will mean 10 dollars and 10 cents in USD.

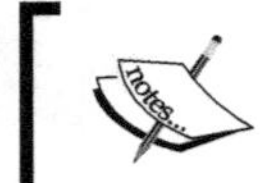

Note that in order for Solr to be able to handle currency exchange between two currencies, we need to provide the direct conversion rate between these two currencies.

If you need to reload the `currencyExchange.xml` file, you will need to reload the core (or collection) for Solr to see the changes. If you use the master-slave deployment, slave servers will reload the core upon finishing fetching the new index and new version of the `currencyExchange.xml` file, which will be loaded (of course, if it is configured to be replicated).

The last thing is the query. As you can see, you can query Solr with currencies different from the one used during indexing. This is possible because of the provided exchange rate file. As you can see, when we use a `range` query for a `price` field, we specify the value, colon character, and currency code after it. Remember that if you provide a currency code unknown to Solr, it will throw an exception saying that the currency is not known.

There's more...

You can also have the exchange rates updated automatically by specifying the currency provider.

Setting up your own currency provider

Specifying the currency exchange rate file is great, but we need to update this file because the exchange rates change constantly. Luckily for us, Solr committers thought about it and gave us the option to provide an exchange rate provider instead of a plain file. The provider is a class responsible for providing the exchange rate data. The default exchange rate provider available in Solr uses exchange rates from `http://openexchangerates.org`, which are updated hourly. In order to use it, we need to modify our `currencyField` field type definition and introduce three new properties (and remove the `currencyConfig` property):

- `providerClass`: This is the class implementing the exchange rates provider, which in our case will be the default available in Solr, which is `solr.OpenExchangeRatesOrgProvider`
- `refreshInterval`: This defines how often to refresh the rates (specified in minutes)
- `ratesFileLocation`: This is the location of the file with rates in an open exchange format

So, the final configuration should look like this:

```
<fieldType name="currencyField" class="solr.CurrencyField"
providerClass="solr.OpenExchangeRatesOrgProvider"
refreshInterval="120" ratesFileLocation="http://192.168.10.10/latest.
json"/>
```

You can download the sample exchange file from the `http://openexchangerates.org` site after creating an account.

3
Analyzing Your Text Data

In this chapter, we will cover the following topics:

- Using the enumeration type
- Removing HTML tags during indexing
- Storing data outside of Solr index
- Using synonyms
- Stemming different languages
- Using nonaggressive stemmers
- Using the n-gram approach to do performant trailing wildcard searches
- Using position increment to divide sentences
- Using patterns to replace tokens

Introduction

The process of data indexing can be divided into parts. One of the parts is data analysis. It's one of the crucial parts of data preparation. It defines how your data will be divided into terms from text, and what type it will be. The Solr data parsing behavior is defined by types. A type's behavior can be defined in the context of the indexing process, query process, or both. Furthermore, the type definition is composed of a tokenizer (or multiple tokenizers, some for querying and some for indexing) and filters (both token and character filters). A **tokenizer** specifies how your data will be preprocessed after it is sent to the appropriate field. An analyzer operates on the whole data that is sent to the field. Types can only have one tokenizer. The result of the tokenizer is a stream of objects called tokens.

Next in the analysis chain are the filters. They operate on the tokens in the token stream. They can do anything with the tokens—changing, removing, or making them lowercase are just a few examples. Types can have multiple filters, which are run one after another.

One additional type of filter is the character filter. It does not operate on tokens from the token stream. It operates on non-tokenized data and is invoked before being sent to the analyzer. This chapter will focus on data analysis and how to handle day-to-day analysis questions and problems. You'll see how to use char filters, tokenizers, and of course, the filters.

Using the enumeration type

Imagine that we use Solr to store information about our environment's state, error, and events related to them—a simple solution that will work as a simple log centralization solution. For our simple use case, we will store the identifier of the message, the information, what type of event it is, and the severity of the event, showing us how important the event is. However, what we will want to be sure of is that the `severity` field contains only values from a given list. To achieve all this, we will use the Solr enumeration type.

How to do it...

To achieve our requirements, we will have to perform the following steps:

1. We will start with the index structure. Our field list from the `schema.xml` file will look as follows:

   ```
   <field name="id" type="string" indexed="true" stored="true"
   required="true" />
   <field name="problem" type="text_general" indexed="true"
   stored="true" />
   <field name="severity" type="enum_type" indexed="true"
   stored="true" />
   ```

2. In addition to this, we will need `enum_type` to be defined. To do this, we add the following entry to the `schema.xml` file:

   ```
   <fieldType name="enum_type" class="solr.EnumField"
   enumsConfig="enumsConfig.xml" enumName="severity"/>
   ```

3. Now, we need to create the `enumsConfig.xml` file to hold our enumeration values. The content of the file will look as follows:

   ```
   <?xml version="1.0" ?>
   <enumsConfig>
    <enum name="severity">
     <value>Ignore</value>
     <value>Low</value>
   ```

```
  <value>Medium</value>
  <value>High</value>
  <value>Critical</value>
 </enum>
</enumsConfig>
```

4. Finally, we can index our test data, which looks as follows:

```
<doc>
  <field name="id">1</field>
  <field name="problem">Service unavailable</field>
  <field name="severity">Critical</field>
 </doc>
 <doc>
  <field name="id">2</field>
  <field name="problem">Logging error</field>
  <field name="severity">Low</field>
 </doc>
 <doc>
  <field name="id">3</field>
  <field name="problem">Disk space low on node1</field>
  <field name="severity">High</field>
 </doc>
</add>
```

5. Now, if we want to search for all the events that have the severity level high or critical, and sort them on this basis, we can run the following query:

```
http://localhost:8983/solr/cookbook/select?q=*:*&sort=severity+des
c&fq=severity:(Critical+OR+High)
```

6. In return, Solr will respond with the following result:

```
<?xml version="1.0" encoding="UTF-8"?>
<response>
 <lst name="responseHeader">
  <int name="status">0</int>
  <int name="QTime">1</int>
  <lst name="params">
   <str name="q">*:*</str>
   <str name="indent">true</str>
   <str name="sort">severity desc</str>
   <str name="fq">severity:(Critical OR High)</str>
  </lst>
 </lst>
```

```
<result name="response" numFound="2" start="0">
 <doc>
  <str name="id">1</str>
  <str name="problem">Service unavailable</str>
  <str name="severity">Critical</str>
  <long name="_version_">1470159603541999616</long></doc>
 <doc>
  <str name="id">3</str>
  <str name="problem">Disk space low on node1</str>
  <str name="severity">High</str>
  <long name="_version_">1470159603544096769</long></doc>
</result>
</response>
```

Now, let's look at how it works.

How it works...

As you can see, our index structure is rather simple. It consists of three fields; the `id` field holds the document identifier, the `problem` field contains event description, and the `severity` field contains information about the event importance. The interesting thing is the `severity` field that is defined using the new `enum_type` type.

Our new `enum_type` type uses `solr.EnumField` as its implementation class. It also tells Solr the enumeration value definition files that should be used (in our case, it is `enumsConfig.xml` stored in the same directory as the rest of the configuration). Finally, we have the `enumName` property, which tells Solr which section of the mentioned `enumsConfig.xml` file to use.

The `enumsConfig.xml` file stores our enumeration values. The root tag called `<enumsConfig>` can store multiple `<enum>` entries, each defined with the `name` property. The value of the `name` property of the `<enum>` tag should be the same as the value of the `enumName` property in our previously defined type. It allows us to handle multiple enumeration types in a single configuration file.

Now, if we look at our data, we can see that the values of the document `severity` field contain one of the values defined in the `enumsConfig.xml` file. If we try to index the document with a value that is not present in the configuration, Solr will throw an error and reject the document. Also, remember that when changing the `enumsConfig.xml` file, you should reindex your data.

Finally, the query shows that the field using the new enumeration type can be used for querying, filtering, and sorting. The sort order will depend on the order of the enumeration value definitions.

Removing HTML tags during indexing

There are many real-life situations when you have to clean your data. Let's assume that you want to index web pages that your client sends you. You don't know anything about the structure of the page; one thing you know is that you must provide a search mechanism that will enable searching through the content of the pages. Of course, you can index the whole page splitting it by whitespaces, but then you will probably hear the client complain about the HTML tags being searchable, and so on. So, before we enable searching on the contents of the page, we need to clean the data. In this recipe, we will see how to remove the HTML tags with Solr.

How to do it...

Now, let's take a look at the steps needed to remove the HTML tags from our data.

1. We start by assuming that our data looks like this:

```
<add>
 <doc>
  <field name="id">1</field>
  <field name="html"><![CDATA[<html><head><title>My page</title></
head><body><p>This is a <b>my</b><i>sample</i> page</body></
html>]]></field>
 </doc>
</add>
```

2. Now, let's take care of the `schema.xml` file. First, we need to add the type definition to the `schema.xml` file:

```
<fieldType name="html_strip" class="solr.TextField">
 <analyzer>
  <charFilter class="solr.HTMLStripCharFilterFactory"/>
  <tokenizer class="solr.WhitespaceTokenizerFactory"/>
  <filter class="solr.LowerCaseFilterFactory"/>
 </analyzer>
</fieldType>
```

3. The next step is to add the following to the field definition part of the `schema.xml` file:

```
<field name="id" type="string" indexed="true" stored="true"
required="true" />
<field name="html" type="html_strip" indexed="true" stored="false"
/>
```

4. We can now index our data and have the HTML tags removed. Let's check this by going to the analysis section of Solr administration pages and passing the <html><head><title>My page</title></head><body><p>This is a <b>my</b><i>sample</i> page</body></html> text to analyze, as shown in the following screenshot:

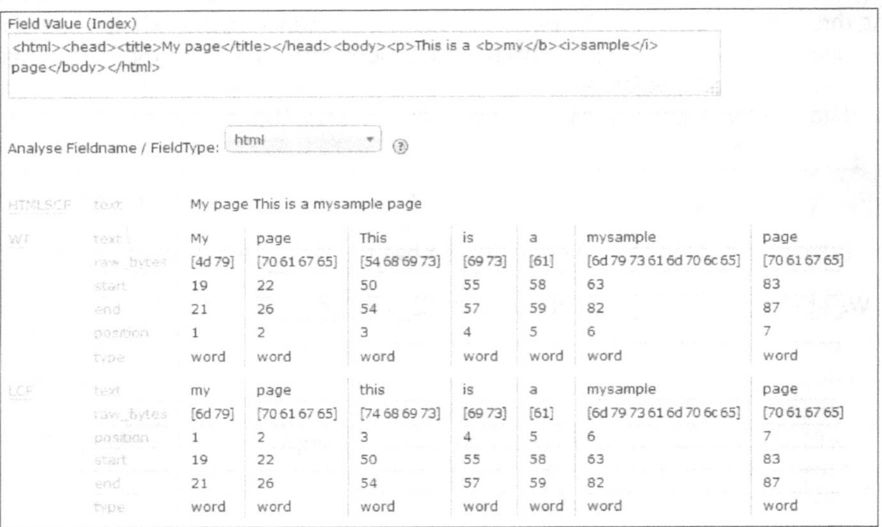

How it works...

First, we have the data example. In the example, we see one file with two fields, the identifier, and some HTML data nested in the CDATA section. You must remember to surround the HTML data with CDATA tags if they are full pages and start from HTML tags, as shown in our example. Otherwise, Solr will have problems parsing the data. However, if you only have some tags present in the data, you shouldn't worry.

Next, we have the html_strip field type definition. It is based on solr.TextField to enable a full-field analysis. Following this we have a character filter that handles the HTML and XML tag stripping. The character filters are invoked before the data is sent to the tokenizer. This way, they can operate on untokenized data. In our case, the character filter strips the HTML and XML tags, attributes, and so on, and then sends the data to the tokenizer that splits it by whitespace characters. The one and only filter defined in our type makes the tokens lowercase to simplify the search.

If you want to check how your data was indexed, remember not to be mistaken when you choose to store the field contents (the stored="true" attribute). The stored value is the original one sent to Solr, so you won't be able to see the filters in action.

If you wish to check the actual data structures, take a look at the Luke utility (a utility that lets you see the index structure and field values and operates on the index). Luke can be found by visiting `http://code.google.com/p/luke`. Instead of using Luke, I decided to use the analysis capabilities of Solr administration pages and see how the `html` field behaves when we pass the example value provided in the example data file.

There's more...

There is one additional thing that I would like to mention, which is mentioned in the following section.

Preserving defined tags

Sometimes, you might want to preserve some of the tags that are part of the input document. To do this, you can include the `escapedTags` property that should contain a comma-separated list of tags we want to preserve. For example, if you want Solr to preserve and escape the `title` tags, our `solr.HTMLStripCharFilterFactory` configuration will look as follows:

```
<charFilter class="solr.HTMLStripCharFilterFactory" escapedTags="a,
title" />
```

See also

Instead of using the char filter factory, we can use the update request processor for removing the HTML tags. It might be useful if you only need to remove HTML tags from some documents. In such cases, you should define multiple update request processor chains, but only one will have the HTML tag removing processor. If you want to do this, refer to the `solr.HTMLStripFieldUpdateProcessorFactory` Javadoc available at `http://lucene.apache.org/solr/4_10_0/solr-core/org/apache/solr/update/processor/HTMLStripFieldUpdateProcessorFactory.html`.

Storing data outside of Solr index

Although Solr allows us to use the partial update API to update a single field of our document, what it does in the background is the complete reindexing of a document. However, there are situations where such reindexing is not possible. For example, we can have an index containing articles about published books, and we can store the information on how many users visited this article and read it. The number of users is so high that we have thousands of updates per second. Sending a high amount of updates can be demanding for Solr; however, we can store such information in external files and use it for boosting or sorting. This recipe will show how to do this.

How to do it...

The following steps are needed to achieve our requirements:

1. First of all, we will create the index structure by adding the following field definition to our `schema.xml` file:

   ```
   <field name="name" type="text_general" indexed="true"
   stored="true" />
   <field name="visits" type="visitsType" />
   ```

2. Next, we will define the `visitsType` field type by adding the following section to the `schema.xml` file:

   ```
   <fieldType name="visitsType" class="solr.ExternalFileField"
   keyField="id" defVal="0" stored="false" indexed="false"
   valType="float"/>
   ```

3. We also need to put a file called `external_visits` to the directory, where the Solr index directory is located (it is usually the `data` directory and not the `data/index` directory). The contents of the `external_visits` file looks like this:

   ```
   1=1.0
   2=5.0
   ```

4. Our example data looks as follows:

   ```
   <add>
    <doc>
     <field name="id">1</field>
     <field name="name">Solr Cookbook released</field>
    </doc>
    <doc>
     <field name="id">2</field>
     <field name="name">Elasticsearch server released</field>
    </doc>
   </add>
   ```

5. Finally, we can run our query, for example a query that returns all the documents with the `released` term in the `name` field, sorted in descending order by the number of visits:

   ```
   http://localhost:8983/solr/cookbook/select?q=name:released&sort=fi
   eld(visits)+desc
   ```

6. The results returned by Solr will be as follows:

```
<?xml version="1.0" encoding="UTF-8"?>
<response>
 <lst name="responseHeader">
  <int name="status">0</int>
  <int name="QTime">15</int>
  <lst name="params">
   <str name="q">name:released</str>
   <str name="sort">field(visits) desc</str>
  </lst>
 </lst>
 <result name="response" numFound="2" start="0">
  <doc>
   <str name="id">2</str>
   <str name="name">Elasticsearch server released</str>
   <long name="_version_">1470198928794189824</long></doc>
  <doc>
   <str name="id">1</str>
   <str name="name">Solr Cookbook released</str>
   <long name="_version_">1470198928742809600</long></doc>
 </result>
</response>
```

Now, let's see how it works.

How it works...

Our index structure is built of three fields; the `id` field holds the unique identifier of our articles, the `name` field holds its name, and the `visits` field holds the number of visits for each document.

The `visits` field is the one we are interested in the most. It uses a new type, the `visitsType` field type. We defined the type by using the `solr.ExternalFileField` class, which tells Solr that we will store the values for this field in an external file. To use this type, we need to provide a few properties specific to the field type:

- `keyField`: This is the name of the field that is used to differentiate documents. Usually, we set the value of the property to the name of the primary key, but in general, it should point Solr to a field that can be used to differentiate documents.
- `defVal`: This is the default value of the field using the field type, when no value for the given document is found in the external field. So, in our case, if a document identifier with a value can't be found in the external field, it will be given a value of `0`.
- `valType`: This is the name of the type that will be used for values in the external field. It can be any float-based field type; in our case, it is one of the default, simple type provided in the example Solr schema.

Finally, we have the `external_visits` file. As I already mentioned, this file needs to be placed in the same directory as the directory in which Solr stores the index for the collection (or core). This is because Solr will load the file during startup and reload along with each searcher reopening (the hard commit with searcher reopening or the soft commit). The naming scheme of the file is really simple; it consists of the constant external part concatenated with the name of the field that uses the external field type; in our case, it is `external_visits`. When it comes to the contents, this is also not complicated; it contains pairs of document identifiers (matching the values from the field defined by the `keyField` property) and the float values, which in our case is the number of visits. The identifier and value must be concatenated with the = character. We don't need to sort the values in the file, but Solr will work slightly faster when the values in the external field are sorted on the basis of the document identifier.

Finally, as you can see in the query result, the data is sorted properly. We can also use the value for boosting, but we can't search on the data stored in the external field type; Solr just doesn't allow this.

Using synonyms

Let's assume we have an e-commerce client and we are providing a search system based on Solr. Our index has thousands of documents that mainly consist of books and everything works fine. Then, one day, someone from the marketing department comes into your office and says that he wants to be able to find books that have the word *machine* when he types *electronics* into the search box. The first thing that comes to mind is "hey, do it in the source and I'll index that". However, this is not an option this time because there can be many documents in the database that have those words. We don't want to change the whole database. This is when synonyms come into play, and this recipe will show you how to use synonyms.

How to do it...

To make the example as simple as possible, I assumed that we only have two fields in our index.

1. Let's start with defining our index structure by adding the following field definition section to the `schema.xml` file:

   ```
   <field name="id" type="string" indexed="true" stored="true"
   required="true" />
   <field name="description" type="text_syn" indexed="true"
   stored="true" />
   ```

2. Now, let's add the `text_syn` field type definition to the `schema.xml` file, as shown in the code snippet:

```
<fieldType name="text_syn" class="solr.TextField">
 <analyzer type="query">
  <tokenizer class="solr.WhitespaceTokenizerFactory"/>
  <filter class="solr.LowerCaseFilterFactory"/>
 </analyzer>
 <analyzer type="index">
  <tokenizer class="solr.WhitespaceTokenizerFactory"/>
  <filter class="solr.SynonymFilterFactory" synonyms="synonyms.
txt" ignoreCase="true" expand="false" />
  <filter class="solr.LowerCaseFilterFactory"/>
 </analyzer>
</fieldType>
```

3. As you noticed, there is a file already mentioned, which is `synonyms.txt`. Let's take a look at its contents:

```
machine => electronics
```

The `synonyms.txt` file should be placed in the same directory as other configuration files are placed in the `conf` directory.

4. Finally, we can look at the analysis page of the Solr administration panel to see if the synonyms are properly recognized and applied:

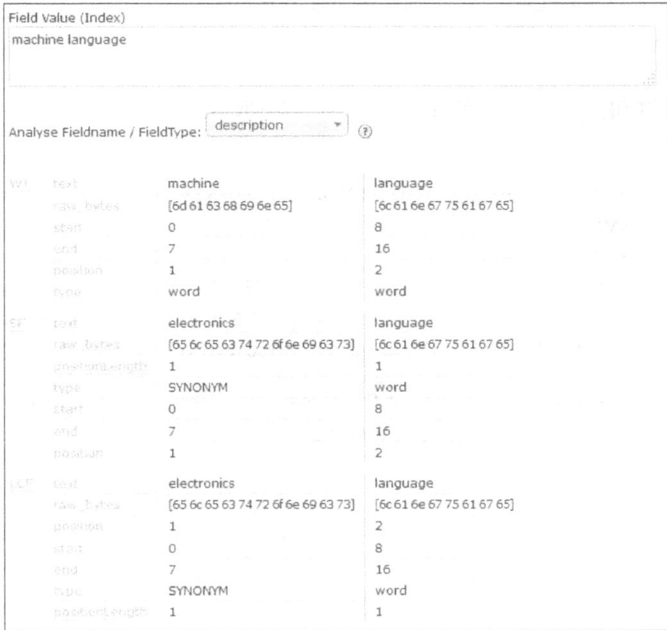

How it works...

First, we have our field definition. There are two fields, identifier (the `id` field) and description (the `description` field). The second field should be our interest right at the moment. It's based on the new field type, `text_syn`, the definition of which is shown in the second listing.

Now the new type, `text_syn`, is based on the `solr.TextField` class, so we will analyze it. Its definition is divided; it behaves in one way while indexing (the `<analyzer type="query">` section) and in a different way while querying (the `<analyzer type="index">` section).

The first thing we see is the query time analyzer definition. It consists of the tokenizer that splits the data on the basis of white space characters (`solr.WhitespaceTokenizerFactory`), and then the lowercase filter makes all the tokens lowercased.

The interesting part is the index time behavior. It starts with the same tokenizer, but then the synonyms filter comes into play. Its definition starts like all the other filters, with the factory definition, which is the `solr.SynonymFilterFactory` class. Next, we have a `synonyms` attribute that defines which file contains the synonyms definition. Following this, we have the `ignoreCase` attribute that tells Solr to ignore the case of the tokens and the contents of the synonyms file (because its value is set to `true`).

The last attribute named `expand` is set to `false`. This means that Solr won't expand the synonyms; all equivalent synonyms will be reduced to the first synonym in the line. If the attribute is set to `true`, all synonyms will be expanded to all equivalent forms. For example, if we have `expand` set to `true`, the synonyms file looks as follows:

```
machine, robot, ai
```

All the words are changed into different words, which means that `machine` is changed into `robot` and `ai`.

The example `synonyms.txt` file tells Solr that when the word `machine` appears in the field based on the `text_syn` type, it should be replaced by `electronics`, but not vice versa. Note that the word `machine` will only be changed during indexing, and not query time. Each synonym rule should be placed in a separate line in the `synonyms.txt` file. Also, remember that the file should be written in UTF-8 file encoding. This is crucial, and you should always remember it because Solr will expect the file to be encoded UTF-8.

As you can see, in the provided screenshot from the Solr administration pages, the defined synonym was properly applied during the indexing phase.

There's more...

There is one more thing connected to using synonyms in Solr, which is described in the following section.

Equivalent synonyms setup

Let's get back to our example for a second. What if the person from the marketing department says that he wants not only to be able to find books that have the word `machine` when entering the word `electronics`, but also all the books that have the word `electronics` to be found when entering the word `machine`. The answer is simple. First, we will set the `expand` attribute (of the filter) to `true`. Then, we will change our `synonyms.txt` file to something like this:

```
machine, electronics
```

As I said earlier, Solr will expand synonyms to equivalent forms.

See also

- If you want to use Solr capabilities for managing resource files, such as the synonyms file that we just discussed, look at the official documentation of Solr available at `https://cwiki.apache.org/confluence/display/solr/Managed+Resources`

Stemming different languages

Stemming is a very common requirement; it is the process of reducing words to their root form (or stems). Let's imagine the book e-commerce store, where you store the books' names and descriptions. We want to be able to find words such as `shown` and `showed` when you type the word `show`, and vice versa. We can achieve this requirement using stemming algorithms. The thing is, there are no general stemmers; they are language-specific. This recipe will show you how to add stemming to your data analysis chain and where to look for a list of stemmers.

How to do it...

To achieve our requirement to stem English, we need to take certain steps:

1. We will start with the index structure. Let's assume that our index consists of three fields that we defined in the `schema.xml` file:

   ```
   <field name="id" type="string" indexed="true" stored="true"
   required="true" />
   <field name="name" type="string" indexed="true" stored="true" />
   <field name="description" type="text_stem" indexed="true"
   stored="true" />
   ```

2. Now, let's define our `text_stem` type, which should look like this:

```
<fieldType name="text_stem" class="solr.TextField">
 <analyzer>
  <tokenizer class="solr.WhitespaceTokenizerFactory"/>
  <filter class="solr.SnowballPorterFilterFactory" />
 </analyzer>
</fieldType>
```

3. Now, we can index our data. For example, let's index the following data:

```
<add>
 <doc>
  <field name="id">1</field>
  <field name="name">Solr cookbook</field>
  <field name="description">This is a book that we show</field>
 </doc>
 <doc>
  <field name="id">2</field>
  <field name="name">Solr cookbook 2</field>
  <field name="description">This is a book I showed</field>
 </doc>
</add>
```

4. After indexing, we can test how our data was analyzed. To do this, let's run the following query:

```
http://localhost:8983/solr/cookbook/select?q=description:show
```

The result we get from Solr is as follows:

```
<?xml version="1.0" encoding="UTF-8"?>
<response>
 <lst name="responseHeader">
  <int name="status">0</int>
  <int name="QTime">1</int>
  <lst name="params">
   <str name="q">description:show</str>
  </lst>
 </lst>
 <result name="response" numFound="2" start="0">
  <doc>
   <str name="id">1</str>
   <str name="name">Solr cookbook</str>
```

```
    <str name="description">This is a book that we show</str>
    <long name="_version_">1468265180046557184</long></doc>
  <doc>
    <str name="id">2</str>
    <str name="name">Solr cookbook 2</str>
    <str name="description">This is a book I showed</str>
    <long name="_version_">1468265180093743104</long></doc>
 </result>
</response>
```

5. We can also use the Solr administration panel to see how the `show` and `showed` words are processed:

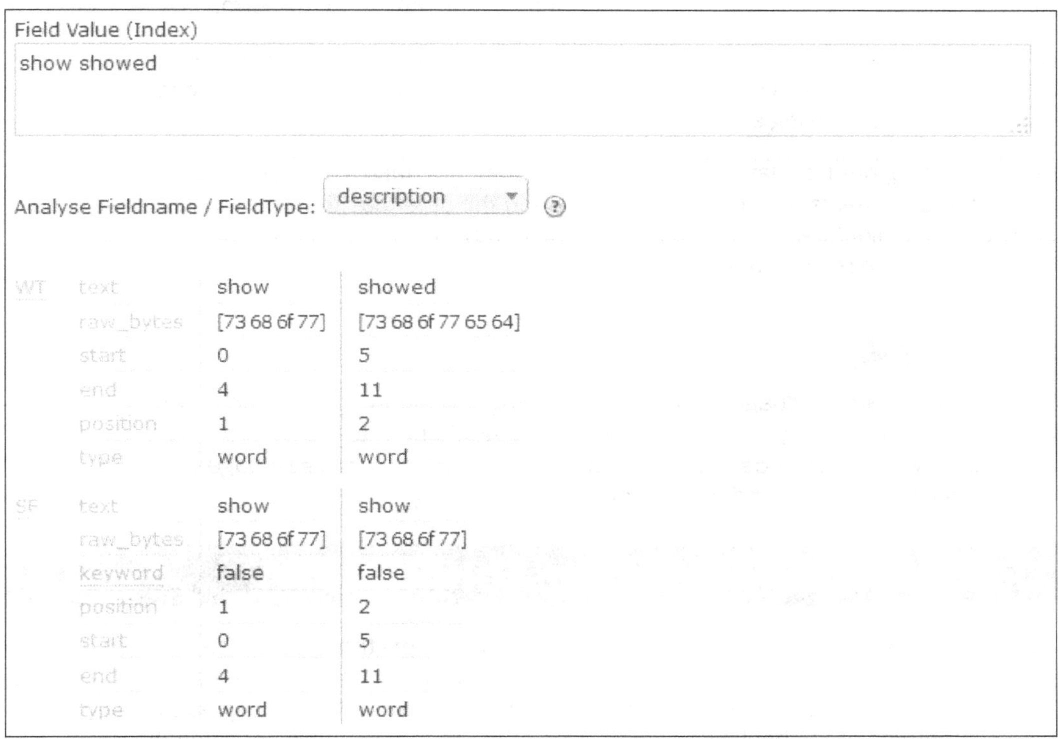

That's right, Solr finds two documents matching the query, which means that our fields and types are working as intended.

How it works...

Our index consists of three fields. The first field holds the unique identifier of the document (the `id` field), the second field holds the name of the document (the `name` field), and the third field holds the document description (the `description` field). The `description` field is the field that will be stemmed.

The stemmed field is based on a Solr text field and has an analyzer that is used at query and indexing time. It is tokenized on the basis of the whitespace characters by using `solr.WhitespaceTokenizerFactory`. Then, the stemming filter (`solr.SnowballPorterFilterFactory`) is used. What does this filter do? It tries to bring the words to its root form, which means that words such as `shows`, `showing`, and `show` will all be changed to `show`, or at least they should be changed to this form.

Note that in order to properly use stemming algorithms, they should be used on query and indexing times. It is a must because of the stemming results, so the same stems are produced during querying and indexing.

As you can see, our test data consists of two documents. Take a look at the descriptions. One of the documents has the word `showed`, and the other has the word `show` in their `description` fields. After indexing and running the sample query, Solr will return two documents in the results, which means that stemming did its job.

There's more...

There are too many languages that have stemming support integrated into Solr to mention them all. If you are using a language other than English, refer to the `https://cwiki.apache.org/confluence/display/solr/Language+Analysis` page of the Solr official documentation to find the appropriate filter.

Using nonaggressive stemmers

Nowadays, it's nice to have stemming algorithms (algorithms that will reduce words to their stem or root forms) in your application, which will allow you to find words such as `cat` and `cats` just by typing `cat`. However, let's imagine that you have a search engine that searches through contents of the books in a library. One of the requirements is changing the plural forms of the words from plural to singular; nothing less, nothing more. Can Solr do this? Yes, Solr can do this, and this recipe will show you how to do it.

How to do it...

1. First, let's start with a simple, two-field index (add the following section to your `schema.xml` file):

```
<field name="id" type="string" indexed="true" stored="true"
required="true" />
<field name="description" type="text_light_stem" indexed="true"
stored="true" />
```

2. Now, let's define the `text_light_stem` field type, which should look like this (add this to your `schema.xml` file):

```
<fieldType name="text_light_stem" class="solr.TextField">
 <analyzer>
  <tokenizer class="solr.WhitespaceTokenizerFactory"/>
  <filter class="solr.EnglishMinimalStemFilterFactory" />
  <filter class="solr.LowerCaseFilterFactory"/>
 </analyzer>
</fieldType>
```

3. Then, let's check the analysis tool of Solr administration pages; you should see that words such as `ways`, `keys`, and `populations` have been changed to their singular forms:

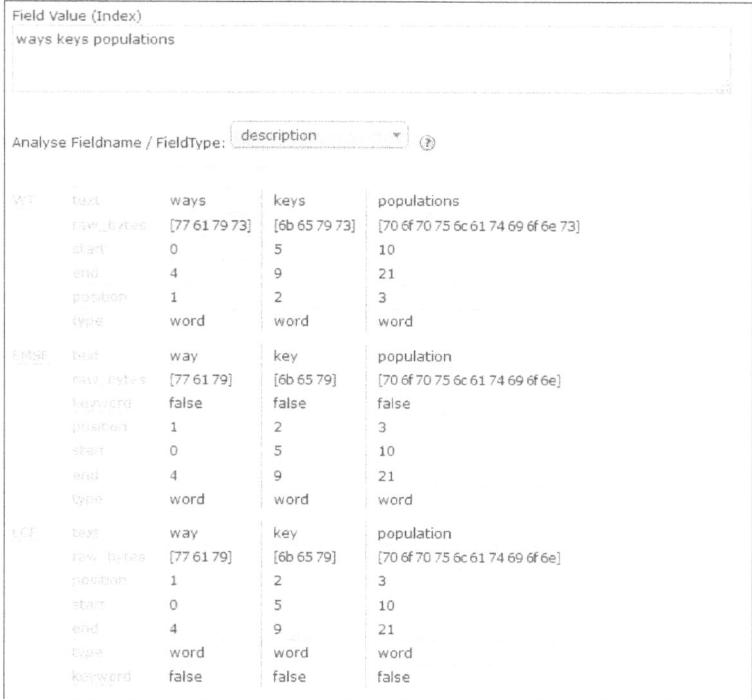

How it works...

First, we need to define the fields in the `schema.xml` file. We do this by adding the contents from the first example into the `schema.xml` file. It tells Solr that our index will consist of two fields—the `id` field that will be responsible for holding information about the unique identifier of the document, and the `description` file that will be responsible for holding the document description.

The `description` field is where the magic is being done. We defined a new field type for this field, and we called it `text_light_stem`. The field definition consists of a tokenizer and two filters. The `solr.WhitespaceTokenizerFactory` tokenizer splits the words on the basis of whitespace characters. The first filter is the one we are interested in. This is the light-stemming filter that we will use to perform minimal stemming. In general, aggressive stemming can and will change the words more, while minimal stemming is usually about removing the plural forms. The class that enables Solr to use this filter is `solr.EnglishMinimalStemFilterFactory`. This filter takes care of the process of light stemming. You can see this by using analysis tools of the Solr administration panel. The second filter, `solr.LowerCaseFilterFactory` is responsible for lowercasing terms.

There's more...

Light stemming supports a number of different languages. To use the light stemmers for your respective language, add the following filters to your type:

Language	Filter
Russian	`solr.RussianLightStemFilterFactory`
Portuguese	`solr.PortugueseLightStemFilterFactory`
French	`solr.FrenchLightStemFilterFactory`
German	`solr.GermanLightStemFilterFactory`
Italian	`solr.ItalianLightStemFilterFactory`
Spanish	`solr.SpanishLightStemFilterFactory`
Hungarian	`solr.HungarianLightStemFilterFactory`
Swedish	`solr.SwedishLightStemFilterFactory`
Finish	`solr.FinnishLightStemFilterFactory`
Indonesian	`solr.IndonesianStemFilterFactory` (with the `stemDerivational="false"` attribute)
Norwegian	`solr.NorwegianLightStemFilterFactory`

In the case of `solr.IndonesianStemFilterFactory`, you need to add the `stemDerivational="false"` attribute in order to have it working as a light stemmer.

Using the n-gram approach to do performant trailing wildcard searches

Many users working with traditional RDBMS systems are used to wildcard searches. The most common among them are the ones using the * characters, which means zero or more characters. If you used SQL databases, you probably saw searches such as this:

```
AND name LIKE 'ABC12%'
```

However, wildcard searchers are not too efficient when it comes to Solr. This is because Solr needs to enumerate all the terms because the query is executed. So, how do we prepare our Solr deployment to handle trailing wildcard characters in an efficient way? This recipe will show you how to prepare your data and make efficient searches.

How to do it...

There are some steps we need to make efficient wildcards using the n-gram approach:

1. The first step is to create a proper index structure. Let's assume we have the following fields defined in the `schema.xml` file:

```
<field name="id" type="string" indexed="true" stored="true"
required="true" />
<field name="name" type="text_wildcard" indexed="true"
stored="true" />
```

2. Now, let's define our `text_wildcard` type, again in the `schema.xml` file:

```
<fieldType name="text_wildcard" class="solr.TextField">
 <analyzer type="index">
  <tokenizer class="solr.WhitespaceTokenizerFactory"/>
  <filter class="solr.EdgeNGramFilterFactory" minGramSize="1"
maxGramSize="25"/>
  <filter class="solr.LowerCaseFilterFactory"/>
 </analyzer>
 <analyzer type="query">
  <tokenizer class="solr.WhitespaceTokenizerFactory"/>
  <filter class="solr.LowerCaseFilterFactory"/>
 </analyzer>
</fieldType>
```

3. The third step is to create an index example data that looks like this:

```
<add>
 <doc>
  <field name="id">1</field>
  <field name="name">XYZ1234ABC12POI</field>
 </doc>
</add>
```

4. Now, send the following query to Solr:

```
http://localhost:8983/solr/cookbook/select?q=name:XYZ1
```

The Solr response for this query is as follows:

```
<?xml version="1.0" encoding="UTF-8"?>
<response>
 <lst name="responseHeader">
  <int name="status">0</int>
  <int name="QTime">0</int>
  <lst name="params">
   <str name="q">name:XYZ1</str>
  </lst>
 </lst>
 <result name="response" numFound="1" start="0">
  <doc>
   <str name="id">1</str>
   <str name="name">XYZ1234ABC12POI</str>
   <long name="_version_">1468270390243491840</long></doc>
 </result>
</response>
```

As you see, the document has been found, so our setup is working as intended.

How it works...

First, let's look at our index structure defined in the `schema.xml` file. We have two fields, one holding the unique identifier of the document (the `id` field) and the second holding the name of the document (the `name` field), which are actually the fields we are interested in.

The `name` field is based on the new type we defined, `text_wildcard`. This type is responsible for enabling trailing wildcards, the ones that will enable running queries similar to `LIKE 'WORD%'` in SQL. As you can see, the field type is divided into two analyzers, one for data analysis during indexing and the other for query processing.

The querying analyzer is straight—it just tokenizes the data on the basis of whitespace characters (using the `solr.WhitespaceTokenizerFactory` tokenizer) and lowercases it (using the `solr.LowerCaseFilterFactory` filter). We don't want the query time analysis to include n-gram because we will provide only a part of the word, the first letters of it. For example, in our case, we passed the `XYZ1` part of the whole `XYZ1234ABC12POI` name.

Now, the indexing time analysis (of course, we are talking about the `name` field) is similar to the query time. During indexing, the data is tokenized on the basis of whitespace characters (using the same `solr.WhitespaceTokenizerFactory` tokenizer), but there is also an additional filter defined. The `solr.EdgeNGramFilterFactory` filter is responsible for generating so called n-grams. In our setup, we tell Solr that the minimum length of an n-gram is `1` (the `minGramSize` attribute) and the maximum length is `25` (the `maxGramSize` attribute). We also use the `solr.LowerCaseFilterFactory` filter to lowercase the n-gram output. So, what will Solr do with our example data? It will create the following tokens from the example text `X`, `XY`, `XYZ`, `XYZ1`, `XYZ12`, and so on. It will create tokens by adding the next character from the string to the previous token, up to the maximum length of n-gram that is given in the filter configuration. As you can see, the `YZ1` term won't match.

So, by typing the example query, we can be sure that the example document will be found because the n-gram filter is defined in the configuration of the field. We also didn't define the n-gram on the querying stage of analysis because we don't want our query to be analyzed in such a way, since that could lead to false positive hits, and we don't want this to happen.

By the way, this functionality, as described, can be successfully used to provide autocomplete (if you are not familiar with the autocomplete feature, take a look at `http://en.wikipedia.org/wiki/Autocomplete`) features for your application.

Remember that using n-grams will make your index a bit larger. As a result of this, you should avoid having n-grams on all the fields in the index; you should carefully decide which fields should use n-grams and which should not.

Using position increment to divide sentences

Imagine that we want to search in the short notes created by our users. We want to have two possibilities—searching inside a single sentence and searching inside the whole content of the note. We also know that our users don't write notes longer than 100 sentences, and each sentence has a maximum of 100 words, giving us a maximum of 10,000 words per note. To achieve this, we will use position increments that allow us to control how data is divided in the same field.

How to do it...

The following steps will allow us to fulfill our requirements:

1. We start with example data, which will look like this:

```
<add>
 <doc>
  <field name="id">1</field>
  <field name="note_line">Support meeting at Monday.</field>
  <field name="note_line">Need to prepare presentation.</field>
 </doc>
</add>
```

2. Now, we need to create an index structure. To do this, we need to add the fields that will be used. We do this by adding the following part to the `schema.xml` file:

```
<field name="id" type="string" indexed="true" stored="true"
required="true" />
<field name="note_line" type="text_general" indexed="true"
stored="true" multiValued="true" />
```

3. Now, add the first field type definition, `text_general`. We do this by adding the appropriate field type definition to the `schema.xml` file:

```
<analyzer type="index">
  <tokenizer class="solr.StandardTokenizerFactory"/>
  <filter class="solr.LowerCaseFilterFactory"/>
 </analyzer>
 <analyzer type="query">
  <tokenizer class="solr.StandardTokenizerFactory"/>
  <filter class="solr.LowerCaseFilterFactory"/>
 </analyzer>
</fieldType>
```

4. To test our functionality, we will start with searching inside the whole note. Once we find the ones that contain the `monday` and `presentation` words, we will run the following query:

```
http://localhost:8983/solr/cookbook/select?q=monday+presentation&d
f=note_line&q.op=AND
```

The result returned by Solr looks as follows:

```
<?xml version="1.0" encoding="UTF-8"?>
<response>
 <lst name="responseHeader">
  <int name="status">0</int>
  <int name="QTime">1</int>
```

```
  <lst name="params">
   <str name="q">monday presentation</str>
   <str name="df">note_line</str>
   <str name="q.op">AND</str>
  </lst>
 </lst>
 <result name="response" numFound="1" start="0">
  <doc>
   <str name="id">1</str>
   <arr name="note_line">
    <str>Support meeting at Monday.</str>
    <str>Need to prepare presentation.</str>
   </arr>
   <long name="_version_">1470163824187277312</long></doc>
 </result>
</response>
```

Our example note is returned, which is as expected.

5. Now, if we want to search for the same words, but only inside a single sentence, we will run the following query:

```
http://localhost:8983/solr/cookbook/select?q="monday presentation"
~100+OR+"presentation monday"~100&df=note_line&q.op=AND
```

The result will be as follows:

```
<?xml version="1.0" encoding="UTF-8"?>
<response>
 <lst name="responseHeader">
  <int name="status">0</int>
  <int name="QTime">1</int>
  <lst name="params">
   <str name="q">"monday presentation"~100 OR "presentation
monday"~100</str>
   <str name="df">note_line</str>
   <str name="indent">true</str>
   <str name="q.op">AND</str>
  </lst>
 </lst>
 <result name="response" numFound="0" start="0">
 </result>
</response>
```

As you can see, no result is returned, which is again as expected.

How it works...

We start with our data, which is quite simple. However, we have to remember one thing. We put each line of the user note in a single field, which is `note_line`. Due to this, we can see that our index structure stored in the `schema.xml` file contains this field, and it is a multivalued field because each note can have more than one sentence. In addition to the mentioned field, we can also see a single additional field, the `id` field, which stores the identifier.

Our `text_general` type is very straightforward, apart from one thing, the `positionIncrementGap` property, which is set to `1000000`. This property specifies the gap between each instance of a field for multivalued fields, in our case the gap between each sentence. The higher the value of the `positionIncrementGap` property, the larger the gap will be, which means a larger phrase slop will be needed to match data between instances of the field. This is needed because we don't want the queries to match between sentences, and the value should be large enough (as shown in the example), so we can even use the phrase slop.

If we look at our first query and the results returned by it, we can see that it matches our note. This is understandable because we just use two term queries (having two words), and we search across all the data in the `note_line` field.

The second query is more interesting. We use a phrase query to limit the searching to a single sentence. We need to include both phrases because we don't know in which order the words were included in the query. However, the interesting thing is the phrase slop for both phrase queries—the `~100` part. As you remember, in the introduction to the recipe, we said that our notes can have a maximum of 100 sentences with a maximum of 100 words each. After looking at our indexing time analysis, we shouldn't have more than 100 tokens per sentence. As a result of this, we tell our phrase queries to include a slop of `100`, which basically means that each token can have a maximum of 100 other tokens between them (including the defined gap). In our case, we set the `positionIncrementGap` property to `1000000` in the field type definition, so the gap between sentences will be higher than 100, and this is why Solr won't match our document.

Using patterns to replace tokens

Let's assume that we want to search inside user blog posts. We need to prepare a simple search returning only the identifier of the documents that were matched. However, we will want to remove some words because of explicit language. Of course, we can do this using the `stop words` functionality, but what if we want to know how many documents have their contents censored with compute statistics on. In such a case, we can't use the `stop words` functionality, we need something more, which means that we need regular expressions. This recipe will show you how to achieve such requirements using Solr and one of its filters.

How to do it...

To achieve our needs, we will use the `solr.PatternReplaceFilterFactory` filter. Let's assume that we want to remove all the words that start with the `word` prefix. These are the steps needed:

1. First, we need to create our index structure, so the fields we add to the `schema.xml` file are as follows:

```
<field name="id" type="string" indexed="true" stored="true"
required="true" />
<field name="post" type="text_ignore" indexed="true"
stored="false" />
```

2. We also need to define the `text_ignore` field type by adding the following section to the `schema.xml` file:

```
<fieldType name="text_ignore" class="solr.TextField"
positionIncrementGap="100">
 <analyzer type="index">
  <tokenizer class="solr.StandardTokenizerFactory"/>
  <filter class="solr.LowerCaseFilterFactory" />
  <filter class="solr.PatternReplaceFilterFactory"
pattern="word[a-zA-Z0-9]*" replacement="[censored]" />
 </analyzer>
 <analyzer type="query">
  <tokenizer class="solr.StandardTokenizerFactory"/>
  <filter class="solr.LowerCaseFilterFactory"/>
 </analyzer>
</fieldType>
```

3. Now, we can index our test data that looks as follows:

```
<add>
 <doc>
  <field name="id">1</field>
  <field name="post">First post</field>
 </doc>
 <doc>
  <field name="id">2</field>
  <field name="post">Second post single word</field>
 </doc>
 <doc>
  <field name="id">3</field>
  <field name="post">Third post and the word1</field>
 </doc>
</add>
```

4. First, before running our query, let's see if we are actually changing tokens starting with the `word` prefix to `[censored]`, just like we want to. We do this using the analysis tool from the Solr admin panel. The result can be seen in the following screenshot:

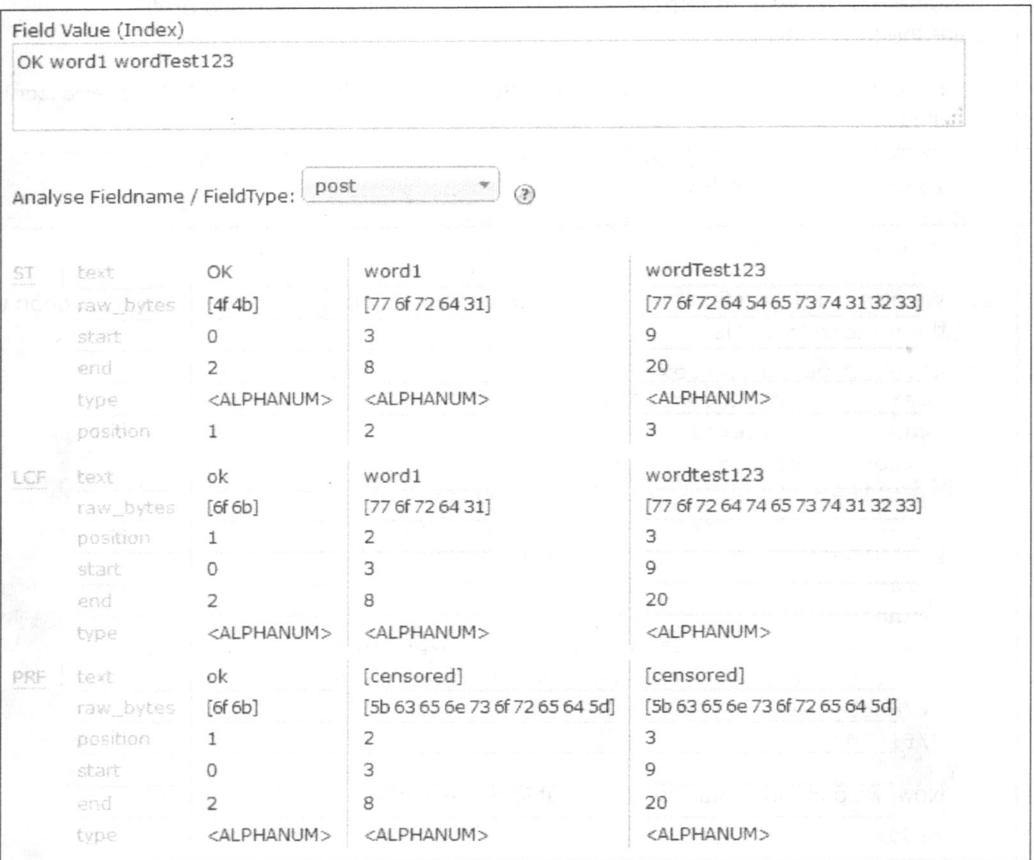

5. Now, let's compute the statistics we are looking for. To do this, we will use the following query:

```
http://localhost:8983/solr/cookbook/select?q=*:*&rows=0&facet=true
&facet.query={!raw f=post}[censored]
```

6. The results returned by Solr are as follows:

```
<?xml version="1.0" encoding="UTF-8"?>
<response>
 <lst name="responseHeader">
  <int name="status">0</int>
```

```
    <int name="QTime">1</int>
    <lst name="params">
     <str name="facet.query">{!raw f=post}[censored]</str>
     <str name="q">*:*</str>
     <str name="rows">0</str>
     <str name="facet">true</str>
    </lst>
   </lst>
   <result name="response" numFound="3" start="0">
   </result>
   <lst name="facet_counts">
    <lst name="facet_queries">
     <int name="{!raw f=post}[censored]">2</int>
    </lst>
    <lst name="facet_fields"/>
    <lst name="facet_dates"/>
    <lst name="facet_ranges"/>
   </lst>
  </response>
```

As we can see, everything works, so now let's look at how all of this was achieved.

How it works...

As we already said, our index structure is very simple. We only need two things; the first is the document identifier, which is held by the `id` field, which we store and return in the results, and the second is the `post` field that holds the post contents.

The `post` field uses our new type, `text_ignore`. The type itself is rather simple, it uses `solr.StandardTokenizerFactory` to tokenize data (both during querying and indexing); we then lowercase the data by using `solr.LowerCaseFilterFactory`. On the indexing side, however, we do one more thing—we use the `solr.PatternReplaceFilterFactory` filter. We use it because it allows us to not only remove some words but also to replace them. Of course, we can use synonyms (described in the *Using synonyms* recipe of this chapter), but they only work on whole words, not on patterns in which we want them to work. Basically, what we do here is replace every word starting with the `word` pattern with the `[censored]` term. We achieve this by specifying a simple regular expression (`pattern="word[a-zA-Z0-9]*"`), telling Solr to match every word starting with the given prefix and followed by characters or numbers (yes, I know that the regex can be more complicated, but this is only an example). In addition to this, we said that we want the matched word to be replaced by the `[censored]` term (`replacement="[censored]"`).

As you can see in the preceding screenshot, our filter is working as it should. During indexing, a term that starts with the `word` prefix is changed to the term `[censored]`.

Now, let's look into our analysis query. We are interested in all the documents that are in our collection (`q=*:*`), and we will use faceting to get the information about the number of documents with the `[censored]` term (`facet.query={!raw f=post}[censored]`). We used the `raw` query parser and sent the facet query against the `post` field (`f=post`) to easily pass a term with the two Lucene special characters– `[` and `]`. As you can see, we got the count in the results–two documents out of three have at least a single word `censored`.

There's more...

There is one additional thing I will like to mention, check the next section.

Using solr.PatternReplaceCharFilterFactory

Sometimes, we want to do an analysis before the field text is actually tokenized. Solr allows us to do this by providing the `solr.PatternReplaceCharFilterFactory` char filter, which can be used to do the analysis on the whole text before it is passed to the tokenizer. If we want our recipe example to use the char filter instead of the token filter, we need to change our `text_ignore` type definition as follows:

```
<fieldType name="text_ignore" class="solr.TextField"
positionIncrementGap="100">
 <analyzer type="index">
  <charFilter class="solr.PatternReplaceCharFilterFactory"
pattern="word[a-zA-Z0-9]*" replacement="[censored]" />
  <tokenizer class="solr.StandardTokenizerFactory"/>
  <filter class="solr.LowerCaseFilterFactory" />
 </analyzer>
 <analyzer type="query">
  <tokenizer class="solr.StandardTokenizerFactory"/>
  <filter class="solr.LowerCaseFilterFactory"/>
 </analyzer>
</fieldType>
```

You might want to follow this method if you need to operate on the whole text and not on the tokens produced by the tokenizer.

4
Querying Solr

In this chapter, we will cover the following topics:

- Understanding and using the Lucene query language
- Using position-aware queries
- Using boosting with autocomplete
- Phrase queries with shingles
- Handling user queries without errors
- Handling hierarchies with nested documents
- Sorting data on the basis of a function value
- Controlling the number of terms needed to match
- Affecting document score using function queries
- Using simple nested queries
- Using the Solr document's query join functionality
- Handling typos with n-grams
- Rescoring query results

Introduction

Creating a simple query is not a hard task, but creating a complex one, with faceting, local params, parameter dereferencing, and phrase queries can be a challenging task. Other than this, you must remember to write your query while keeping the performance factors in mind. This is why something that is simple at first sight can turn into something more challenging, such as writing a good, complex query. This chapter will try to guide you through some of the tasks you might encounter during your everyday work with Solr.

Understanding and using the Lucene query language

As you know, Solr is built using the Apache Lucene library. Due to this, some of the query parsers available in Solr allow us to fully leverage the query language of Lucene, giving us great flexibility to understand how our queries work and with what documents they match. In this recipe, we will discuss an example usage of the Lucene query language by looking at a book search site that gives its users the possibility of defining complex Boolean queries that contain phrases.

How to do it...

Let's perform the following steps to achieve this:

1. The first step is to prepare our index to handle data. To do this, we add the following entries to the `schema.xml` file:

```
<field name="id" type="string" indexed="true" stored="true"
required="true" />
<field name="title" type="text_general" indexed="true"
stored="true" />
<field name="description" type="text_general" indexed="true"
stored="true" />
<field name="published" type="int" indexed="true" stored="true" />
```

2. Now, let's index some sample book data. The data that we want to index looks as follows:

```
<doc>
  <field name="id">1</field>
  <field name="title">Solr 4.0 cookbook</field>
  <field name="description">The book is totally focused on the 4.0
version of Apache Solr enterprise search server. The content is
divided into ten thematic chapters, just like with the previous
version of the book</field>
  <field name="published">2012</field>
 </doc>
 <doc>
  <field name="id">2</field>
  <field name="title">Solr 3.1 cookbook</field>
```

```
  <field name="description">The book is focused on the 3.1 version
of Solr. The content is divided into ten chapters, each of which
consists of a few to several recipes.</field>
  <field name="published">2011</field>
 </doc>
</add>
```

3. Let's assume that our user wants to find the books that have the term `solr` in their title and `book` in their description. In addition, our user wants to see the books that were published between 2011 and 2013 (inclusive of 2011). However, this is not all. Our user also says that he doesn't want books that have the term `3.1` or the `book is focused` phrase in their description. The query seems a bit complicated, but Solr can easily handle it. A request that handles all the requirements looks as follows:

   ```
   http://localhost:8983/solr/cookbook/select?q=title:solr AND
   description:book AND published:[2011+TO+2013} NOT (description:3.1
   OR description:"book is focused")
   ```

4. The results returned by Solr are as follows:

   ```
   <?xml version="1.0" encoding="UTF-8"?>
   <response>
    <lst name="responseHeader">
     <int name="status">0</int>
     <int name="QTime">64</int>
     <lst name="params">
      <str name="q">title:solr AND description:book AND
   published:[2011 TO 2013} NOT (description:3.1 OR description:"book
   is focused")</str>
     </lst>
    </lst>
    <result name="response" numFound="1" start="0">
     <doc>
      <str name="id">1</str>
      <str name="title">Solr 4.0 cookbook</str>
      <str name="description">The book is totally focused on the 4.0
   version of Apache Solr enterprise search server. The content is
   divided into ten thematic chapters, just like with the previous
   version of the book</str>
      <int name="published">2012</int>
      <long name="_version_">1471367306831462400</long></doc>
    </result>
   </response>
   ```

As we can see, Solr returned the document we were after, so now let's see how it works.

How it works...

Our index is very simple; it contains four fields:

- The first field is the one responsible for the unique identifier of the book (the `id` field)
- The second field is the title of the book (the `title` field)
- The third field is the description of the book (the `description` field)
- The fourth field holds the publication year (the `published` field)

By default, Solr uses the standard query parser that supports the full Lucene query language. This means that we can search in a particular field, use phrase and range queries, use Boolean operators, and so on.

Our particular query says that we want the documents that have `solr` in the `title` field (`title:solr`), `book` in the `description` field (`description:book`), and the publication date between `2011` and `2013`, including `2011` (`published:[2011 TO 2013}`).These three parts of the query are connected to each other with the Boolean operator `AND`. Both sides of the operator must match for the document to be considered a match; in our case, all three conditions must be met. The Lucene query language provides us with the possibility of using three Boolean operators: `AND` (requires both operands to be matched), `OR` (any operant can be a match), and `NOT` (the operand after the operator can't match). After the operands are concatenated with the `AND` operator, we have the `NOT` operator, which means that the section in the parenthesis can't be a match for the document to be returned in the search results (`(description:3.1 OR description:"book is focused")`). This basically means that the description of the book can't have the `3.1` term or the `book is focused` phrase.

Of course, the logical operators are not everything that is present in the query. We have the sections specifying that we want a particular value in a field, for example, `title:solr`. We have the range query run against the `published` field and say that we want all documents with a value between `2011` and `2013` (exclusive) in this field. One thing to remember when it comes to the range query is that using `[` or `]` means that we want the value to be inclusive, while using `{` or `}` means that the value will be exclusive. Finally, we have the phrase query that we construct by surrounding the phrase with the `"` character.

Note that the query shown in the example is suboptimal. Some parts of it should be moved to filter queries (such as the section about publication year) because of performance reasons. However, for the purpose of demonstrating the Lucene query language, I decided to go for the simplest example. The more optimal version of the query looks as follows:

```
http://localhost:8983/solr/cookbook/select?q=title:solr AND
description:book NOT (description:3.1 OR description:"book is focused"
)&fq=published:[2011+TO+2013}
```

See also

- Of course, the recipe doesn't show all the possibilities of the Lucene query language (for example, it doesn't mention the `-`, `+`, and `!` operators). If you want to know more, look at the Javadoc of the classic Lucene query parser available at `http://lucene.apache.org/core/4_10_0/queryparser/org/apache/lucene/queryparser/classic/package-summary.html`.

Using position aware queries

Most of the queries exposed by Lucene and Solr are not position-aware, which means that the query doesn't care about the place in the document where the word comes from. Of course, we have phrase queries that we can use for phrase searching, and even introduce the phrase slop, but this is not always enough. Sometimes, we might want to search for words with their positions in the searched documents. Let's assume that we allow our users to search for book titles and descriptions and specify how these words should be positioned related to each other. Solr provides us with such functionalities, and this recipe will show you how to use them.

How to do it...

Let's start with a simple index structure. For the purpose of this recipe, we will use the following fields:

1. Add the following sections to the `schema.xml` file:

```
<field name="id" type="string" indexed="true" stored="true"
required="true" />
<field name="title" type="text_general" indexed="true"
stored="true" />
<field name="description" type="text_general" indexed="true"
stored="true" />
```

2. After this, we index our sample data, which looks as follows:

```
<add>
 <doc>
  <field name="id">1</field>
  <field name="title">Solr 4.0 cookbook</field>
  <field name="description">The book is totally focused on the 4.0
version of Apache Solr enterprise search server. The content is
divided into ten thematic chapters, just like with the previous
version of the book</field>
 </doc>
 <doc>
```

```
  <field name="id">2</field>
  <field name="title">Solr 3.1 cookbook</field>
  <field name="description">The book is focused on the 3.1 version
of Solr. The content is divided into ten chapters, each of which
consists of a few to several recipes.</field>
 </doc>
</add>
```

Let's assume that our user wants to find books that have the words `chapters` and `solr` not more than 10 times apart from each other (no matter the order). In addition to this, he only wants documents with the word `book` followed by the word `solr`. However, the word `solr` should not be further than 8 words from it and, in addition to this, the word `solr` should be no more than 3 words from the word `3.1`. Of course, all the mentioned requirements are about the documents that were indexed. The query that fulfills this requirement looks as follows:

```
http://localhost:8983/solr/cookbook/select?q={!surround}
(10n(chapters,solr) AND 8w(book,3n(solr,3.1)))&df=description
```

The result returned by Solr looks as follows:

```
<?xml version="1.0" encoding="UTF-8"?>
<response>
 <lst name="responseHeader">
  <int name="status">0</int>
  <int name="QTime">0</int>
  <lst name="params">
   <str name="q">{!surround}(10n(chapters,solr) AND
8w(book,3n(solr,3.1)))</str>
   <str name="df">description</str>
  </lst>
 </lst>
 <result name="response" numFound="1" start="0">
  <doc>
   <str name="id">2</str>
   <str name="title">Solr 3.1 cookbook</str>
   <str name="description">The book is focused on the 3.1 version of
Solr. The content is divided into ten chapters, each of which consists
of a few to several recipes.</str>
   <long name="_version_">1471273737021030400</long></doc>
 </result>
</response>
```

Solr returns the only book that matches user requirements, so now let's see how it works.

How it works...

We start with the index structure, which is quite simple. It contains three fields:

- One field holds the identifier of the document (the `id` field)
- One field holds the title of the book (the `title` field)
- The last field holds the description of the book (the `description` field)

Our example data is also very simple; it contains two books and their descriptions.

The query is the thing that we are interested in. First, the last part of the query says that the default search field is the `description` field; we've specified this using the `df` query property (`df=description`). To use position-aware queries in Solr, we need to use the Surround query parser; we do this by adding `{!surround}` to our query. The whole query is surrounded by parentheses, so we tell Solr that the whole query should be processed by the query parser that we choose.

Before we continue, it is crucial to know the operators that are supported by the Surround query parser; they are `AND`, `OR`, `NOT`, `W`, and `N`. The first three operators were discussed in the *Understanding and using the Lucene query language* recipe earlier in this chapter; the `W` and `N` operators are new. `W` and `N` are position operators; the `W` operator is unordered, which means that words can be in any order; the `N` operator is ordered, so word order matters. The positional operators require distance to be specified, and assume `1` when none is provided; the value can be from `2` to `99` and is specified as a prefix. For example, `2n(solr, cookbook)` means that the query should match documents that have the words `solr` and `cookbook`, the second one no further than two positions away from each other (up to one term between them). For example, `solr 3.1 cookbook` will match, while `solr 3.1 updated edition cookbook` won't.

Now, as we know how the surround query parser works, let's discuss what we told Solr to do. The `10n(chapters,solr)` part of the query says that we want documents having the words `chapters` and `solr` up to 10 positions from each other, no matter the order. The `8w(book,3n(solr,3.1))` part of the query specifies that we want the word `book` present up to 8 positions before the span query defined by the `3n(solr,3.1)` part. The `3n(solr,3.1)` part tells Solr to create a span query that matches documents having the `solr` word up to 3 positions from the word `3.1` in whatever order.

As you can see, with the use of the Surround query parser and its ability to create span queries using the `N` and `W` operators, we can create queries that match documents using not only terms but also the information on where they are in the document, in other words, their positions.

There are a few things one should remember when using span queries. First of all, the queries are much more demanding when it comes to CPU usage because they not only need to match terms but also check their positions. The second limitation of span queries is that they are not analyzed at all, so you need to provide the terms that match the ones that were indexed, else the documents won't match.

There's more...

There is one additional thing I would like to mention, as mentioned in the following section.

Too many generated queries

Sometimes, Surround query parsers can generate too many internal queries that will result in no documents being returned for the query. We can overwrite this behavior by specifying the `maxBasicQueries` property for the Surround query parser with a high value. For example, our example query might look as follows:

```
http://localhost:8983/solr/cookbook/select?q={!surroundmaxBasicQueri
es=20000}(10n(chapters,solr) AND 8w(book,3n(solr,3.1)))&df=description
```

Using boosting with autocomplete

Autocomplete is very good when it comes to our user search experience. It is especially useful for showing users' data that we want to promote or the data that is of value to the users. In general, in e-commerce, the deployment of the autocomplete functionality means more profit. However, there are situations where we want to promote certain products or documents, for example, the currently top-selling books or financial reports, which are the most important ones. This recipe will show you how to boost certain documents when using the n-gram-based autocomplete functionality.

How to do it...

Let's perform the following steps to boost certain documents using the n-gram-based autocomplete function:

1. We start with creating the index structure for our use case; we just put the following section to the `schema.xml` file:

   ```
   <field name="id" type="string" indexed="true" stored="true"
   required="true"/>
   <field name="title" type="text_general" indexed="true"
   stored="true"/>
   <field name="title_ac" type="text_general_edge_ngram"
   indexed="true" stored="false"/>
   ```

2. Next, we define the `text_general_edge_ngram` type by adding the following section to the `schema.xml` file:

```
<fieldType name="text_general_edge_ngram" class="solr.TextField"
positionIncrementGap="100">
 <analyzer type="index">
  <tokenizer class="solr.StandardTokenizerFactory"/>
  <filter class="solr.LowerCaseFilterFactory"/>
  <filter class="solr.EdgeNGramFilterFactory" minGramSize="2"
maxGramSize="45"/>
 </analyzer>
 <analyzer type="query">
  <tokenizer class="solr.StandardTokenizerFactory"/>
  <filter class="solr.LowerCaseFilterFactory"/>
 </analyzer>
</fieldType>
```

3. The next step is to add a copy field definition so that the `title_ac` field is automatically populated by the data from the `title` field. We do this by adding the following to the `schema.xml` file:

```
<copyField source="title" dest="title_ac" />
```

4. Imagine that one of our documents, the one with identifier `2`, is the most valuable one for us and we would like to show it on top in searches and autocomplete. To achieve this, our example data looks as follows:

```
<add>
 <doc>
  <field name="id">1</field>
  <field name="title">Financial report 2014</field>
 </doc>
 <doc boost="1000">
  <field name="id">2</field>
  <field name="title">Financial marketing report 2014</field>
 </doc>
 <doc>
  <field name="id">3</field>
  <field name="title">Excluded financials in 2014 - internal
report</field>
 </doc>
</add>
```

5. Now, let's run our autocomplete query, which looks as follows:

```
http://localhost:8983/solr/cookbook/select?q=financial
repor&df=title_ac&q.op=AND
```

6. The results returned by Solr looks as follows:

```
<?xml version="1.0" encoding="UTF-8"?>
<response>
 <lst name="responseHeader">
  <int name="status">0</int>
  <int name="QTime">1</int>
  <lst name="params">
   <str name="q">financial repor</str>
   <str name="df">title_ac</str>
   <str name="q.op">AND</str>
  </lst>
 </lst>
 <result name="response" numFound="3" start="0">
  <doc>
   <str name="id">2</str>
   <str name="title">Financial marketing report 2014</str>
   <long name="_version_">1471236319725223936</long></doc>
  <doc>
   <str name="id">1</str>
   <str name="title">Financial report 2014</str>
    <long name="_version_">1471236319670697984</long></doc>
  <doc>
   <str name="id">3</str>
   <str name="title">Excluded financials in 2014 - internal
report</str>
   <long name="_version_">1471236319726272512</long></doc>
 </result>
</response>
```

As we can see, we got the required results. Now, let's see how it works.

How it works...

Our index structure is very simple. We have a field responsible for holding the unique identifier of the document (the `id` field). We also have two fields that are used to hold the title of the document:

- The `title` field (used for searching)
- The `title_ac` field (used for autocomplete)

The next thing is the definition of the `text_general_edge_ngram` type. At query time, (`<analyzer type="query">`), we use the `solr.StandardTokenizerFactory` tokenizer and the `solr.LowerCaseFilterFactory` filter to divide the phrase and lowercase it. The index time analysis (`<analyzer type="index">`) is more important. During indexing, we not only repeat the same steps as during query time, we also use the `solr.EdgeNGramFilterFactory` filter to divide tokens into grams to implement the autocomplete functionality. We want to return the document containing the term `financial` when the user enters `finan` into the search box. The screenshot from the analysis section of the Solr administration panel shows how the filter works:

ENGTF	text	fi	fin	fina	finan	financ	financi	financia	financial
	raw_bytes	[66 69]	[66 69 6e]	[66 69 6e 61]	[66 69 6e 61 6e]	[66 69 6e 61 6e 63]	[66 69 6e 61 6e 63 69]	[66 69 6e 61 6e 63 69 61]	[66 69 6e 61 6e 63 69 61 6c]
	start	0	0	0	0	0	0	0	0
	end	9	9	9	9	9	9	9	9
	positionLength	1	1	1	1	1	1	1	1
	position	1	1	1	1	1	1	1	1
	type	word	word	word	word	word	word	word	word

Finally, the last thing about the `schema.xml` file is the copy field. We added it, so we tell Solr that it should copy the contents of the `title` field to the `title_ac` field because we need a different analysis for the `title_ac` field.

As you can see in the example data, the document with the `id` field equaling `2` is a bit different when compared to the rest of the documents. In its definition, it has the boost property included (`<doc boost="1000">`). It tells Solr to add boost to the document during indexing. The default boost value given to every document is `1`, so when we set the boost value to `1000`, we inform Solr that the document is much more important than the ones with the default boost.

We can see the difference in the results of our query. The document with an `id` of `2` is on the top of the results list, although, from the scoring algorithm point of view, the best match is the document with the identifier of `1`. Since we set the boost value during indexation, Solr is informed that our boosted document is more important, and it increases its score accordingly.

Phrase queries with shingles

Imagine that you have an application that searches within millions of documents that are generated by a law company. One of the requirements is to search boost the documents that have either a search phrase or part of the phrase in their title. So, is it possible to achieve it using Solr? Yes, and this recipe will show you how to do this.

How to do it...

Let's follow these steps to achieve this:

1. Let's start with our index structure; we configure it by adding the following section to the `schema.xml` file:

```
<field name="id" type="string" indexed="true" stored="true"
required="true" />
<field name="title" type="text_general" indexed="true"
stored="true" />
```

2. The second step is to create example data that looks like this:

```
<doc>
  <field name="id">1</field>
  <field name="title">Financial report 2014</field>
 </doc>
 <doc>
  <field name="id">2</field>
  <field name="title">Financial marketing report 2014</field>
 </doc>
 <doc>
  <field name="id">3</field>
  <field name="title">Excluded financials in 2014 - internal
report</field>
 </doc>
</add>
```

3. Let's assume our users want to find documents with the terms `financial report 2014` in the `title` field. However, we also want boost and partial phrases so the documents with query terms closer to each other have a higher boost. To do this, make the following query to Solr:

```
http://localhost:8983/solr/cookbook/select?q=financial report
2014&defType=edismax&qf=title&pf=title&pf2=title&pf3=title
```

The result should look like this:

```
<?xml version="1.0" encoding="UTF-8"?>
<response>
 <lst name="responseHeader">
  <int name="status">0</int>
  <int name="QTime">11</int>
  <lst name="params">
```

```
      <str name="q">financial report 2014</str>
      <str name="defType">edismax</str>
      <str name="qf">title</str>
      <str name="pf">title</str>
      <str name="pf3">title</str>
      <str name="pf2">title</str>
    </lst>
  </lst>
  <result name="response" numFound="3" start="0">
    <doc>
      <str name="id">1</str>
      <str name="title">Financial report 2014</str>
      <long name="_version_">1471162075046739968</long></doc>
    <doc>
      <str name="id">2</str>
      <str name="title">Financial marketing report 2014</str>
      <long name="_version_">1471162075092877312</long></doc>
    <doc>
      <str name="id">3</str>
      <str name="title">Excluded financials in 2014 - internal report</
str>
      <long name="_version_">1471162075092877313</long></doc>
  </result>
</response>
```

The debug query (the `debugQuery=on` parameter) shows us how the Lucene query was made:

```
<str name="parsedquery">(+(DisjunctionMaxQuery((title:financial)) Di
sjunctionMaxQuery((title:report)) DisjunctionMaxQuery((title:2014)))
DisjunctionMaxQuery((title:"financial report 2014")) (DisjunctionMa
xQuery((title:"financial report")) DisjunctionMaxQuery((title:"repo
rt 2014"))) DisjunctionMaxQuery((title:"financial report 2014")))/
no_coord</str>
```

As you can see, we got the documents we wanted, and in the right order. Now, let's see why this happened.

How it works...

For this recipe, I chose a very simple index. It contains only two fields:

- The identifier of the document (the `id` field)
- The title of the document (the `title` field)

The query is the part that we should be most interested in. We start by sending the terms in the `q` parameter (`q=financial report 2014`). This means that all our example documents will be matched. We also specify that we want to use the extended `dismax` query parser (`defType=edismax`). We define the field that we want to search on by specifying the `qf=title` parameter. This part of the query satisfies one of our requirements—the one that forces us to match the terms in the `title` field. Notice that the default logical operator is `OR` in our case. Because of that, even if only a single term from the query will be present in a document, it will be returned in the results of the query.

The second requirement is to boost the documents with the phrase query. We can add the phrase query to the `q` parameter, but instead we use the `pf` parameter. By specifying `pf=title`, we say that the query parser should make the phrase query using the values in the `q` parameter. We can see this in the debug query output, `DisjunctionMaxQuery((title:"financial report 2014"))`. In the results, we can see that the document matching the phrase query is at the top of the results.

The third requirement is the inclusion of the partial phrases, again using the value of the `q` parameter. The `pf2` parameter will take the value of the `q` parameter and create pairs and phrase queries out of them. So, in our case, it will create the `financial report` and `report 2014` phrases. We can see `DisjunctionMaxQuery((title:"financial report"))` and `DisjunctionMaxQuery((title:"report 2014"))` in the debug query. The `pf3` parameter will do a similar thing to `pf2`, but instead of constructing pairs, it will create triples. In our case, it will create the `financial report 2014` phrase. Again, we can see this in the debug query.

All the queries constructed by Solr using the `pf`, `pf2`, and `pf3` parameters are added to the query and will boost the documents that match them. We can see this in the results returned by Solr.

See also

- The Simple query parser allows us to use a subset of the default Lucene query language. The full documentation on a Simple query parser can be found at `https://cwiki.apache.org/confluence/display/solr/The+Extended+DisMax+Query+Parser`.

Handling user queries without errors

When building an application that uses Solr, we usually pass the query that the user sent to Solr. Sometimes, we even allow users to send complex queries that contain Lucene special characters. Due to this, there are situations where the user provides malformed queries, and thus, Solr throws an exception when running such queries. We can alter this behavior by using a new query parser called **Simple**. This recipe will show you how to do this.

Getting ready

Before continuing to read this recipe, I suggest reading the *Understanding and using the Lucene query language* recipe from this chapter.

How to do it...

Let's look into how to handle user queries without errors using the following steps:

1. We start by creating a simple index structure that will allow us to easily illustrate the example. To do this, we place the following section in the `schema.xml` file:

   ```
   <field name="id" type="string" indexed="true" stored="true"
   required="true" />
   <field name="title" type="text_general" indexed="true"
   stored="true"/>
   <field name="author" type="text_general" indexed="true"
   multiValued="true" />
   ```

2. In addition to this, we index an example data that looks as follows:

   ```
   <doc>
     <field name="id">1</field>
     <field name="title">Apache Solr 3.1 Cookbook</field>
     <field name="author">Rafał Kuć</field>
    </doc>
    <doc>
     <field name="id">2</field>
     <field name="title">Apache Solr 4.0 Cookbook</field>
     <field name="author">Rafał Kuć</field>
    </doc>
    <doc>
     <field name="id">3</field>
     <field name="title">Elasticsearch Server book</field>
     <field name="author">Rafał Kuć</field>
     <field name="author">Marek Rogoziński</field>
    </doc>
   </add>
   ```

3. Now, let's assume that our user runs the `"Apache Cookbook` query. So, the query using the default Solr query parser will look as follows:

   ```
   http://localhost:8983/solr/cookbook/select?q="Apache
   Cookbook&qf=title author
   ```

4. The result returned by such a query will look like the following:

```
<?xml version="1.0" encoding="UTF-8"?>
<response>
 <lst name="responseHeader">
  <int name="status">400</int>
  <int name="QTime">2</int>
  <lst name="params">
   <str name="q">"Apache Cookbook</str>
   <str name="qf">title author</str>
  </lst>
 </lst>
 <lst name="error">
  <str name="msg">org.apache.solr.search.SyntaxError: Cannot parse
'"Apache Solr': Lexical error at line 1, column 13.  Encountered:
&lt;EOF&gt; after : "\"Apache Solr"</str>
  <int name="code">400</int>
 </lst>
</response>
```

5. We see an error, so let's use the Simple query parser. To do this, we run the following query:

```
http://localhost:8983/solr/cookbook/select?q="ApacheCookbook&qf=ti
tle author&defType=simple
```

6. The results for this query look like the following:

```
<?xml version="1.0" encoding="UTF-8"?>
<response>
 <lst name="responseHeader">
  <int name="status">0</int>
  <int name="QTime">4</int>
  <lst name="params">
   <str name="q">"Apache Cookbook</str>
   <str name="defType">simple</str>
   <str name="qf">title author</str>
  </lst>
 </lst>
 <result name="response" numFound="2" start="0">
  <doc>
   <str name="id">1</str>
```

```
    <str name="title">Apache Solr 3.1 Cookbook</str>
    <arr name="author">
     <str>Rafał Kuć</str>
    </arr>
    <long name="_version_">1471151647034966016</long></doc>
   <doc>
    <str name="id">2</str>
    <str name="title">Apache Solr 4.0 Cookbook</str>
    <arr name="author">
     <str>Rafał Kuć</str>
    </arr>
    <long name="_version_">1471151647089491968</long></doc>
  </result>
</response>
```

As we can see, the results were returned without an error. Let's see how it works.

How it works...

Our index structure is very simple. It contains three fields:

- The document identifier (the `id` field)
- The book title (the `title` field)
- The authors of the book (the `author` field)

The data is very simple as well, so let's just skip discussing it.

The first query uses a standard Solr query parser and produces an error. This is because the query is not proper; there is no closing " character. This is only an example, and we can expect way more errors with user queries. If we want Solr to take care of such errors, we can use the Simple query parser, which we do in the second query. As you can see, the second query produces results for our query without an error. Of course, a phrase query is not run because the query was not properly constructed. However, we get results in spite of the fact that the query contains errors.

See also

- The Simple query parser allows us to use a subset of the default Lucene query language. The full documentation on Simple query parsers can be found at `https://cwiki.apache.org/confluence/display/solr/Other+Parsers#OtherParsers-SimpleQueryParser`.

Handling hierarchies with nested documents

In the real world, data is not flat, it contains many hierarchies that we need to handle. Sometimes it is not possible to flatten the data, but still we want to avoid cross and false matches. For example, let's assume that we have articles and comments to these articles, for example, news sites or blogs. Imagine that we want to search for articles and comments at the same time. To do this, we will use the Solr nested documents; this recipe will show you how to do this.

How to do it...

To handle hierarchies with nested documents, follow these steps:

1. We start by defining the index structure. To do this, we add the following fields to our `schema.xml` file:

```
<field name="id" type="string" indexed="true" stored="true"
required="true" />
<field name="title" type="text_general" indexed="true"
stored="true"/>
<field name="content" type="text_general" indexed="true"
stored="true"/>
<field name="author" type="text_general" indexed="true"
stored="true"/>
<field name="parent" type="boolean" indexed="true" stored="true"
multiValued="false" />
```

2. For the functionality of the nested documents, we need to define the `_root_` field in the `schema.xml` file. We do this by adding the following section to it:

```
<field name="_root_" type="string" indexed="true" stored="false"
/>
```

3. We also need a special cache defined, which is called `perSegFilter`. To define it, we need to add the following section to the `solrconfig.xml` file:

```
<cache name="perSegFilter" class="solr.search.LRUCache"
size="10" initialSize="0" autowarmCount="10" regenerator="solr.
NoOpRegenerator" />
```

4. Our example data looks as follows:

```
<add>
 <doc>
  <field name="id">1</field>
  <field name="title">Next-gen consoles announced</field>
  <field name="parent">true</field>
```

```
    <doc>
     <field name="id">10001</field>
     <field name="content">Great, can't wait!</field>
     <field name="author">annon</field>
     <field name="parent">false</field>
    </doc>
    <doc>
     <field name="id">10002</field>
     <field name="content">When they'll be out?</field>
     <field name="author">marel</field>
     <field name="parent">false</field>
    </doc>
   </doc>
   <doc>
    <field name="id">2</field>
    <field name="title">Next-gen consoles announced will be
  announced</field>
    <field name="parent">true</field>
    <doc>
     <field name="id">20001</field>
     <field name="content">New Mario, super!</field>
     <field name="author">ralf</field>
     <field name="parent">false</field>
    </doc>
   </doc>
  </add>
```

5. Let's look at the query now. Let's assume that we want to find articles with the `next-gen consoles` term in their title and the `out` term in one of the comments. This way, we should only match our first article. The query to achieve this looks as follows:

```
http://localhost:8983/solr/cookbook/select?q=title:(Next-gen
consoles)+_query_:"{!parent which=parent:true}content:out"&q.
op=AND
```

The results returned by Solr will be as follows:

```
<?xml version="1.0" encoding="UTF-8"?>
<response>
 <lst name="responseHeader">
  <int name="status">0</int>
  <int name="QTime">1</int>
  <lst name="params">
```

```
    <str name="q">title:(Next-gen consoles) _query_:"{!parent
which=parent:true}content:out"</str>
    <str name="q.op">AND</str>
   </lst>
  </lst>
  <result name="response" numFound="1" start="0">
   <doc>
    <str name="id">1</str>
    <str name="title">Next-gen consoles announced</str>
    <bool name="parent">true</bool>
    <long name="_version_">1471146160561324032</long></doc>
  </result>
 </response>
```

As we can see, everything works as it should, so let's see how it works.

How it works...

We start with the index structure. Since the parent and nested documents are stored in the same index (or collection), we have their fields defined in the same `schema.xml` file. Our parent document is described by the following:

- The `id` field that holds the identifier
- The `title` field that holds the title of the article

The children documents are described by the `id` field holding the identifier, the `content` field holding comment contents, the `author` field providing the author with the comment, and the special field called `_root_` that allows Solr to store the parent document identifier. Finally, we also have the `parent` field, which will hold information about whether the document is a parent or nested document.

The cache we defined in the `solrconfig.xml` file is a special cache used by Solr to provide nested document support. It needs to be called `perSegFilter` (`name="perSegFilter"`). It is constructed for each Lucene segment, so it is near real-time friendly. Like all the other caches Solr uses, we can set the `perSegFilter` cache's initial size (`initialSize="0"`), its maximum size (`size="10"`), and the auto warm count (`autowarmCount="10"`).

The example data is where things get interesting. As you can see, the parent documents look exactly the same. They contain the identifier, title, and information that they are the parent (`<field name="parent">true</field>`). However, in addition to the standard field information, we also included the nested documents inside the parent documents. Yes, that's right, we just nest the parent documents.

This is needed because the nested documents in Solr rely on only the Lucene block-join functionality, which means that we need to index the parent and nested documents in the same segment. In the children documents (the nested ones), we also index the information that there are children (`<field name="parent">false</field>`).

The query is the second interesting thing that we encounter in the recipe. The first query part, `title:(Next-gen consoles)`, is responsible for searching in the parent documents. We just search in the `title` field for the provided phrase. The next part of the query (`_query_:"{!parent which=parent:true}content:out"`) is the part with the nested documents query. We specify that we want to use the parent query parser (`{!parent`), which performs matching on the children documents and returns the parent documents. By adding the `which=parent:true` parameter, the parent query parser knows which documents are the parent ones (in our case, they are the ones with the `parent` field equal to `true`). The last part of the query is the standard field search (`content:out`); we just search the `content` field for the `out` term.

Finally, we tell Solr that we want all the query parts to be mandatory, by specifying the default Boolean query operator to `AND` and specifying `q.op=AND`.

There's more...

There is one more thing to remember when it comes to nested document support in Solr.

Returning children documents in the query

Of course, in addition to returning the parent documents, Solr can also return the children documents. We can do this using the `child` parser instead of the `parent` one that we used in our query. So, to return all the children documents for the parent document matching `Next-gen consoles` in the `title` field, we will run the following query:

```
http://localhost:8983/solr/cookbook/select?q={!child of=parent:true}
title:(Next-gen consoles)&q.op=AND
```

Sorting data on the basis of a function value

Suppose we have a search application that stores information about companies. Every company is described by a name and two floating point numbers that represent the geographical location of the company. One day your boss comes to your room and says that he wants the search results to be sorted by distance from the user's location. What's more, he wants us to force our search engine to return the distance from a user location to each of the returned companies. This recipe will show you how to achieve this requirement.

How to do it...

Let's perform the following steps to sort data on the basis of a function value:

1. For this recipe, we will begin with the following index structure (add the following entries to your `schema.xml`file):

   ```
   <field name="id" type="string" indexed="true" stored="true"
   required="true" />
   <field name="name" type="text_general" indexed="true"
   stored="true"/>
   <field name="location" type="location" indexed="true"
   stored="true" />
   <dynamicField name="*_coordinate" type="tdouble" indexed="true"
   stored="false" />
   ```

2. We also need to define the location type in our `schema.xml` file, so we add the following section to it:

   ```
   <fieldType name="location" class="solr.LatLonType"
   subFieldSuffix="_coordinate"/>
   ```

   I assume that the user location will be provided from the application that is making the query.

3. Now, let's index our example data file, which looks as follows:

   ```
   <add>
    <doc>
     <field name="id">1</field>
     <field name="name">Company 1</field>
     <field name="location">56.4,40.2</field>
    </doc>
    <doc>
     <field name="id">2</field>
     <field name="name">Company 2</field>
     <field name="location">50.1,48.9</field>
    </doc>
    <doc>
     <field name="id">3</field>
     <field name="name">Company 3</field>
     <field name="location">23.18,39.1</field>
    </doc>
   </add>
   ```

4. So, our user stands at the North Pole and uses our search application. Now, let's assume that we want to get the companies sorted in a way that the ones that are nearest to the user are at the top of the result list. In addition to this, we want to return the distance from the user's location to each of the companies. The query that matches our requirements will look as follows:

```
http://localhost:8983/solr/cookbook/select?q=name:company&sort=geo
dist(location,0.0,0.0)+asc&fl=*,distance:geodist(location,0.0,0.0)
```

The results of this query will look like this:

```
<?xml version="1.0" encoding="UTF-8"?>
<response>
 <lst name="responseHeader">
  <int name="status">0</int>
  <int name="QTime">1</int>
  <lst name="params">
   <str name="q">name:company</str>
   <str name="fl">*,distance:geodist(location,0.0,0.0)</str>
   <str name="sort">geodist(location,0.0,0.0) asc</str>
  </lst>
 </lst>
 <result name="response" numFound="3" start="0">
  <doc>
   <str name="id">3</str>
   <str name="name">Company 3</str>
   <str name="location">23.18,39.1</str>
   <long name="_version_">1471140606301437952</long>
   <double name="distance">4946.836542733629</double></doc>
  <doc>
   <str name="id">1</str>
   <str name="name">Company 1</str>
   <str name="location">56.4,40.2</str>
   <long name="_version_">1471140606244814848</long>
   <double name="distance">7227.258357265134</double></doc>
  <doc>
   <str name="id">2</str>
   <str name="name">Company 2</str>
   <str name="location">50.1,48.9</str>
   <long name="_version_">1471140606300389376</long>
   <double name="distance">7234.322642147299</double></doc>
 </result>
</response>
```

If you want to calculate the distance by hand, you will see that the results are sorted as they should be.

How it works...

As you can see in the index structure and data, every company is described by three fields:

- `id`: This is the unique identifier
- `name`: This is the company name
- `location`: This is the latitude and longitude of the company location

I'll skip commenting on how the actual location of the company is stored; if you want to read more about it, refer to the *Indexing multiple geographical points* recipe from *Chapter 2, Indexing Your Data*.

We wanted to get the companies that match the given query and are sorted in ascending order from the North Pole. To do this, we run a simple query that asks for companies with the term `company` in the `name` field. The second thing is the sorting order. We included a function there, the `geodist` function, which calculates the distance between points. In our example, the function takes three parameters:

- The first parameter specifies the field in the index that should be used to calculate the distance
- The second parameter is the latitude value of the point from which the distance will be calculated
- The third parameter is the longitude value of the point from which the distance will be calculated

After the function, there is the order of the sort, which in our case is `asc`, which means it is in ascending order.

Finally, we modified the fields returned for each document in the result. We did this by specifying the `fl=*,distance:geodist(location,0.0,0.0)` parameter. It basically means to return all the stored fields for a document (the `*` value), and in addition to this, includes the value of the function query—the same that we used for distance calculation and sorting. However, we did one more thing—we told Solr to return the calculated distance in the field called `distance` (of course, the field is not present in our index structure). We did this by appending the function name with the name of the pseudo field and the `:` character, in our case, `distance:`. This forced Solr to return the distance, not in a field called `geodist(location,0.0,0.0)`, but in one called `distance`. Of course, this is not needed, but it is convenient and easier to read.

Controlling the number of terms needed to match

Imagine a situation where you have an e-commerce bookstore and you want to make a search algorithm that tries to bring the best search results to your customers. However, you notice that many of your customers tend to make queries with too many words, which results in an empty result list. So, you decide to make a query that will require a maximum of two of the words, which the user entered, to be matched. This recipe will show you how to do it.

Getting ready

Before we continue, it is crucial to mention that the following method can only be used with the `dismax` or `edismax` query parser. For the list of available query parsers, refer to `http://wiki.apache.org/solr/QueryParser`.

How to do it...

Follow these steps to control the number of terms needed to match:

1. Let's begin with creating our index structure. For our simple use case, we will only have documents with the identifier (the `id` field) and title (the `title` field). We define the index structure by adding the following section to the `schema.xml` file:

```
<field name="id" type="string" indexed="true" stored="true"
required="true" />
<field name="title" type="text" indexed="true" stored="true" />
```

2. Now, let's look at the example data:

```
<add>
 <doc>
  <field name="id">1</field>
  <field name="title">Solrcook book revised</field>
 </doc>
 <doc>
  <field name="id">2</field>
  <field name="title">Some book that was revised</field>
 </doc>
 <doc>
  <field name="id">3</field>
  <field name="title">Another revised book</field>
 </doc>
</add>
```

3. The third step is to make a query that will satisfy the requirements. For example, let's imagine that we want 100 percent of the terms matched for queries that have three or fewer terms in them, and only 25 percent of the terms matched for queries that have four or more terms. Such a query might look like this:

```
http://localhost:8983/solr/cookbook/select?q=book+revised+another+
different+word+that+doesnt+count&defType=dismax&mm=3<25%25
```

This query will return the following results:

```
<?xml version="1.0" encoding="UTF-8"?>
<response>
 <lst name="responseHeader">
  <int name="status">0</int>
  <int name="QTime">1</int>
  <lst name="params">
   <str name="mm">3&lt;25%</str>
   <str name="q">book revised another different word that doesnt
count</str>
   <str name="defType">dismax</str>
  </lst>
 </lst>
 <result name="response" numFound="3" start="0">
  <doc>
   <str name="id">3</str>
   <str name="title">Another revised book</str>
   <long name="_version_">1470445837694795776</long></doc>
  <doc>
   <str name="id">2</str>
   <str name="title">Some book that was revised</str>
   <long name="_version_">1470445837693747200</long></doc>
  <doc>
   <str name="id">1</str>
   <str name="title">Solrcook book revised</str>
   <long name="_version_">1470445837648658432</long></doc>
 </result>
</response>
```

On the other hand, let's look at the following query:

```
http://localhost:8983/solr/cookbook/select?q=book+revised+another&defT
ype=dismax&mm=3<25%25
```

This query will return the following results:

```
<?xml version="1.0" encoding="UTF-8"?>
<response>
 <lst name="responseHeader">
  <int name="status">0</int>
  <int name="QTime">1</int>
  <lst name="params">
   <str name="mm">3&lt;25%</str>
   <str name="q">book revised another</str>
   <str name="defType">dismax</str>
  </lst>
 </lst>
 <result name="response" numFound="1" start="0">
  <doc>
   <str name="id">3</str>
   <str name="title">Another revised book</str>
   <long name="_version_">1470445837694795776</long></doc>
 </result>
</response>
```

As you can see, only a single document was returned. Now, let's see how it works.

How it works...

The index structure and data are fairly simple. Every book is described by using two fields:

- The unique identifier
- The title

The data itself is not complicated, so let's skip discussing it.

The query is the thing that we are interested in. The first query sends eight terms in the `q` parameter. However, since we are using the `dismax` query parser (the `defType=dismax` parameter) and added the mysterious `mm` parameter, Solr returned three documents. This is because we specified `mm=3<25%25` (which is in fact `mm=3<25%`, but we needed to URL-encode it). It tells Solr to enforce matching all the query terms. If there are three or fewer terms present in the query, they must all match. If there are more terms in the query, at least 25 percent of the query terms must be found in a document for it to be considered a match.

Now, if we look at the second query, we notice that it has three terms in it, and it only returns a single document, the one with all three terms matched. Apart from the `q` parameter, all the others, especially the `mm` parameter stayed the same. As you remember, we set the `mm` parameter so that queries that have three or less terms must have all of them matched in a document for that document to be returned in the results. And this is the case in the second example.

Before we finish, let's get back to the first query and its results. Note that the document that has three words matched is at the top of the list. The relevance algorithm is still there, which means that the documents that have more words that matched the query will be higher on the result list than those that have less words that match the query.

See also

- The documentation on the `mm` parameter can be found at `http://lucene.apache.org/solr/4_10_0/solr-core/org/apache/solr/util/doc-files/min-should-match.html`

Affecting document score using function queries

There are many situations where you would like to have an influence on how the score of the documents is calculated. For example, you would like to boost the documents on the basis of the purchases of it. As in, as an e-commerce bookstore, you would like to be showed relevant results, but you would also like to influence them by adding yet another factor to their score. Is this possible? Yes, and this recipe will show you how to do it.

How to do it...

Let's see how the document score is affected using function queries and the following steps:

1. Let's start by defining the index structure by adding the following section to the `schema.xml` file:

```
<field name="id" type="string" indexed="true" stored="true"
required="true" />
<field name="title" type="text_general" indexed="true"
stored="true" />
<field name="sold" type="int" indexed="true" stored="true" />
```

2. The second step will be the example data, which looks like this:

```
<add>
 <doc>
  <field name="id">1</field>
  <field name="title">Solrcook book revised</field>
  <field name="sold">5</field>
 </doc>
 <doc>
```

```
  <field name="id">2</field>
  <field name="title">Some book revised</field>
  <field name="sold">200</field>
 </doc>
 <doc>
  <field name="id">3</field>
  <field name="title">Another revised book</field>
  <field name="sold">60</field>
 </doc>
</add>
```

3. After indexing our data, we can try to boost our documents using function queries. Our user types `revised` into the search box, and we want to return the most relevant results. Our simple query looks as follows:

   ```
   http://localhost:8983/solr/cookbook/select?defType=dismax&qf=title
   &q=revised&fl=*,score
   ```

   The results will look like the following:

   ```
   <?xml version="1.0" encoding="UTF-8"?>
   <response>
    <lst name="responseHeader">
     <int name="status">0</int>
     <int name="QTime">1</int>
     <lst name="params">
      <str name="q">revised</str>
      <str name="defType">dismax</str>
      <str name="qf">title</str>
      <str name="fl">*,score</str>
     </lst>
    </lst>
    <result name="response" numFound="3" start="0"
   maxScore="0.35615897">
     <doc>
      <str name="id">1</str>
      <str name="title">Solrcook book revised</str>
      <int name="sold">5</int>
      <long name="_version_">1470467358823809024</long>
      <float name="score">0.35615897</float></doc>
     <doc>
      <str name="id">2</str>
      <str name="title">Some book revised</str>
      <int name="sold">200</int>
   ```

```
    <long name="_version_">1470467358872043520</long>
    <float name="score">0.35615897</float></doc>
   <doc>
    <str name="id">3</str>
    <str name="title">Another revised book</str>
    <int name="sold">60</int>
    <long name="_version_">1470467358873092096</long>
    <float name="score">0.35615897</float></doc>
  </result>
</response>
```

4. Now let's add another factor to our scoring mechanism. What we would like to do is affect the score of the document on the basis of how many books were sold. Basically, we want the score affected by the contents of the `sold` field. To do that, we add the following parameter to our query:

```
bf=product(sold)
```

So, our modified query will look like this:

http://localhost:8983/solr/cookbook/select?defType=dismax&qf=title&q=revised&fl=*,score&bf=product(sold)

The results for the preceding query will look like this:

```
<?xml version="1.0" encoding="UTF-8"?>
<response>
 <lst name="responseHeader">
  <int name="status">0</int>
  <int name="QTime">0</int>
  <lst name="params">
   <str name="q">revised</str>
   <str name="defType">dismax</str>
   <str name="bf">product(sold)</str>
   <str name="qf">title</str>
   <str name="indent">true</str>
   <str name="fl">*,score</str>
  </lst>
 </lst>
 <result name="response" numFound="3" start="0"
maxScore="163.1048">
  <doc>
   <str name="id">2</str>
   <str name="title">Some book revised</str>
   <int name="sold">200</int>
   <long name="_version_">1470467358872043520</long>
   <float name="score">163.1048</float></doc>
  <doc>
   <str name="id">3</str>
```

```
    <str name="title">Another revised book</str>
    <int name="sold">60</int>
    <long name="_version_">1470467358873092096</long>
    <float name="score">49.07608</float></doc>
   <doc>
    <str name="id">1</str>
    <str name="title">Solrcook book revised</str>
    <int name="sold">5</int>
    <long name="_version_">1470467358823809024</long>
    <float name="score">4.279089</float></doc>
  </result>
</response>
```

As you see, adding the parameter changes the whole result list. Now, let's see why this happened.

How it works...

The `schema.xml` file is simple. It contains three fields:

- `id`: This is responsible for holding the unique identifier of the book
- `title`: This is the book title
- `sold`: This is the number of books that have been sold during the last month

Our example data is very simple, but let's discuss it. We have three example books and each of the books has the same number of words in the `title` field. This is why, when typing the first query, all documents get the same score. As you see, the first book is the one with the least pieces sold, and this is not what we want to achieve.

This is why we added the `bf` parameter. It tells Solr what function to use to affect the scoring computation (in this case, the result of the function will be added to the score of the document). In our case, it is the `product` function, which returns the product of the values we provide as its arguments; in our case, the one and only argument of the function will be the value of the book's `sold` field.

The result list of the modified query clearly shows how the scoring was affected by the function. In the first place on the results list, we have the book that was the most popular during the last week. The next book is the one that was less popular than the first book, but more popular than the last book. The last book on the results list is the least popular.

See also

- If you want to know more about the functions available in Solr, go to the Solr wiki page at `https://cwiki.apache.org/confluence/display/solr/Function+Queries`

Using simple nested queries

Imagine a situation where you need a query nested inside another query. For example, you want to run a query using the standard request handler, but you need to embed a query that is parsed by the `dismax` query parser inside it. For example, we will like to find all the books having a certain phrase in their title, and boost the ones that have a part of the phrase present. This recipe will show you how to do this.

How to do it...

Let's start with a simple index that has the following structure:

1. You need to put the following section to the `schema.xml` file:

```
<field name="id" type="string" indexed="true" stored="true"
required="true" />
<field name="title" type="text_general" indexed="true"
stored="true" />
```

2. The next step is data indexing. Our example data looks as follows:

```
<add>
 <doc>
  <field name="id">1</field>
  <field name="title">Revised solrcookbook</field>
 </doc>
 <doc>
  <field name="id">2</field>
  <field name="title">Some book revised</field>
 </doc>
 <doc>
  <field name="id">3</field>
  <field name="title">Another revised little book</field>
 </doc>
</add>
```

3. Now, let's prepare a query that matches our initial requirements. Let's assume we are searching for the terms `book` and `revised` in the `title` field, but we would also like to boost the books that have the `revised little` phrase and terms in the same `title` field. Such a query would look like this:

```
http://localhost:8983/solr/cookbook/select?q=book+revised+_
query_:"{!dismax qf=title pf=title^10 v=$qq}"&qq=revised+little&df
=title
```

The results of this query should look like this:

```
<?xml version="1.0" encoding="UTF-8"?>
<response>
 <lst name="responseHeader">
  <int name="status">0</int>
  <int name="QTime">2</int>
  <lst name="params">
   <str name="qq">revised little</str>
   <str name="q">book revised _query_:"{!dismax qf=title
pf=title^10 v=$qq}"</str>
   <str name="df">title</str>
  </lst>
 </lst>
 <result name="response" numFound="3" start="0">
  <doc>
   <str name="id">3</str>
   <str name="title">Another revised little book</str>
   <long name="_version_">1470513872076013568</long></doc>
  <doc>
   <str name="id">2</str>
   <str name="title">Some book revised</str>
   <long name="_version_">1470513872074964992</long></doc>
  <doc>
   <str name="id">1</str>
   <str name="title">Revised solr cookbook</str>
   <long name="_version_">1470513872027779072</long></doc>
 </result>
</response>
```

As you can see, the results list was sorted exactly the way we wanted. Now, let's see how it works.

How it works...

As you can see, our index is very simple. It consists of two fields:

- One field holds the unique identifier (the `id` field)
- Another field holds the title of the book (the `title` field)

The query is what we are interested in. The `q` parameter is built using two parts. The first part, `book+revised`, is just a usual query composed from two terms. The second part of the query starts with a strange-looking expression, `_query_`. This expression tells Solr that another query should be made that will affect the results list. Notice that the expression is surrounded with `"` characters.

Then, we see the expression telling Solr to use the `dismax` query parser (the `!dismax` part) and the parameters that will be passed to the parser (`qf` and `pf`). The `v` parameter is an abbreviation for value, and it is used to pass the value of the `q` parameter. The value passed to the `dismax` query parser will be `revised+little` in our case. Why? You can see something that is called **parameter dereferencing**. By the use of the `$qq` expression, we tell Solr to use the value of the `qq` parameter. Of course, we can pass the value to the `v` parameter, but I wanted to show you how to use the dereferencing mechanism. The `qq` parameter (it can take any other name you choose) is set to `revised+little` and used by Solr as a parameter for the query that was passed to the `dismax` query parser. The last parameter, `df=title`, tells Solr which field should be used as the default search field. Remember that using parameter dereferencing allows us to simplify the queries sent to Solr and save common parts of queries in the request handler configuration.

As we can see in the result list, Solr returns all the documents for the first part of the query and boosts the document matching the second query.

Using the Solr document query join functionality

When using Solr, you will probably be used to having a flat structure of documents without any relationships. However, there are situations where decomposing relationships is a cost we can't bear. Due to this, Solr 4.0 comes with a join functionality that lets us use some basic relationships. For example, imagine that our index consists of books and workbooks, and we want to use this relationship. This recipe will show you how to do this.

How to do it...

Let's perform the following steps:

1. First of all, let's assume that we have the following index structure (just place the following entries in your `schema.xml` file):

```
<field name="id" type="string" indexed="true" stored="true"
required="true" multiValued="false" />
<field name="name" type="text_general" indexed="true"
stored="true" multiValued="false"/>
<field name="type" type="string" indexed="true" stored="true"/>
<field name="book" type="string" indexed="true" stored="true"/>
```

2. Now, let's index our test data that looks as follows:

```
<add>
 <doc>
  <field name="id">1</field>
```

```
    <field name="name">Book 1</field>
    <field name="type">book</field>
   </doc>
   <doc>
    <field name="id">2</field>
    <field name="name">Book 2</field>
    <field name="type">book</field>
   </doc>
   <doc>
    <field name="id">3</field>
    <field name="name">Workbook A</field>
    <field name="type">workbook</field>
    <field name="book">1</field>
   </doc>
   <doc>
    <field name="id">4</field>
    <field name="name">Workbook B</field>
    <field name="type">workbook</field>
    <field name="book">2</field>
   </doc>
  </add>
```

3. Let's assume we want to get all the books that have workbooks. Also, we want to narrow the books we have to search, since we are searching only for those that have the character `2` in their names. In order to do this, we run the following query:

   ```
   http://localhost:8983/solr/cookbook/select/?q={!join from=book
   to=id}type:workbook&fq=name:2
   ```

   The Solr response for this query is as follows:

   ```
   <?xml version="1.0" encoding="UTF-8"?>
   <response>
    <lst name="responseHeader">
     <int name="status">0</int>
     <int name="QTime">1</int>
     <lst name="params">
      <str name="q">{!join from=book to=id}type:workbook</str>
      <str name="fq">name:2</str>
     </lst>
    </lst>
    <result name="response" numFound="1" start="0">
     <doc>
      <str name="id">2</str>
      <str name="name">Book 2</str>
   ```

```
        <str name="type">book</str>
        <long name="_version_">1471154992469508096</long></doc>
      </result>
    </response>
```

As you can see, the returned document is exactly the one we expected.

How it works...

Although the example index structure is simple, I would like to comment on it. The `id` field is responsible for holding the unique identifier of the document, the `name` field is the document name, the `type` field holds documents types, and the `book` field is optional and specifies the identifier of the parent document. So, you can see that in our example data, we have two parent documents (those with `id` field values of `1` and `2`) and two child documents (those with `id` field values of `3` and `4`).

Now, let's stop for a bit before looking at the query and look at our example data. If you query only for workbooks, you will get documents with identifiers `3` and `4`. The parent for the document with an `id` field equal to `3` is `1`, and the parent for the document with the `id` field equal to `4` is `2`. If we filter `1` and `2` with the `fq=name:2` filter, we should only get the document with the `id` field equal to `2` as the result. So, looking at the query result, it works as intended, but how does the query actually work?

I'll begin the description from the join part—`q={!join from=book to=id} type:workbook`. As you can see, we used local parameters to choose different types of query parsers, such as the join query parser (the `!join` part of the query). We specified that children documents should use the `book` field (the `from` parameter) and join it with the `id` field (the `to` parameter). The `type:workbook` part specifies the query we run; we want only those documents that have the `workbook` value in their `type` field. The `fq` parameter, which narrows the result set to only those documents that have the value `2` in the `name` field, is applied after the join is executed, so we only apply it to the parent documents.

Note that the Solr pseudo join results only contain the parent's documents, not children, which is a bit different from the join of relational databases.

Handling typos with n-grams

Sometimes, there are situations where you would like to have some kind of functionality that allows you to give your user the search results even though he made a typo, perhaps even more than one typo. In Solr, there are multiple ways to do this—use the Spellchecker component and try to correct the user's mistake, use fuzzy queries, or use the n-gram approach. This recipe will concentrate on the third approach and show you how to use n-grams to handle user typos.

How to do it...

For this recipe, let's assume that our index is built of four fields: `identifier`, `name`, `description`, and `description_ngram`, which will be processed with the n-gram filter.

1. So, let's start with the definition of our index structure that can look like this (we will place the following entries in the `schema.xml` file):

```
<field name="id" type="string" indexed="true" stored="true"
required="true" multiValued="false" />
<field name="name" type="text_general" indexed="true"
stored="true"/>
<field name="description" type="text_general" indexed="true"
stored="true" />
<field name="description_ngram" type="text_ngram" indexed="true"
stored="false" />
```

2. Since we want to use the n-gram approach, we will include the following filter in our `text_ngram` field type definition:

```
<filter class="solr.NGramFilterFactory" minGramSize="2"
maxGramSize="2" />
```

The filter will be responsible for dividing the indexed data and queries into two bi-grams. To better illustrate what I mean, look at the following screenshot, which shows how the mentioned filter worked for the word `multiple`:

NGTF	text	mu	ul	lt	ti	ip	pl	le
	raw_bytes	[6d 75]	[75 6c]	[6c 74]	[74 69]	[69 70]	[70 6c]	[6c 65]
	start	0	0	0	0	0	0	0
	end	8	8	8	8	8	8	8
	positionLength	1	1	1	1	1	1	1
	position	1	1	1	1	1	1	1
	type	word	word	word	word	word	word	word

So, the whole `text_ngram` type definition will look like this:

```
<fieldType name="text_ngram" class="solr.TextField"
positionIncrementGap="100">
 <analyzer>
  <tokenizer class="solr.StandardTokenizerFactory"/>
  <filter class="solr.LowerCaseFilterFactory"/>
  <filter class="solr.NGramFilterFactory" minGramSize="2"
maxGramSize="2" />
 </analyzer>
</fieldType>
```

3. We also need to add the copy field definition to our `schema.xml` file to automatically copy the value of the `description` field to the `description_ngram` field. To copy the field definition, use the following code:

   ```
   <copyField source="description" dest="description_ngram" />
   ```

4. Now, we can index our data. For this recipe, I used the following data sample:

   ```
   <add>
    <doc>
     <field name="id">1</field>
     <field name="name">Solr Cookbook 4.0</field>
     <field name="description">Solr Cookbook 4.0 contains multiple
   recipes helping you with your everyday work with Solr :)</field>
    </doc>
    <doc>
     <field name="id">2</field>
     <field name="name">Elasticsearch Server second edition</field>
     <field name="description">A nice book about Elasticsearch for
   novice and intermediate users</field>
    </doc>
   </add>
   ```

5. After indexing it, I decided to test if my query can handle a single typo in each of the words provided to the query, so I sent the following query to Solr:

   ```
   http://localhost:8983/solr/cookbook/select?q=description:(kontains
   +multyple) description_ngram:"kontains+multyple"&q.op=OR
   ```

The words I am interested in are `contains` and `multiple`. The result of the query is as follows:

```
<?xml version="1.0" encoding="UTF-8"?>
<response>
 <lst name="responseHeader">
  <int name="status">0</int>
  <int name="QTime">3</int>
  <lst name="params">
   <str name="q">description:(kontains multyple) description_
ngram:"kontains multyple"</str>
   <str name="q.op">OR</str>
  </lst>
 </lst>
 <result name="response" numFound="1" start="0">
  <doc>
   <str name="id">1</str>
```

```
    <str name="name">Solr Cookbook 4.0</str>
    <str name="description">Solr Cookbook 4.0 contains multiple recipes
helping you with your everyday work with Solr :)</str>
    <long name="_version_">1471155870918246400</long></doc>
  </result>
</response>
```

As you can see, the document we are interested in is found. So, let's see how this works.

How it works...

As you can see from the index structure, we have two fields, `name` and `description`, defined to use the `text_ngram` field. We want these fields to support returning search results even when users enter a typo of some kind.

To allow this, we use the `solr.NGramFilterFactory` filter with two attributes defined, the `minGramSize` attribute that sets the minimum size of the produced n-gram, and the `maxGramSize` attribute that sets the maximum size of the produced n-gram. With both of those attributes set to `2`, we configure the `solr.NGramFilterFactory` filter to produce the so-called **2-grams**, which are tokens that are built of two characters. The third attribute of the `filter` tag, the `class` attribute, specifies the filter factory class we want to use.

Let's concentrate on the previous screenshot to discuss how the `solr.NGramFilterFactory` filter works in our case. As I wrote earlier, we want the n-gram filter to produce grams built of two characters. You can see how the filter we chose works. From the `multiple` word, it created the following bi-grams (n-grams built from 2 characters):

```
mu ul lttiippl le
```

So the idea of the algorithm is quite simple—divide the word so that we take the first character and the character after it and make a bi-gram from it. Then, we take the second character and the next character to create the second bi-gram, and so on, until we can't make any more bi-grams.

Now, if you look at the query, there are two words we are looking for, and both of them have a typo in them. The `kontains` word will be `contain` without a typo, and the `multyple` word will be `multiple` without a typo. However, we assume that our user made the typo. Our query also specifies the logical query operator we want to use, which is the `OR` operator. We use it because we want to match all documents with even a single match to any bi-gram. If we turn the `kontainsmultyple` tokens into bi-grams, we will get the following (I'll use the | character to separate the words from each other):

```
ko on nt ta ai in ns | mu ul lt ty yppl le
```

If we turn the `contains multiple` tokens into bi-grams, we will get the following:

```
co on nt ta ai in ns | mu ul lttiippl le
```

If you compare these bi-grams, you will see that only three of them differ between the proper words and the ones with typos. The rest of them are the same. As a result of this, our query finds the document we indexed. You might wonder why we queried both the `description` and `description_ngram` fields. We did this because we don't know if the client's query is one with typos or without. If it is without, we want the documents with better matches to be higher in the results list than the ones that are not perfectly matched. Notice that we used the phrase query against the `description_ngram` field; we need to do this, otherwise the second of our documents will also be matched because it has similar bi-grams just on different positions and not close to each other.

Of course, all of this doesn't come without some downsides. One of the major downsides of this approach is the growth of the index size because of the number of tokens produced by the n-gram filter. The second downside is the number of results produced as a result of such an approach; there will be many more results than you are used to, and that's why we queried both the `description` and `description_ngram` fields because we want to increase the score of the perfectly matched documents (you can also boost the `description` field during query). You can also try the same approach with the `edismax` query parser, and the minimum should match the `mm` parameter, but this is beyond the scope of this recipe.

Rescoring query results

Imagine a situation in which your score calculation is affected by numerous function queries, which makes the score calculation very CPU-intensive. This is not a problem for small result sets, but it is for larger ones. Starting from Solr 4.9, this great search engine gives us the possibility of rerank results. This means that Solr will get some results from our initial query and will apply another query only on those results. The query that is applied modifies the score of the documents. This recipe will show you how this can be done.

How to do it...

Let's say that we have a use case where we want to show the latest books added to our index and boost them on the basis of some additional query. To do this, we will need to take the following steps:

1. Let's start with a simple index structure. Our index will be built of three fields that look as follows (please put the following entries to the `schema.xml` file):

```
<field name="id" type="string" indexed="true" stored="true"
required="true" />
<field name="title" type="text_general" indexed="true"
stored="true" />
<field name="added" type="date" indexed="true" stored="true" />
```

2. Next, we index our example data that looks as follows:

```
<add>
 <doc>
  <field name="id">1</field>
  <field name="title">Solr 4.0 cookbook</field>
  <field name="added">2012-01-12T23:59:59Z</field>
 </doc>
 <doc>
  <field name="id">2</field>
  <field name="title">Solr 3.1 cookbook</field>
  <field name="added">2011-07-01T23:59:59Z</field>
 </doc>
 <doc>
  <field name="id">3</field>
  <field name="title">Elasticsearch Server</field>
  <field name="added">2012-03-01T23:59:59Z</field>
 </doc>
 <doc>
  <field name="id">4</field>
  <field name="title">Elasticsearch Server second edition</field>
  <field name="added">2014-04-01T23:59:59Z</field>
 </doc>
 <doc>
  <field name="id">5</field>
  <field name="title">Mastering Elasticsearch</field>
  <field name="added">2013-11-01T23:59:59Z</field>
 </doc>
</add>
```

3. Let's assume that our standard query looks as follows:

```
http://localhost:8983/solr/cookbook/select?q={!boost%20
b=recip(ms(NOW,added),3.16e-11,1,1)}*:*+OR+_query_:"title:solr+tit
le:cookbook"&fl=*,score
```

4. The results returned by Solr looks like this (note that your score for the documents might be different because of the time):

```
<?xml version="1.0" encoding="UTF-8"?>
<response>
<lst name="responseHeader">
  <int name="status">0</int>
  <int name="QTime">3</int>
  <lst name="params">
```

```
    <str name="q">{!boost b=recip(ms(NOW,added),3.16e-11,1,1)}*:*
OR _query_:"title:solr title:cookbook"</str>
    <str name="fl">*,score</str>
  </lst>
</lst>
<result name="response" numFound="5" start="0"
maxScore="0.35659808">
  <doc>
    <str name="id">1</str>
    <str name="title">Solr 4.0 cookbook</str>
    <date name="added">2012-01-12T23:59:59Z</date>
    <long name="_version_">1487144228514430976</long>
    <float name="score">0.35659808</float></doc>
  <doc>
    <str name="id">2</str>
    <str name="title">Solr 3.1 cookbook</str>
    <date name="added">2011-07-01T23:59:59Z</date>
    <long name="_version_">1487144228588879872</long>
    <float name="score">0.31378558</float></doc>
  <doc>
    <str name="id">4</str>
    <str name="title">Elasticsearch Server second edition</str>
    <date name="added">2014-04-01T23:59:59Z</date>
    <long name="_version_">1487144228589928448</long>
    <float name="score">0.12536839</float></doc>
  <doc>
    <str name="id">5</str>
    <str name="title">Mastering Elasticsearch</str>
    <date name="added">2013-11-01T23:59:59Z</date>
    <long name="_version_">1487144228590977024</long>
    <float name="score">0.10079001</float></doc>
  <doc>
    <str name="id">3</str>
    <str name="title">Elasticsearch Server</str>
    <date name="added">2012-03-01T23:59:59Z</date>
    <long name="_version_">1487144228588879873</long>
    <float name="score">0.056244835</float></doc>
</result>
</response>
```

5. Of course, this is only an example. To see the actual difference in query execution time, we need to have way more documents indexed than the five shown in the example. However, let's assume that the query is being run for a longer period of time. The modified query that scores only the top documents looks as follows:

   ```
   http://localhost:8983/solr/cookbook/select?q=*:*&rq={!rerank reRan
   kQuery=$rerankQueryreRankDocs=100 reRankWeight=10}&rerankQuery=tit
   le:solr+title:cookbook&sort=added+desc&fl=score,*
   ```

6. The results are as follows:


```
<?xml version="1.0" encoding="UTF-8"?>
<response>
 <lst name="responseHeader">
  <int name="status">0</int>
  <int name="QTime">1</int>
  <lst name="params">
   <str name="q">*:*</str>
   <str name="rerankQuery">title:solr title:cookbook</str>
   <str name="fl">score,*</str>
   <str name="sort">added desc</str>
   <str name="rq">{!rerank reRankQuery=$rerankQuery reRankDocs=100
reRankWeight=10}</str>
  </lst>
 </lst>
 <result name="response" numFound="5" start="0"
maxScore="11.68315">
  <doc>
   <str name="id">1</str>
   <str name="title">Solr 4.0 cookbook</str>
   <date name="added">2012-01-12T23:59:59Z</date>
   <long name="_version_">1471421442477260800</long>
   <float name="score">11.68315</float></doc>
  <doc>
   <str name="id">2</str>
   <str name="title">Solr 3.1 cookbook</str>
   <date name="added">2011-07-01T23:59:59Z</date>
   <long name="_version_">1471421442543321088</long>
   <float name="score">11.68315</float></doc>
  <doc>
   <str name="id">3</str>
   <str name="title">Elasticsearch Server</str>
   <date name="added">2012-03-01T23:59:59Z</date>
```

```
    <long name="_version_">1471421442544369664</long>
    <float name="score">1.0</float></doc>
   <doc>
    <str name="id">4</str>
    <str name="title">Elasticsearch Server second edition</str>
    <date name="added">2014-04-01T23:59:59Z</date>
    <long name="_version_">1471421442544369665</long>
    <float name="score">1.0</float></doc>
   <doc>
    <str name="id">5</str>
    <str name="title">Mastering Elasticsearch</str>
    <date name="added">2013-11-01T23:59:59Z</date>
    <long name="_version_">1471421442545418240</long>
    <float name="score">1.0</float></doc>
  </result>
</response>
```

As we can see, the results changed, and believe me, so did the execution time. Now, let's see how it works.

How it works...

Our index structure is very simple; it contains the following:

- The book identifier (the `id` field)
- The book title (the `title` field)
- The date the book was added into our application (the `added` field)

The example data is also very simple, so let's skip discussing it.

Our initial query asks for all documents in the index and boosts the documents that were added recently (`{!boost%20b=recip(ms(NOW,added),3.16e-11,1,1)}*:*`). We also boost the documents by adding an `OR` query (`_query_:"title:solr+title:cookbook"`). The results returned by Solr shows that the query works as it should.

The `recip(field_name, m, a, b)` is a reciprocal function that implements `a/(m*x+b)`, where `m`, `a`, and `b` are constants, and `x` is the value stored in `field_name`. For a description of available functions, refer to the official Solr documentation available at `https://cwiki.apache.org/confluence/display/solr/Function+Queries`.

The thing is that we are calculating the score of the documents for all of the documents that match the query, and for some use cases, this is not the best way, it might be too resource-heavy. This is why we modified our query. It also queries for all the documents (`q=*:*`); however, it first sorts the document on the basis of the date they were added (`sort=added+desc`). In this way, we have the newest documents at the top of the results set, so we are sure we will use them to score calculations using our reranking.

Instead of calculating the score for all the documents, we decided to use the Solr rerank functionality. We specified the query that should be used for boosting (`rerankQuery=title:solr+title:cookbook`) and included the rerank functionality. To do this, we used the `rq` parameter and rerank query parser (`!rerank`). It allows us to specify the rerank query by dereferencing the query itself; we said that Solr should take the query stored in the `rerankQuery` parameter (`reRankQuery=$rerankQuery`). We also said that we only want the score to be calculated on the top 100 documents returned by our query (`reRankDocs=100`) and the rerank weight to be set to `10` (`reRankWeight=10`). The best thing about the second query is that the score using the boosting query will only be given for the top 100 documents because of the `reRankDocs` property. If you look at the results, you can see that the score was properly calculated.

The thing to keep in mind is that this method can't be used every time, for every query, and every use case. If you need to score all the documents and show only the top ones among them, you can't use this method. In our case, we were able to change the boosting on date for date sorting because we are only interested in the newest documents, but remember that this is not always the case.

5
Faceting

In this chapter, we will cover the following topics:

- Getting the number of documents with the same field value
- Getting the number of documents with the same value range
- Getting the number of documents matching the query and subquery
- Removing filters from faceting results
- Using decision tree faceting
- Calculating faceting for relevant documents in groups
- Improving faceting performance for low cardinality fields

Introduction

One of the advantages of Solr is its ability to calculate statistics from your data. Solr faceting mechanism provides functionalities that can help us in several tasks that we do every day. From getting the number of documents with the same values in a field (for example, companies from the same city) through the ability of date and range faceting, to the autocomplete features based on the faceting mechanism. This chapter will show you how to handle some of the common tasks when using the faceting mechanism.

Getting the number of documents with the same field value

Imagine a situation where you have to return the number of documents with the same field value besides the search results. For example, you have an application that allows your user to search for companies in Europe and your client wants to have the number of companies in the cities where the companies that were found by the query are located. To do this, you can of course run several queries, but Solr provides a mechanism called faceting that can do this for you. This recipe will show you how to use it.

How to do it...

1. Let's start by assuming that we have the following fields present in the `schema.xml` file:

   ```
   <field name="id" type="string" indexed="true" stored="true"
   required="true" />
   <field name="name" type="text_general" indexed="true"
   stored="true" />
   <field name="city" type="string" indexed="true" stored="true" />
   ```

2. The next step is to index the following example data:

   ```
   <add>
    <doc>
     <field name="id">1</field>
     <field name="name">Company 1</field>
     <field name="city">New York</field>
    </doc>
    <doc>
     <field name="id">2</field>
     <field name="name">Company 2</field>
     <field name="city">New Orleans</field>
    </doc>
    <doc>
     <field name="id">3</field>
     <field name="name">Company 3</field>
     <field name="city">New York</field>
    </doc>
   </add>
   ```

3. Suppose that our hypothetical user searches for the word `company`. Apart from the query results, we would also like to return the number of documents with the same city. The query that will give us what we want should look as follows:

```
http://localhost:8983/solr/cookbook/select?q=name:company&facet=tr
ue&facet.field=city
```

   The result of the preceding query should be as follows:

```
<?xml version="1.0" encoding="UTF-8"?>
<response>
 <lst name="responseHeader">
  <int name="status">0</int>
  <int name="QTime">1</int>
  <lst name="params">
   <str name="q">name:company</str>
   <str name="facet.field">city</str>
   <str name="facet">true</str>
  </lst>
 </lst>
 <result name="response" numFound="3" start="0">
  <doc>
   <str name="id">1</str>
   <str name="name">Company 1</str>
   <str name="city">New York</str>
   <long name="_version_">1471068544442564608</long></doc>
  <doc>
   <str name="id">2</str>
   <str name="name">Company 2</str>
   <str name="city">New Orleans</str>
   <long name="_version_">1471068544491847680</long></doc>
  <doc>
   <str name="id">3</str>
   <str name="name">Company 3</str>
   <str name="city">New York</str>
   <long name="_version_">1471068544492896256</long></doc>
 </result>
 <lst name="facet_counts">
  <lst name="facet_queries"/>
  <lst name="facet_fields">
   <lst name="city">
    <int name="New York">2</int>
```

```
        <int name="New Orleans">1</int>
      </lst>
    </lst>
    <lst name="facet_dates"/>
    <lst name="facet_ranges"/>
  </lst>
</response>
```

As you can see, besides the normal results list, we got faceting results with the numbers that we wanted. Now let's see how that happened.

How it works...

The index structure and the data are pretty simple and make the example easier to understand. Each company is described by three fields. We are particularly interested in the `city` field. This is the field that we want to use to get the number of companies that have the same value in this field, which basically means that they are in the same city. The `city` field is configured to use the `string` type—the one that is not analyzed—the value that we pass in the field will be indexed without any additional processing by Solr. This is because field faceting works on the indexed tokens. If we analyze the field, faceting will be calculated for each token and not for the whole field value (which is the city name in our case).

To get the desired results, we run a query to Solr and inform the query parser that we want the documents that have the word `company` in the `name` field. Additionally, we can say that we want to enable faceting mechanism—we can say that using the `facet=true` parameter. The `facet.field` parameter tells Solr which field to use to calculate faceting numbers. You can specify the `facet.field` parameter multiple times to get faceting numbers for different fields in the same query.

As you can see in the results list, the results of all types of faceting are grouped in the list with the `name="facet_counts"` attribute. The field-based faceting is grouped under the list with the `name="facet_fields"` attribute. Every field that you specified using the `facet.field` parameter has its own list that has the attribute `name` the same as the value of the parameter in the query—in our case, it is `city`. Then, finally, you can see the results that we are interested in—the pairs of value (the `name` attribute) and how many documents have the value in the specified field.

There's more...

There are two more things that I would like to show you about field faceting.

How to show facets with counts greater than zero

The default behavior of Solr is to show all the faceting results, no matter what the counts are. If you want to show only the facets with counts greater than zero, then you should add the `facet.mincount=1` parameter to the query (you can set this parameter to another value if you are interested in any arbitrary value).

Lexicographical sorting of the faceting results

If you want to sort the faceting results lexicographically, not by the highest count (which is the default behavior), then you need to add the `facet.sort=index` parameter.

Getting the number of documents with the same value range

Imagine that you have an application where users can search the index to find a car for rent. One of the requirements of the application is to show a navigation panel, where the user can choose the price range for the cars they are interested in. To do this in an efficient way, we will use range faceting and this recipe will show you how to do it.

How to do it...

Let's begin with the following index structure:

1. Add the following fields definition to our `schema.xml` file:

```
<field name="id" type="string" indexed="true" stored="true"
required="true" />
<field name="name" type="text_general" indexed="true"
stored="true" />
<field name="price" type="float" indexed="true" stored="true" />
```

2. The example data that we will use looks as follows:

```
<add>
 <doc>
  <field name="id">1</field>
  <field name="name">Super Mazda</field>
  <field name="price">50</field>
 </doc>
 <doc>
  <field name="id">2</field>
  <field name="name">Mercedes Benz</field>
  <field name="price">210</field>
```

```
  </doc>
  <doc>
   <field name="id">3</field>
   <field name="name">Bentley</field>
   <field name="price">290</field>
  </doc>
  <doc>
   <field name="id">2</field>
   <field name="name">Super Honda</field>
   <field name="price">99.90</field>
  </doc>
</add>
```

3. Now, as you recall, our requirement was to show the navigation panel with the price ranges. To do that, we need to get that data from Solr. We also know that the minimum price for car rent is 1 dollar and the maximum is 400 dollars. To get the price ranges from Solr, we send the following query:

   ```
   http://localhost:8983/solr/cookbook/select?q=*:*&rows=0&facet=true
   &facet.range=price&facet.range.start=0&facet.range.end=400&facet.
   range.gap=100
   ```

   The preceding query would result in the following result list:

   ```
   <?xml version="1.0" encoding="UTF-8"?>
   <response>

    <lst name="responseHeader">
     <int name="status">0</int>
     <int name="QTime">43</int>
     <lst name="params">
      <str name="facet.range">price</str>
      <str name="q">*:*</str>
      <str name="facet.range.gap">100</str>
      <str name="rows">0</str>
      <str name="facet">true</str>
      <str name="facet.range.start">0</str>
      <str name="facet.range.end">400</str>
     </lst>
    </lst>
    <result name="response" numFound="3" start="0">
    </result>
    <lst name="facet_counts">
     <lst name="facet_queries"/>
     <lst name="facet_fields"/>
   ```

```
    <lst name="facet_dates"/>
    <lst name="facet_ranges">
     <lst name="price">
      <lst name="counts">
       <int name="0.0">2</int>
       <int name="100.0">0</int>
       <int name="200.0">1</int>
       <int name="300.0">0</int>
      </lst>
      <float name="gap">100.0</float>
      <float name="start">0.0</float>
      <float name="end">400.0</float>
     </lst>
    </lst>
   </lst>
  </response>
```

As you can see in the results, we only got the faceting results. So here we got exactly what we wanted. Now let's see how it works.

How it works...

As you can see, the index structure is simple. There are three fields:

- One is responsible for the unique identifier (the `id` field)
- One is responsible for the car name (the `name` field)
- The last one is responsible for the price of rent (the `price` field)

The query is where all the magic happens. As we are not interested in the search results, we ask for all documents in the index (the `q=*:*` parameter), and we tell Solr not to return the search results (the `rows=0` parameter). Then, we tell Solr that we want the faceting mechanism to be enabled for the query (the `facet=true` parameter). We will not be using the standard faceting mechanism—the field-based faceting. Instead, we will be using the range faceting, which is optimized to work with ranges. So, we tell Solr which field will be used to range faceting by adding the `facet.range` parameter with the `price` value. This means that the `price` field will be used for the range faceting calculation. Then, we specify the lower boundary from where the range faceting calculation will begin. We do this by adding the `facet.range.start` parameter—in our example, we set it to `0`. Next, we have the `facet.range.end` parameter which tells Solr when to stop the calculation of the range faceting. The last parameter (`facet.range.gap`) informs Solr about the length of the periods that will be calculated.

Remember that when using the range faceting mechanism, you must specify the three parameters:

- `facet.range.start`
- `facet.range.end`
- `facet.range.gap`

If these are not specified, the range faceting mechanism won't work.

In the faceting results, you can see the periods and the number of documents that were found in each of them. The first period can be found under the `<int name="0.0">` tag. This period consists of prices ranging from 0 to 100 (in mathematical notation, it would be `<0; 100>`). It contains two cars. The next period can be found under the `<int name="100.0">` tag and consists of prices ranging from 100 to 200 (in mathematical notation, it would be `<100; 200>`), and so on.

Getting the number of documents matching the query and subquery

Imagine a situation where you have an application that has a search feature for cars. One of the requirements is not only to show the search results, but also to show the number of cars with the price period chosen by the user. There is also another thing—these queries must be fast because of the number of queries that will be running. Can Solr handle this? The answer is yes. This recipe will show you how to do it.

How to do it...

Let's start with creating an index with a very simple index structure that looks as follows:

1. Add the following definition to your `schema.xml`:

```
<field name="id" type="string" indexed="true" stored="true"
required="true" />
<field name="name" type="text_general" indexed="true"
stored="true" />
<field name="price" type="float" indexed="true" stored="true" />
```

2. Now, let's index the following sample data:

```
<add>
 <doc>
  <field name="id">1</field>
  <field name="name">Car 1</field>
  <field name="price">70</field>
```

```
  </doc>
  <doc>
   <field name="id">2</field>
   <field name="name">Car 2</field>
   <field name="price">101</field>
  </doc>
  <doc>
   <field name="id">3</field>
   <field name="name">Car 3</field>
   <field name="price">201</field>
  </doc>
  <doc>
   <field name="id">4</field>
   <field name="name">Car 4</field>
   <field name="price">99.90</field>
  </doc>
</add>
```

Now, as you recall, our requirement is to show cars that match the query (let's suppose that our user typed `car`) and to show the counts in the chosen price periods. For the purpose of this recipe, let's assume that the user has chosen two periods of prices:

- 10-80
- 90-300

3. The query to achieve such requirements should look as follows:

```
http://localhost:8983/solr/cookbook/select?q=name:car&facet=true&f
acet.query=price:[10 TO 80]&facet.query=price:[90 TO 300]
```

The result list of the preceding query should look as follows:

```
<?xml version="1.0" encoding="UTF-8"?>
<response>
 <lst name="responseHeader">
  <int name="status">0</int>
  <int name="QTime">1</int>
  <lst name="params">
   <arr name="facet.query">
    <str>price:[10 TO 80]</str>
    <str>price:[90 TO 300]</str>
   </arr>
   <str name="q">name:car</str>
   <str name="facet">true</str>
  </lst>
```

```
 </lst>
 <result name="response" numFound="4" start="0">
  <doc>
   <str name="id">1</str>
   <str name="name">Car 1</str>
   <float name="price">70.0</float>
   <long name="_version_">1471069733520408576</long></doc>
  <doc>
   <str name="id">2</str>
   <str name="name">Car 2</str>
   <float name="price">101.0</float>
   <long name="_version_">1471069733568643072</long></doc>
  <doc>
   <str name="id">3</str>
   <str name="name">Car 3</str>
   <float name="price">201.0</float>
   <long name="_version_">1471069733569691648</long></doc>
  <doc>
   <str name="id">4</str>
   <str name="name">Car 4</str>
   <float name="price">99.9</float>
   <long name="_version_">1471069733570740224</long></doc>
 </result>
 <lst name="facet_counts">
  <lst name="facet_queries">
   <int name="price:[10 TO 80]">1</int>
   <int name="price:[90 TO 300]">3</int>
  </lst>
  <lst name="facet_fields"/>
  <lst name="facet_dates"/>
  <lst name="facet_ranges"/>
 </lst>
</response>
```

Solr returned the results in the form that we wanted them to be, so now let's take a look at how it works.

How it works...

As you can see, the index structure is quite simple. There are three fields:

- One is responsible for the unique identifier (the `id` field)
- One is responsible for the car name (the `name` field)
- The last one is responsible for the price (the `price` field)

Next, we have the query. First, you can see a standard query, where we tell Solr that we want to get all the documents that have `car` word in the `name` field (the `q=name:car` parameter). Next, we can say that we want to use the faceting mechanism by adding the `facet=true` parameter to the query. This time we will use the query faceting type. This means that we can pass the query to the faceting mechanism and as a result, we will get the number of documents that match the given query. In our example, we wanted to know the prices:

- One is from the price of 10 to 80
- Another from the price of 90 to 300

This is achieved by adding the `facet.query` parameter with the appropriate value. The first period is defined as a standard range query to the `price` field—`price:[10 TO 80]`. The second query is very similar, it has just different values. The value passed to the `facet.query` parameter should be a Lucene query written using the default query syntax.

As you can see in the results, the query faceting results are grouped under the `<lst name="facet_queries">` XML tag with the names exactly as in the queries sent to Solr. You can see that Solr has correctly calculated the number of cars in each of the periods, which means that this is a perfect solution for us, when we can't use the range faceting mechanism.

Removing filters from faceting results

Let's assume for the purpose of this recipe, you have an application that can search for companies within a city and a state. However, the requirements say that not only should you show the search results, but also the number of companies in each city and the number of companies in each state (to say in the Solr way—you want to exclude the filter query from the faceting results). Can Solr do this efficiently ? Sure it can, and this recipe will show you how to do it.

Getting ready

Before you start reading this recipe, let's take a look at the *Getting the number of documents with the same field value* recipe of this chapter.

How to do it...

1. As usual we start with a very simple index structure that contains four fields. We do this by adding the following section to the `schema.xml` file:

```
<field name="id" type="string" indexed="true" stored="true"
required="true" />
<field name="name" type="text_general" indexed="true"
stored="true" />
<field name="city" type="string" indexed="true" stored="true" />
<field name="state" type="string" indexed="true" stored="true" />
```

2. The second step would be to index the following example data:

```
<add>
 <doc>
  <field name="id">1</field>
  <field name="name">Company 1</field>
  <field name="city">New York</field>
  <field name="state">New York</field>
 </doc>
 <doc>
  <field name="id">2</field>
  <field name="name">Company 2</field>
  <field name="city">New Orleans</field>
  <field name="state">Luiziana</field>
 </doc>
 <doc>
  <field name="id">3</field>
  <field name="name">Company 3</field>
  <field name="city">New York</field>
  <field name="state">New York</field>
 </doc>
 <doc>
  <field name="id">4</field>
  <field name="name">Company 4/field>
  <field name="city">New York</field>
  <field name="state">New York</field>
 </doc>
</add>
```

3. Let's suppose that our hypothetical user searches for the word `company`, and we tell our application that the user needs the companies matching the word in the state of `New York`. However, we would like to show the number of documents matching the word `company` in all the states and in the cities of all the states. In that case, the query that will fulfill our requirement should look as follows:

```
http://localhost:8983/solr/cookbook/select?q=name:company&facet=tr
ue &fq={!tag=stateTag}state:"New York"&facet.field={!ex=stateTag}
city&facet.field={!ex=stateTag}state
```

The result for the preceding query will look as follows:

```
<?xml version="1.0" encoding="UTF-8"?>
<response>
 <lst name="responseHeader">
  <int name="status">0</int>
  <int name="QTime">1</int>
```

```
  <lst name="params">
   <str name="q">name:company</str>
   <arr name="facet.field">
    <str>{!ex=stateTag}city</str>
    <str>{!ex=stateTag}state</str>
   </arr>
   <str name="fq">{!tag=stateTag}state:"New York"</str>
   <str name="facet">true </str>
  </lst>
 </lst>
 <result name="response" numFound="3" start="0">
  <doc>
   <str name="id">1</str>
   <str name="name">Company 1</str>
   <str name="city">New York</str>
   <str name="state">New York</str>
   <long name="_version_">1471070665204301824</long></doc>
  <doc>
   <str name="id">3</str>
   <str name="name">Company 3</str>
   <str name="city">New York</str>
   <str name="state">New York</str>
   <long name="_version_">1471070665210593280</long></doc>
  <doc>
   <str name="id">4</str>
   <str name="name">Company 4</str>
   <str name="city">New York</str>
   <str name="state">New York</str>
   <long name="_version_">1471070665210593281</long></doc>
 </result>
 <lst name="facet_counts">
  <lst name="facet_queries"/>
  <lst name="facet_fields">
   <lst name="city">
    <int name="New York">3</int>
    <int name="New Orleans">1</int>
   </lst>
   <lst name="state">
    <int name="New York">3</int>
    <int name="Luiziana">1</int>
   </lst>
  </lst>
  <lst name="facet_dates"/>
  <lst name="facet_ranges"/>
 </lst>
</response>
```

Now let's see how it works.

How it works...

The index structure is pretty simple—it contains four fields that describe the company. The search will be performed against the `name` field, while the filtering and the faceting will be done with the use of the `state` and the `city` fields.

So, let's get on with the query. As you can see, we have some typical elements there. First of all we have the `q` parameter, which just tells Solr where and what to search for. Then, the `facet=true` parameter enables the faceting mechanism. Following that you have a strange looking filter query (the `fq` parameter) with the value of `fq={!tag=stateTag}state:"New York"`. It tells Solr to only show those results that have both `New York` in the `state` field, but not the results that have either of them. By adding the `{!tag=stateTag}` part, we basically gave that filter query a name (`stateTag`) that we will use further.

Now look at the two `facet.field` parameters. Our requirement was to show the number of companies in all states and in all cities. The only thing that was preventing us from getting those numbers was the filter query that we added to the query. So, let's exclude it from the faceting results. How do we do it? It's simple—just add `{!ex=stateTag}` to the beginning of each of the `facet.field` parameters like this: `facet.field={!ex=stateTag}city`. It tells Solr to exclude the filter with the passed name.

As you can see in the results list, we got the numbers correctly, which means that the exclude works as intended.

Using decision tree faceting

Imagine that in our store we have products divided into categories. In addition to this, we store information about the stock of the items. Now, we want to show our crew how many of the products in the categories are in stock and how many are missing. The first thing that comes to mind is to use the faceting mechanism and some additional calculation. But why bother, when Solr 4.0 and later can do that calculation for us with the use of so-called pivot faceting? This recipe will show you how to use it.

How to do it...

1. We start with defining the index structure that we can easily use. We do this by adding the following field definitions to the `schema.xml` file:

```
<field name="id" type="string" indexed="true" stored="true"
required="true" />
<field name="name" type="text_general" indexed="true"
stored="true" />
<field name="category" type="string" indexed="true" stored="true"
/>
<field name="stock" type="boolean" indexed="true" stored="true" />
```

2. Now, let's index the following example data:

```
<add>
 <doc>
  <field name="id">1</field>
  <field name="name">Book 1</field>
  <field name="category">books</field>
  <field name="stock">true</field>
 </doc>
 <doc>
  <field name="id">2</field>
  <field name="name">Book 2</field>
  <field name="category">books</field>
  <field name="stock">true</field>
 </doc>
 <doc>
  <field name="id">3</field>
  <field name="name">Workbook 1</field>
  <field name="category">workbooks</field>
  <field name="stock">false</field>
 </doc>
 <doc>
  <field name="id">4</field>
  <field name="name">Workbook 2</field>
  <field name="category">workbooks</field>
  <field name="stock">true</field>
 </doc>
</add>
```

3. Let's assume that we are running a query from the administration panel of our shop and we are not interested in the documents at all. We only want to know how many documents are in stock and how many are not for each of the categories. The query implementing this logic should look as follows:

```
http://localhost:8983/solr/cookbook/select?q=*:*&rows=0&facet=true
&facet.pivot=category,stock
```

The response to the preceding query is as follows:

```
<?xml version="1.0" encoding="UTF-8"?>
<response>
 <lst name="responseHeader">
  <int name="status">0</int>
  <int name="QTime">1</int>
  <lst name="params">
   <str name="q">*:*</str>
```

```
    <str name="facet.pivot">category,stock</str>
    <str name="rows">0</str>
    <str name="facet">true</str>
   </lst>
  </lst>
  <result name="response" numFound="4" start="0">
  </result>
  <lst name="facet_counts">
   <lst name="facet_queries"/>
   <lst name="facet_fields"/>
   <lst name="facet_dates"/>
   <lst name="facet_ranges"/>
   <lst name="facet_pivot">
    <arr name="category,stock">
     <lst>
      <str name="field">category</str>
      <str name="value">books</str>
      <int name="count">2</int>
      <arr name="pivot">
       <lst>
        <str name="field">stock</str>
        <bool name="value">true</bool>
        <int name="count">2</int>
       </lst>
      </arr>
     </lst>
     <lst>
      <str name="field">category</str>
      <str name="value">workbooks</str>
      <int name="count">2</int>
      <arr name="pivot">
       <lst>
        <str name="field">stock</str>
        <bool name="value">false</bool>
        <int name="count">1</int>
       </lst>
       <lst>
        <str name="field">stock</str>
        <bool name="value">true</bool>
        <int name="count">1</int>
       </lst>
      </arr>
     </lst>
    </arr>
   </lst>
  </lst>
 </response>
```

As you can see, we've achieved what we wanted, now let's see how it works.

How it works...

Our data is very simple. As you can see in the field definition section of the schema.xml file and the example data, every document is described by four fields:

- id
- name
- category
- stock

I think that their names speak for themselves and I don't need to discuss them.

The interesting bit starts with the query. We specified that we want the query to match all the documents (the q=*:* parameter), but we don't want to see any documents in the response (the rows=0 parameter). In addition to this, we want to have faceting calculation enabled (the facet=true parameter) and we will use the decision tree faceting—aka pivot faceting. We do this by specifying which fields should be included in the tree faceting. In our case, we want the top-level of the pivot facet to be calculated on the basis of the category field and the second level (the one nested in the category field calculation) should be based on the values available in the stock field. Of course, if you would like to have another value of another field nested under the stock field, you can do that by adding another field to the facet.pivot query parameter. Assuming that you would like to see faceting on field price nested under the stock field, your facet.pivot parameter would look like this: facet.pivot=category,stock,price.

As you can see in the response, each nested faceting calculation result is written inside the <arr name="pivot"> XML tag. So, let's look at the response structure. The first level of your facet pivot tree is based on the category field. You can see that there are two books (<int name="count">2</int>) in the books category (<str name="value">books</str>) and all these books have the stock field (<str name="field">stock</str>) set to true (<bool name="value">true</bool>). For the workbooks category, the situation is a bit different because you can see two different sections there—one for documents with the stock field equal to false and the other with the stock field set to true. However, in the end the calculation is correct and that's what we wanted!

Calculating faceting for relevant documents in groups

If you have ever used the field-collapsing functionality of Solr, you might be wondering whether there is a possibility of using that functionality and faceting. Of course, there is, but the default behavior still works and so you get the faceting calculation on the basis of documents and not on document groups. In this recipe, we will learn how to query Solr so that it returns facets calculated for the most relevant document in each group.

Getting ready

Before reading the following recipe, let's take a look at *Grouping documents by the field value*, *Grouping documents by the query value*, and *Grouping documents by the function value* recipes in *Chapter 8, Using Additional Functionalities*. Also if you are not familiar with faceting functionality, read the first three recipes of this chapter.

How to do it...

1. In the first step, we need to create an index. For the purpose of this recipe, let's assume that we have the following index structure (just add the following section to your `schema.xml` file):

```
<field name="id" type="string" indexed="true" stored="true"
required="true" />
<field name="name" type="text_general" indexed="true"
stored="true" />
<field name="category" type="string" indexed="true" stored="true"
/>
<field name="stock" type="boolean" indexed="true" stored="true" />
```

2. The second step is to index the data. We will use an example data, which looks as follows:

```
<add>
 <doc>
  <field name="id">1</field>
  <field name="name">Book 1</field>
  <field name="category">books</field>
  <field name="stock">true</field>
 </doc>
 <doc>
  <field name="id">2</field>
  <field name="name">Book 2</field>
  <field name="category">books</field>
  <field name="stock">true</field>
 </doc>
 <doc>
  <field name="id">3</field>
  <field name="name">Workbook 1</field>
  <field name="category">Workbooks</field>
  <field name="stock">false</field>
 </doc>
 <doc>
```

```
    <field name="id">4</field>
    <field name="name">Workbook 2</field>
    <field name="category">Workbooks</field>
    <field name="stock">true</field>
  </doc>
</add>
```

3. So, now it's time for our query. Let's assume that we want our results to be grouped on the values of the `category` field and we want the faceting to be calculated on the `stock` field. Also remember that we are only interested in the most relevant document from each result group when it comes to faceting. So, the query that would tell Solr to do what we want should look as follows:

   ```
   http://localhost:8983/solr/cookbook/select?q=*:*&facet=true&facet.
   field=stock&group=true&group.field=category&group.truncate=true
   ```

   The results for the preceding query would look as follows:

   ```
   <?xml version="1.0" encoding="UTF-8"?>
   <response>
   <lst name="responseHeader">
     <int name="status">0</int>
     <int name="QTime">1</int>
     <lst name="params">
       <str name="q">*:*</str>
       <str name="facet.field">stock</str>
       <str name="group.truncate">true</str>
       <str name="facet">true</str>
       <str name="group.field">category</str>
       <str name="group">true</str>
     </lst>
   </lst>
   <lst name="grouped">
     <lst name="category">
       <int name="matches">4</int>
       <arr name="groups">
         <lst>
           <str name="groupValue">books</str>
           <result name="doclist" numFound="2" start="0">
             <doc>
               <str name="id">1</str>
               <str name="name">Book 1</str>
               <str name="category">books</str>
               <bool name="stock">true</bool>
   ```

```
            <long name="_version_">1487145087213240320</long></
doc>
        </result>
      </lst>
      <lst>
        <str name="groupValue">Workbooks</str>
        <result name="doclist" numFound="2" start="0">
          <doc>
            <str name="id">3</str>
            <str name="name">Workbook 1</str>
            <str name="category">Workbooks</str>
            <bool name="stock">false</bool>
            <long name="_version_">1487145087281397760</long></
doc>
        </result>
      </lst>
    </arr>
  </lst>
</lst>
<lst name="facet_counts">
  <lst name="facet_queries"/>
  <lst name="facet_fields">
    <lst name="stock">
      <int name="false">1</int>
      <int name="true">1</int>
    </lst>
  </lst>
  <lst name="facet_dates"/>
  <lst name="facet_ranges"/>
  <lst name="facet_intervals"/>
</lst>
</response>
```

As you can see, everything has worked as it should have. Now let's see how it works in detail.

How it works...

Our data is very simple. As you can see in the field definition section of the `schema.xml` file and the example data, every document is described by four fields:

- `id`
- `name`
- `category`
- `stock`

I think that their names speak for themselves and I don't need to discuss them.

When it comes to the query, we fetch all the documents from the index (the `q=*:*` parameter). Next, we say that we want to use faceting and want it to be calculated on the `stock` field. We want the grouping mechanism to be active and also want to group documents on the basis of the `category` field (all the query parameters responsible for defining faceting and grouping behavior are described in the appropriate recipes in this book, so take a look at those if you are not familiar with those parameters). And finally, something new—the `group.truncate` parameter is set to `true`. If it is set to `true`, like in our case, facet counts will be calculated using only the most relevant document in each of the calculated groups. So, in our case for the group with the `category` field equal to `books`, we have the `true` value in the `stock` field and for the second group we have `false` in the `stock` field. Of course, we are looking at the most relevant documents, so the first ones in our case. As you can easily see, we've got two facet counts for the `stock` field both having a count of `1`, which is what we would expect.

Improving faceting performance for low cardinality fields

Although Solr faceting is very fast, there are times when the default configuration values are not as fast as they can be. There are a few cases where we can tune Solr faceting mechanism and make it work faster. This recipe will show you how to tune the faceting mechanism.

Getting ready

Before you start reading this recipe, take a look at the *Getting the number of documents with the same field value* recipe of this chapter.

How to do it...

For the purpose of this recipe, we will assume that we have the following index structure:

1. Add the following section to your `schema.xml` file:

   ```
   <field name="id" type="string" indexed="true" stored="true"
   required="true" />
   <field name="tag" type="string" indexed="true" stored="true" />
   ```

2. We've used the following bash script to index the data (note that we are indexing two million documents here and are sending them one by one. So it might take a long time to index the data):

   ```
   #!/bin/sh
   URL=http://localhost:8983/solr/cookbook/update/
   ```

```
for i in {1..2000000}
do
  if [ $(( $i % 2 )) -eq 0 ]; then
    curl $URL --data-binary "<add><doc><field name=\"id\">$i</
field><field name=\"tag\">tag1</field></doc></add>" -H 'Content-
type:application/xml'
  else
    curl $URL --data-binary "<add><doc><field name=\"id\">$i</
field><field name=\"tag\">tag2</field></doc></add>" -H 'Content-
type:application/xml'
  fi
done

curl $URL --data-binary '<commit/>' -H 'Content-type:application/
xml'
echo
```

3. Our initial query looked as follows:

   ```
   http://localhost:8983/solr/cookbook/select?q=*:*&facet=true&facet.
   field=tag
   ```

   The results returned by the query are not important—we are just interested in the query execution time, which was about `350` milliseconds.

4. If we consider that the `tag` field on which calculate facet is a low cardinality field (contains a low number of unique values), we can change the faceting calculation method. Our changed query will look as follows:

   ```
   http://localhost:8983/solr/cookbook/select?q=*:*&facet=true&facet.
   field=tag&facet.method=enum
   ```

   If you would run the query in the same controlled environment, you will see that the query execution time was lowered—in this case, it was about 20 percent, but the improvement is highly data- and environment-dependent.

Let's now see how it works.

How it works...

Our index structure is very simple:

- We only have an `id` field that holds the unique identifier of the document
- The `tag` field that holds the tag

I've chosen the data to be as simple as it can be, so the whole picture of how the improvement works can be clearly seen.

The indexing script is also very simple as it runs a loop for 2 million iterations. If the `i` variable is even, then we put the `tag1` value into the `tag` field for that document. Otherwise, we put the `tag2` value. This is how we end up with million documents with `tag1` in the `tag` field and one million documents with the `tag2` value.

By default, when calculating field faceting, Solr will use the field cache method (`facet.method=fc`) and iterate over the documents summing up the terms for the documents matching the query. However, this might not be the most effective way of calculating fields that have a low number of unique terms—the low cardinality fields. For such fields, we can chose the default faceting method that Solr uses for Boolean fields—`facet.method=enum`. What it does is it enumerates the terms for that field and calculates the intersection of the two sets—the one with documents matching the query and the second one that contains documents with a given term. We only have two unique terms in our field (`tag1` and `tag2`) and because of that we've experienced performance improvements. One thing to remember is that we have to be careful not to use that method for high cardinality fields as it might drastically lower the field faceting performance for such fields.

There's more...

There are two more things that I would like to mention when it comes to faceting.

Using per segment field cache for faceting calculation

As mentioned previously, Solr uses global field cache for faceting calculation by default. However, for near real-time use cases, this might not be the best way. The `facet.method=fcs` method works pretty much in the same way as `facet.method=fc`; however, instead of using a global cache structure, it uses a per segment cache for faceting calculation. When using the `facet.method=fcs` field faceting method, Solr rebuilds the faceting cache only for new segments, which might result in faceting query performance improvements, especially for rapidly changing indices.

Our query using the `facet.method=fcs` field faceting would look as follows:

```
http://localhost:8983/solr/cookbook/select?q=*:*&facet=true&facet.
field=tag&facet.method=fcs
```

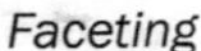

Specifying the number of faceting threads

In addition to what we've discussed, starting from Version 4.5, Solr allows you to define the maximum number of threads that will be used to load field information used in faceting calculation. By using the `facet.threads` parameter we can say that Solr can use up to `N` threads running in parallel and gather data for faceting calculation. For example, if we would like to use up to 10 threads for faceting, we can specify `facet.threads=10` in our query. Omitting this parameter or setting its value to `0` will tell Solr to use the default behavior, which is using only the called thread. Note that the `facet.threads` parameter only works with field faceting for now. A higher number of faceting threads can be very useful during the query warm-up process as it tends to speed up complicated warming queries, including many facet fields.

6
Improving Solr Performance

In this chapter, we will cover the following topics:

- Handling deep paging efficiently
- Configuring the document cache
- Configuring the query result cache
- Configuring the filter cache
- Improving Solr query performance after the start and commit operations
- Lowering the memory consumption of faceting and sorting
- Speeding up indexing with Solr segment merge tuning
- Avoiding caching of rare filters to improve the performance
- Controlling the filter execution to improve expensive filter performance
- Configuring numerical fields for high-performance sorting and range queries

Introduction

The performance of an application is one of the most important factors. Of course, there are other factors such as usability and availability—we can recite much more, but one of the most crucial and major factors is the performance. Even if our application is perfectly done in terms of usability, the users won't be able to use it if they have to wait for minutes for the search results.

The standard Solr deployment is fast enough, but sooner or later a time will come when you will have to optimize your deployment. The recipes in this chapter will try to help you optimize Solr deployment.

If your business depends on Solr, you should keep monitoring it even after optimization. You can see how your environment works, the state of Solr nodes, the number of queries that run, its speed, and so on. There are numerous solutions available on the market, from the generic and open sourced ones such as **Ganglia** (`http://ganglia.sourceforge.net/`) to specific ones such as *SPM Performance Monitoring & Alerting* (`http://www.sematext.com/spm/index.html`) from the Sematext group.

Handling deep paging efficiently

In most cases, the top results returned to the user should be what they are looking for. The top results should be the most relevant ones and the ones we want to show. However, there are use cases where this is not enough. Sometimes we want to get all the results—in the worst case, we want to get all the documents stored in the collection and do something with them. When you are requesting a high number of pages, you will see that the performance will start suffering. This is because Solr needs to build the results list for each request and discard the first *N* ones to get to the requested page. Of course, there are better ways to handle such cases, and Solr allows you to use one of those methods that we will discuss in this recipe.

How to do it...

1. The actual index structure doesn't matter, but for the purpose of this recipe, let's assume that we have the following index structure (we just put the field's definition in the `schema.xml` file):

   ```
   <field name="id" type="string" indexed="true" stored="true"
   required="true" />
   <field name="title" type="text_general" indexed="true"
   stored="true" />
   ```

2. Of course, we also need some data for this example to work. It would be perfect if we had hundreds of thousands of documents to illustrate the performance gains, but for the purpose of the book, we will be using only a few documents to illustrate how cursor-based paging works. Our example data looks as follows:

   ```
   <add>
    <doc>
     <field name="id">1</field>
     <field name="title">Solr 4.0 cookbook</field>
    </doc>
    <doc>
   ```

```
  <field name="id">2</field>
  <field name="title">Solr 3.1 cookbook</field>
 </doc>
 <doc>
  <field name="id">3</field>
  <field name="title">ElasticSearch Server</field>
 </doc>
 <doc>
  <field name="id">4</field>
  <field name="title">Mastering Elasticsearch</field>
 </doc>
 <doc>
  <field name="id">5</field>
  <field name="title">Elasticsearch Server Second Edition</field>
 </doc>
</add>
```

3. Now we can start sending the queries. Assuming that we want to scroll through the results starting from the first one and ending on the last, and we want two documents per page of the results. We start by sending the following query:

   ```
   q=*:*&rows=2&sort=score+desc,id+asc&cursorMark=*
   ```

   The results returned by Solr are as follows:

   ```
   <?xml version="1.0" encoding="UTF-8"?>
   <response>
    <lst name="responseHeader">
     <int name="status">0</int>
     <int name="QTime">1</int>
     <lst name="params">
      <str name="q">*:*</str>
      <str name="cursorMark">*</str>
      <str name="sort">score desc,id asc</str>
      <str name="rows">2</str>
     </lst>
    </lst>
    <result name="response" numFound="5" start="0">
     <doc>
      <str name="id">1</str>
      <str name="title">Solr 4.0 cookbook</str>
      <long name="_version_">1475631480903303168</long></doc>
     <doc>
   ```

```
    <str name="id">2</str>
    <str name="title">Solr 3.1 cookbook</str>
    <long name="_version_">1475631480954683392</long></doc>
  </result>
  <str name="nextCursorMark">AoIIP4AAACEy</str>
</response>
```

Of course, we got the documents we wanted, but we are not only interested in them. We should also look at the value of `nextCursorMark` returned along with the results by Solr. In our case, its value is `AoIIP4AAACEy`, and we will use this value in the next query that will give us the next page of results.

4. The query to give us the second page of results looks as follows:

   ```
   q=*:*&rows=2&sort=score+desc,id+asc&cursorMark=AoIIP4AAACEy
   ```

   The results returned by Solr are as follows:

   ```
   <?xml version="1.0" encoding="UTF-8"?>
   <response>
    <lst name="responseHeader">
     <int name="status">0</int>
     <int name="QTime">3</int>
     <lst name="params">
      <str name="q">*:*</str>
      <str name="cursorMark">AoIIP4AAACEy</str>
      <str name="sort">score desc,id asc</str>
      <str name="rows">2</str>
     </lst>
    </lst>
    <result name="response" numFound="5" start="0">
     <doc>
      <str name="id">3</str>
      <str name="title">ElasticSearch Server</str>
      <long name="_version_">1475631480954683393</long></doc>
     <doc>
      <str name="id">4</str>
      <str name="title">Mastering Elasticsearch</str>
      <long name="_version_">1475631480955731968</long></doc>
    </result>
    <str name="nextCursorMark">AoIIP4AAACE0</str>
   </response>
   ```

   And we got the next two results and the new value of the `nextCursorMark` parameter.

5. Finally, to get the last pages of the results, we will run the following query:

   ```
   q=*:*&rows=2&sort=score+desc,id+asc&cursorMark=AoIIP4AAACE0
   ```

   The results are as follows:

   ```
   <?xml version="1.0" encoding="UTF-8"?>
   <response>
    <lst name="responseHeader">
     <int name="status">0</int>
     <int name="QTime">1</int>
     <lst name="params">
      <str name="q">*:*</str>
      <str name="cursorMark">AoIIP4AAACE0</str>
      <str name="sort">score desc,id asc</str>
      <str name="rows">2</str>
     </lst>
    </lst>
    <result name="response" numFound="5" start="0">
     <doc>
      <str name="id">5</str>
      <str name="title">Elasticsearch Server Second Edition</str>
      <long name="_version_">1475631480956780544</long></doc>
    </result>
   <str name="nextCursorMark">AoIIP4AAACE1</str>
   </response>
   ```

Now let's take a look at how it works.

How it works...

I'll skip discussing the index structure and the data itself, because it is very simple and really doesn't matter in this recipe. They are just here so that we are able to query Solr and get results back.

Before we go into the details on how the scroll method works, you need to remember that Solr is almost stateless when it comes to querying. Of course, there are some caches, but still for a given request Solr creates the result set from scratch for almost each request. When sending a query with `start=0` and `rows=10`, Solr needs to sort all the documents matching the query and return the 10 values on the top. Now imagine that we pass `start=1000000` and `rows=10`. Solr needs to sort all the documents, discard the first 1,000,000, and return the ones on positions 1,000,001 to 1,000,010. This doesn't sound too efficient, and it isn't. The cursor paging method allows you to overcome this by giving Solr the query state information in an encoded value provided by the `cursorMark` parameter. The con of such an approach is the need of getting one page after another—we cannot randomly choose which page we want.

So starting with our first query—we said that we want all documents to be matched (`q=*:*`), we want Solr to return two documents on a single page of results (`rows=2`), and we want the results to be sorted on the basis of score (`sort=score+desc,id+asc`). Finally, we have the `cursorMark` parameter. Because this is the first page of results, we pass `*` as its value.

> Note that until Solr 4.10, one needs to explicitly define the sorting of document identifiers for Solr so that it can properly handle results sorting using the cursor paging method.

As you can see, in addition to the standard results, Solr returned one additional thing—the `nextCursorMark` property. We take the value of this property and use it as the value of the `cursorMark` parameter in the next query. This is needed to get to the next page of results. In our case, the value of the `cursorMark` parameter should be set to `AoIIP4AAACEy`. Of course, you can expect the value of the `nextCursorMark` property to be different after each page of results.

As you can see, the second query is almost the same as the first one, with one change—the value of the `cursorMark` parameter. We set the value of this parameter to the one returned by the `nextCursorMark` property just as I described. And as you can see, Solr returned the second page of results. We did exactly the same for the third query, but of course we set the value of the `cursorMark` parameter to the one returned by the `nextCursorMark` property in the second page of results (which was `AoIIP4AAACE0` in our case).

See also

- If you are interested in performance measurements, refer to the blog post written by Chris Hostetter available at `http://searchhub.org/2013/12/12/coming-soon-to-solr-efficient-cursor-based-iteration-of-large-result-sets/`

Configuring the document cache

Cache can play a major role in your deployment's performance. One of the caches that you can use to configure when setting up Solr is the document cache. It is responsible for storing Lucene internal documents that have been fetched from the disk. The proper configuration of this cache can save precious I/O calls and therefore boost the whole deployment performance. This recipe will show you how to properly configure the document cache.

Getting ready

Remember that the cache usage depends on your queries, update rates, searcher reopening, and on many other things. In this recipe, you will see cache configuration based on some assumptions; however, you will see the logic behind choosing the right cache configuration. You can use the same logic to adjust caches in your Solr deployment.

Also remember that the document cache in Solr is a top-level cache, so whenever a searcher is reopened, the cache is invalidated. This might cause your cache to be almost useless for rapidly changing data, and it is sometimes better to disable the cache completely by removing its configuration from the `solrconfig.xml` file.

How to do it...

For this recipe, I assumed that we are dealing with the deployment of Solr where we have about 100,000,000 documents. In our case, a single Solr instance gets a maximum of 100 concurrent queries and the maximum number of documents that the query can fetch is 256.

With the preceding parameters, our document cache should look somewhat similar to this (add this to the `solrconfig.xml` configuration file):

```
<documentCache
   class="solr.LRUCache"
   size="25600"
   initialSize="25600"/>
```

You can see that we didn't specify the `autowarmCount` parameter—this is because the document cache uses Lucene's internal ID to identify documents. These identifiers can't be copied between the index changes and thus we cannot automatically warm this cache.

How it works...

The document cache configuration is simple. We define it in the `documentCache` XML tag and specify a few parameters that define the document cache behavior. First of all, we define the `class` parameter that tells Solr which Java class to use for implementation. In our example, we use the `solr.LRUCache` parameter because we think that we will be adding more information into the cache than we will getting from the cache. When you see that you are getting more information than you add, consider using the `solr.FastLRUCache` parameter. The next parameter tells Solr about the maximum size of the cache (the `size` parameter). As the Solr documentation says, we should always set this value higher than the maximum number of results returned by the query multiplied by the maximum concurrent queries that we think will be sent to the Solr instance. This will ensure that we always have enough space in the cache, so that Solr will not have to fetch the data from the index multiple times during a single query.

The last parameter tells Solr about the initial size of the cache (the `initialSize` parameter). I tend to set it to the same value as the `size` parameter to ensure that Solr won't be wasting its resources on cache resizing.

Of course, we can't automatically warm the document cache, because it stores internal Lucene document identifiers and those changes with the searcher reopening. Hence it doesn't make sense to use the `autowarmCount` parameter.

There is one thing to remember. The more fields marked as `stored` in the index structure you have, the higher the memory usage of this cache will be.

Remember that the values used in the recipe are examples, which worked for that particular data. You should always observe your Solr instance and act when you see that your cache is acting in the wrong way. Remember that having very large cache with very low hit rate can be worse than having no cache at all.

Like all things, you should pay attention to your cache usage as your Solr instances work. If there are any evictions, then it might be a signal that your caches are too small. If you have very poor cache hit rate, it's advisable to turn off the cache sometimes. Cache setup is one of those things in Apache Solr that is very dependent on your data, queries, and users; so I'll repeat once again—keep an eye on your caches and don't be afraid to react and change them. The information regarding the cache hit rate can be found in the Solr administration panel or in good monitoring software.

Configuring the query result cache

The major role of Solr in a typical e-commerce website is handling the user queries. Of course, users of the site can type multiple queries into the search box and we can't easily predict how many unique queries there might be. However, using the logs that Solr gives us, we can check how many different queries there were on the last day, week, month, or year. Using this information, we can configure the query result cache to suit our needs in the most optimal way, and this recipe will show you how to do it.

Getting ready

Remember that the cache usage is dependent on your queries, update rates, searcher reopening, and so on. In this recipe, you will see cache configuration based on some assumptions; however, you will see the logic behind choosing the right cache configuration. You can use the same logic to adjust caches in your Solr deployment.

Also remember that the query result cache in Solr is a top-level cache, so whenever the searcher is reopened, the cache is invalidated. This might cause your cache to be almost useless for rapidly changing data, and it is sometimes better to disable the cache completely by removing its configuration from the `solrconfig.xml` file.

How to do it...

For the purpose of the recipe, let's assume that one Solr instance of our e-commerce website is handling about 10 to 15 queries per second. Each query can be sorted by four different fields (the user can choose by which field). The user can also choose the order of sort. By analyzing the logs for the past three months, we know that there are about 2,000 unique queries that users tend to type in the search box of our application. We also saw that our users don't usually use the paging mechanism, so the documents users are looking for are at the top of the results.

On the basis of the preceding information, we configured our query results cache as follows (add this to the `solrconfig.xml` configuration file):

```
<queryResultCache
   class="solr.LRUCache"
   size="16000"
   initialSize="16000"
   autowarmCount="4000"/>
```

How it works...

Adding the query result cache to the `solrconfig.xml` file is a simple task. We define it in the `queryResultCache` XML tag and specify a few parameters that define the query result cache behavior. First of all, the `class` parameter tells Solr which Java class to use as the implementation. In our example, we use the `solr.LRUCache` parameter because we think that we will be putting more information into the cache than we will get from the cache. When you see that you are getting more information than you put, consider using `solr.FastLRUCache`. The next parameter tells Solr about the maximum size of the cache (the `size` parameter). This cache should be able to store the ordered identifiers of the objects that were returned by the query with its `sort` parameter and the range of documents requested. This means that we should take the number of unique queries, multiply it by the number of `sort` parameters and the number of possible orders of sort. In our example, the size should be at least the result of this equation:

```
size = 2000 * 4 * 2
```

So the `size` property should be 16,000 in our case.

I tend to set the initial size of this cache set to the maximum size, so in our case, I set the `initialSize` parameter to a value of `16000`. This is done to avoid resizing of the cache and save some CPU cycles.

The last parameter (the `autowarmCount` parameter) says how many entries should be copied when Solr is invalidating caches, which is done after searcher opening (for example, after a soft commit operation). I tend to set this parameter to a quarter of the maximum size of the cache. This is done because I want the caches not to be warming too long. However, remember that the autowarming time depends on your deployment and the `autowarmCount` parameter should be adjusted. Sometimes you can afford higher `autowarmCount` values, sometimes it needs to be low.

Remember that while using the values shown in the example, you can always observe your Solr instance and act when you see that your cache is acting in the wrong way.

Like all things, you should pay attention to your cache usage as your Solr instances work. If there are any evictions, then it might be a signal that the caches are too small. If you have very poor hit rate, it's sometimes better to turn off the cache. Cache setup is one of those things in Apache Solr that is very dependent on your data, queries, and users, so I'll repeat once again—keep an eye on your caches and don't be afraid to react and change them.

Configuring the filter cache

During consulting engagements, I tend to see that Solr users forget or simply don't know how to use filter queries or simple filters. People tend to add another clause with a logical operator to the main query—they forget how efficient filters can be, at least when used wisely. That's why whenever I can, I tell people using Solr to use filter queries. However, when using filter queries, it is nice to know how to set up a cache that is responsible for holding the filter results—the filter cache. This recipe will show you how to properly set up the filter cache.

Getting ready

Remember that the cache usage is dependent on your queries, update rates, searcher reopening, and so on. In this recipe, you will see cache configuration based on some assumptions; however, you will see the logic behind choosing the right cache configuration. You can use the same logic to adjust caches in your Solr deployment.

Also remember that the filter cache in Solr is a top-level cache, so whenever the searcher is reopened, the cache is invalidated. This might cause your cache to be almost useful for rapidly changing data, and it is sometimes better to disable the cache completely by removing its configuration from the `solrconfig.xml` file.

How to do it...

For the purpose of this recipe, let's assume that we have a single Solr slave instance to handle all the queries coming from the application. We took the logs from the last three months and analyzed them. From that, we know that our queries are making about 2,000 different filter queries. By getting this information, we can set up the filter cache for our instance. This configuration should look like the one shown here (add this to the `solrconfig.xml` configuration file):

```
<filterCache
   class="solr.FastLRUCache"
   size="2000"
   initialSize="2000"
   autowarmCount="1000"/>
```

And that's it. Now let's see what those values mean.

How it works...

As you might have noticed, adding the filter cache to the `solrconfig.xml` file is a simple task; you just need to know how many unique filters your Solr instance is receiving. We define it in the `filterCache` XML tag and specify a few parameters that define the query result cache behavior. First of all, the `class` parameter tells Solr which Java class to use as the implementation. In our example, we use `solr.FastLRUCache` because we think that we will get more information than what we will put into the cache. The next parameter tells Solr about the maximum size of the cache (the `size` parameter). In our case, we said that we have about 2,000 unique filters and we set the maximum size to that value. This is done because each entry of the filter cache stores the unordered sets of Solr document identifiers that match the given filter. This way, after the first use of the filter, Solr can use the filter cache to apply filters and thus save the I/O operations.

The next parameter—`initialSize`— tells Solr about the initial size of the filter cache. I tend to set it to the same value as the `size` parameter to avoid cache resize. So in our example, we set the value to `2000`.

The last parameter (the `autowarmCount` parameter) says how many entries should be copied when Solr is invalidating caches (for example, after a commit operation). I tend to set this parameter to a quarter of the maximum size of the cache. This is done because I did not want the caches to be warming too long. However, remember that the autowarming time depends on your deployment and the `autowarmCount` parameter should be adjusted if needed.

Remember that when using the values shown in the example, you should always observe your Solr instance and act when you see that your cache is either too small or too large.

Like with all things, you should pay attention to your cache usage as your Solr instances work. If you see evictions, then this might be a signal that your caches are too small. If you have very poor hit rate, it's sometimes better to turn off the cache. Cache setup is one of those things in Apache Solr that is very dependent on your data, queries, and users, so I'll repeat once again—keep an eye on your caches and don't be afraid to react and change them. For example, take a look at the following screenshot that shows you that the filter cache is probably too small because evictions are happening (this is a screenshot of the Solr administration panel):

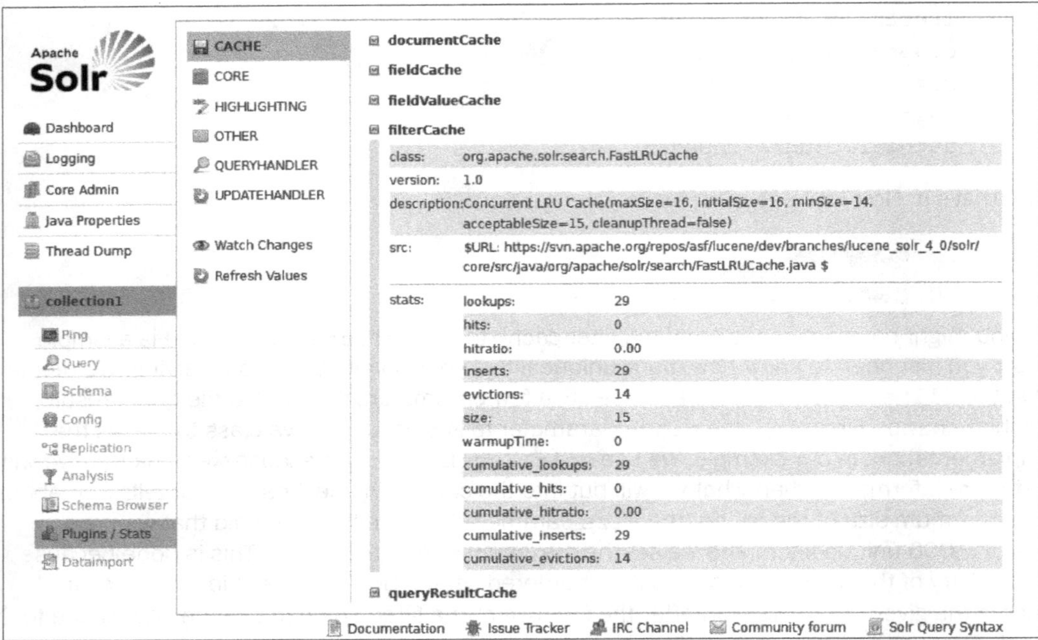

Improving Solr query performance after the start and commit operations

Almost everyone who has some experience with Solr would have noticed one thing—right after startup or searcher reopening (such as a soft autocommit), Solr doesn't have such query performance as after running for a while. This is happening because Solr doesn't have any information stored in caches, the I/O is not optimized, and so on. Can we do something about it? Of course we can, and this recipe will show you how to do it.

How to do it...

1. First of all, we need to identify the most common and the heaviest queries that we send to Solr. I have two ways of doing this: first, I analyze the logs that Solr produces and see how queries are behaving. I tend to choose those queries that are run often and those that run slowly. The second way of choosing the right queries is analyzing the applications that use Solr and see what queries they produce, what queries will be the most crucial, and so on. Based on my experience, the log-based approach is usually much faster and can be done with the use of self-written scripts.

   However, let's assume that we have identified the following queries as good candidates:

   ```
   q=cats&fq=category:1&sort=title+desc,value+desc,score+desc
   q=cars&fq=category:2&sort=title+desc
   q=harry&fq=category:4&sort=score+desc
   ```

2. What we will do next is just add so-called warming queries to the `solrconfig.xml` file. So the `listener` XML tag definition in the `solrconfig.xml` file should look similar to this:

   ```
   <listener event="firstSearcher" class="solr.QuerySenderListener">
    <arr name="queries">
     <lst><str name="q">cats</str><str name="fq">category:*</
   str><str name="sort">title desc,value desc,score desc</str><str
   name="start">0</str><str name="rows">20</str></lst>
     <lst><str name="q">cars</str><str name="fq">category:*</
   str><str name="sort">title desc</str><str name="start">0</str><str
   name="rows">20</str></lst>
    </arr>
   </listener>
   ```

Basically, what we did is added the so-called warming queries to the startup of Solr. Now let's see how it works.

How it works...

By adding the preceding fragment of configuration to the `solrconfig.xml` file, we told Solr that we want it to run those queries whenever a `firstSearcher` event occurs. The `firstSearcher` event is fired whenever a new searcher object is prepared and there is no searcher object available in the memory. Basically, the `firstSearcher` event occurs right after Solr startup.

So what happens after Solr starts up? After adding the preceding fragment, Solr runs each of the defined queries. By doing that, the caches are populated with the entries that are significant for the queries that we identified. This means that if we did the job right, we'll have Solr configured and it is ready to handle the most common and heavy queries right after its start.

Maybe a few words about what the configuration options mean. The warm-up queries are always defined under the `listener` XML tag. The `event` parameter tells Solr what event should trigger the queries—in our case, it is the `firstSearcher` event. The `class` parameter is the Java class that implements the listener mechanism. Next, we have an array of queries that are bound together by the `array` tag with the `name="queries"` parameter. Each of the warming queries is defined as a list of parameters that are grouped by the `lst` tag.

The thing to remember is choosing the warming queries wisely. You don't need to choose the queries with all the values in the `q` parameter, but warm your common filter queries, your `sort` parameter values, and so on. Also remember that warming is not only about Solr itself. During warm-up, Lucene segments are read by the operating system and are cached. This results in commonly used index parts being placed in the memory and thus can be accessed very fast.

There's more...

There is one more recipe that I would like to cover.

Improving Solr performance after committing operations

If you are interested in improving the performance of your Solr instance, you should also look at the `newSearcher` event. This event occurs whenever a commit operation is performed by Solr (for example, after replication). Assuming that we identified the same queries as before as good candidates to warm the caches, we should add the following entries to the `solrconfig.xml` file:

```
<listener event="newSearcher" class="solr.QuerySenderListener">
 <arr name="queries">
  <lst><str name="q">cats</str><str name="fq">category:*</
str><str name="sort">title desc,value desc,score desc</str><str
name="start">0</str><str name="rows">20</str></lst>
  <lst><str name="q">cars</str><str name="fq">category:*</
str><str name="sort">title desc</str><str name="start">0</str><str
name="rows">20</str></lst>
 </arr>
</listener>
```

Remember that the warming queries are especially important for the caches that can't be automatically warmed.

Lowering the memory consumption of faceting and sorting

Faceting and sorting might require a large amount of RAM memory for large volumes of documents. For sorting or faceting, Solr needs to un-invert the values in the index and keep such information in memory—in the field cache. This might require a significant amount of memory when your data is large enough. Of course, you can scale out, have more nodes, and spread the collection among them so that a single Solr instance is put under less pressure. However, Lucene introduced a special structure called **doc values**, which can work as fast as field cache, but doesn't require as much memory. This recipe will show you how to use this.

How to do it...

For the purpose of this recipe, let's assume that we have a bookstore and we allow a user to sort on the title of the book:

1. Our initial index structure (the field's definition section from the `schema.xml` file) looks as follows:

```
<field name="id" type="string" indexed="true" stored="true"
required="true" />
<field name="title" type="text_general" indexed="true"
stored="true" />
<field name="title_sort" type="string" indexed="true"
stored="false" />
```

2. Our sample data looks as follows:

```
<add>
 <doc>
  <field name="id">1</field>
  <field name="title">Solr 4.0 cookbook</field>
 </doc>
 <doc>
  <field name="id">2</field>
  <field name="title">Solr 3.1 cookbook</field>
 </doc>
 <doc>
  <field name="id">3</field>
  <field name="title">ElasticSearch Server</field>
 </doc>
</add>
```

3. Of course, we also need a copy field definition so that Solr automatically copies data from the `title` field to the `title_sort` field (again we add the following to the `schema.xml` file):

```
<copyField source="title" dest="title_sort" />
```

4. To use doc values for the `title_sort` field, we will change its definition so it looks as follows:

```
<field name="title_sort" type="string" indexed="false"
stored="false" docValues="true" />
```

5. So our final field's definition in the `schema.xml` file looks as follows:

```
<field name="id" type="string" indexed="true" stored="true"
required="true" />
<field name="title" type="text_general" indexed="true"
stored="true" />
<field name="title_sort" type="string" indexed="false"
stored="false" docValues="true" />
```

And that's all—if we reindex the data now, the `title_sort` field would use doc values instead of the field cache.

How it works...

By default, the data in a Lucene index is stored in a so-called **inverted index**—a structure that allows very fast terms searching. In our example, the `title` field, the simplified inverted index structure, will look as follows:

term	count	doc
3.1	1	<2>
4.0	1	<1>
cookbook	2	<1, 2>
elastic	1	<3>
search	1	<3>
server	1	<3>
solr	2	<1, 2>

Such a structure is highly efficient when it comes to searching, but requires un-inverting for sorting and faceting. However, this is where doc values comes in—it un-inverts the field during indexing and stores that in the index.

Configuring the field to use doc values is very simple. As you can see, our initial index structure is very simple—it contains three fields: the identifier, the title of the book, and the `title_sort` field, which is not analyzed so we can sort on it.

To enable doc values, we added the `docValues="true"` property for the `title_sort` field and we reindexed the data. Also note that we set the field to not be indexed (`indexed="false"`) and not to be stored (`stored="false"`). The doc values don't require the field to be indexed and stored, and because we have another copy of it in the `title` field, we can omit those.

Note that doc values are only available for specific types—single and multivalued `solr.StrField` based fields, single and multivalued tier-based fields (such as `solr.TrieLongField` based fields), and UUID fields.

Speeding up indexing with Solr segment merge tuning

During indexing, Solr (actually Lucene) creates a series of new index files—the segments. Each segment is written once and read many times, which means that once it is written, it cannot be changed (although some data can be changed, such as delete document markings or numerical doc values). After some time, Solr will try to merge multiple small segments into bigger ones. This is because the more segments the index is built of, the slower the queries will be. Of course, we have the ability to force segment merge (by running the `force merge` command), but such an operation is resource intensive, because Lucene will rewrite the index segments. Because of that, Solr allows you to tune the segment merge process to match our needs, and this recipe will show you how to do that.

How to do it...

The **merge policy** is what controls how merges are done in Apache Lucene and thus in Solr. By default, the merge policy in not explicitly defined in Solr and reasonable defaults are used. This means that by default, Solr will use `org.apache.lucene.index.TieredMergePolicy`:

1. The first and the only step is to add the merge policy configuration to our `solrconfig.xml` file. The following section should be added to the `indexConfig` section of the mentioned configuration file:

```
<mergePolicy class="org.apache.lucene.index.TieredMergePolicy">
 <int name="maxMergeAtOnce">30</int>
 <int name="segmentsPerTier">30</int>
 <int name="maxMergedSegmentMB">20000</int>
</mergePolicy>
```

Now, after restarting Solr, we should see fewer segments than we were seeing previously.

How it works...

Let's start by saying what segment merge is. As we know, a Lucene index is built of pieces—segments. Each segment is a write-once, read many times structure, which means that once written, it can't be altered. Each segment is also a miniature Lucene index by itself. The segment merging process builds a new, larger segment using two or more smaller ones. The new segment will contain the merged information from the old segments. During the segment merge process, deleted documents are physically removed—so no deleted documents will be present in the newly created segment. You have to remember that during delete, Lucene only marks the document for deletion and doesn't remove it from the segment itself.

Now let's get back to our Solr configuration. First of all, we changed the `solrconfig.xml` file to include the explicitly defined merge policy. As I already mentioned, the merge policy is the logic that is responsible for telling Lucene when to start segment merging. We decided to use the default `org.apache.lucene.index.TieredMergePolicy` merge policy; you can read more about it at `http://lucene.apache.org/core/4_10_0/core/org/apache/lucene/index/TieredMergePolicy.html`. In general, Lucene will divide the segments into tiers of similar size and will try to merge them.

We decided to set the `maxMergeAtOnce` property to `30`. This tells how many segments should be merged at once during the normal merge process (by *normal* we mean not forced by calling Solr's `optimize` command). We also set the `segmentsPerTier` property to `30` as well. This property tells Lucene how many segments per chosen tier are allowed. The default value is `10`—smaller values means more merges, but smaller segments number. Higher values that are equal to or higher than the `maxMergeAtOnce` property mean less frequent merges at the cost of the more segments present. We also set the `maxMergedSegmentMB` property to `20000` (which translates to about 20 GB). This property specifies the maximum segment size Lucene is allowed to produce during the normal merge process. If a merge process will result in a segment larger than this value, the merge policy will merge fewer segments to keep the size limiting.

There's more...

There are two more things I would like to mention.

Increasing the RAM buffer size to improve the indexing throughput

In addition to what was written about the segment merging tuning, we can also modify the `ramBufferSizeMB` property and increase it from the default 100 MB to 512 MB. The value of this property controls the amount of memory Lucene can use to store documents before they are flushed to disk (or rather to the `Directory` implementation). If your documents are large, the default `ramBufferSizeMB` value may result in many small segments being created, because the amount of buffer space won't be enough.

However, remember that you need to have enough memory for Solr to be able to work with such buffer size. To change the `ramBufferSizeMB` value, you need to add the following section to the `solrconfig.xml` file (in the `indexConfig` section):

```
<ramBufferSizeMB>512</ramBufferSizeMB>
```

Speeding up querying with merge policy tuning

Of course, we are not only allowed to speed up indexing by allowing more segments in the index. We can also lower the number of segments the index is built on and have a slightly higher query performance at the cost of more often and more intensive merging. To do this, we can try using the following merge policy configuration:

```
<mergePolicy class="org.apache.lucene.index.TieredMergePolicy">
 <int name="maxMergeAtOnce">3</int>
 <int name="segmentsPerTier">3</int>
 <int name="maxMergeAtOnceExplicit">30</int>
</mergePolicy>
```

See also

- If you would like to see how the merge process looks like in real time and how the segments change, I encourage you to read a great post about visualizing Lucene segment merges by Mike McCandless available at `http://blog.mikemccandless.com/2011/02/visualizing-lucenes-segment-merges.html`

Avoiding caching of rare filters to improve the performance

Imagine that some of the filters you use in your queries are not good candidates for caching. You might wonder why—for example, do those filters have date and time with seconds or are spatial filters scattered all over the world? Such filters are quite unique, and thus when they are put into the cache, they are very rarely reused and thus they are more or less useless. Caching such filters is a waste of memory and CPU cycles. Is there something you can do to avoid filter queries caching? Yes, there is a way, and this recipe will show you how to do it.

How to do it...

Let's assume we have the following query being used to get the information we need:

```
q=solr+cookbook&fq=category:books&fq=date:[2014-06-
12T13:22:12Z+TO+2014-07-11T11:24:54Z]
```

The filter query we don't want to cache is the one filtering our documents on the basis of the `date` field. Of course, even though we don't want that filter to be cached, we still want the filtering to be done. In order to turn off caching, we need to add the `{!cache=false}` line to our filter that filters on the basis of the `date` field. After the change, our query should look as follows:

```
q=solr+cookbook&fq=category:books&fq={!cache=false}date:[2014-06-12T13:22:12Z+TO+2014-07-11T11:24:54Z]
```

So now let's take a look at how that works.

How it works...

The first query is very simple; we just search for the document that has the words `solr cookbook` and we want the result set to be narrowed to the `books` category. We also want to narrow the results further to only those that fall into the range of `2014-06-12T13:22:12Z` to `2014-07-11T11:24:54Z` in the `date` field.

As you can imagine, if we have many filters with such dates as the one in the query, the filter cache can be filled very fast. And in addition to that, if you don't reuse the same value in that field, the entry in the field cache is pretty useless. That's why, by adding the `{!cache=false}` part to the filter query, we tell Solr that we don't want those filter query results to be put into the filter cache. With such an approach, we won't pollute the filter cache and thus save some CPU cycles and memory.

There is one more thing when it comes to querying. The filters that are not cached will be executed in parallel with the query, so this can be an additional improvement to your query execution time.

Controlling the filter execution to improve expensive filter performance

If you use filter queries extensively, which isn't a bad thing at all, you might be wondering whether there is something you can do to improve the execution time of some of your filter queries. For example, if you have some filter queries that use heavy function queries, you might want to have them executed only on the documents that passed all the other filters. Let's see how to do that.

Getting ready

Before continuing reading, read the *Avoiding caching of rare filters to improve performance* recipe in this chapter.

How to do it...

1. Let's assume that we have the following query being used to get the documents we are interested in:

```
q=solr+cookbook&fq=category:books&fq={!frange l=10 u=100}log(sum(s
qrt(popularity),100))&fq={!frange l=0 u=10}if(exists(price_a),
sum(0,price_a),sum(0,price))
```

2. For the purpose of this recipe, let's assume that `fq={!frange l=10 u=100} log(sum(sqrt(popularity),100))` and `fq={!frange l=0 u=10}if(exists(price_a),sum(0,price_a),sum(0,price))` are the filter queries that are heavy and we would like to optimize their execution. They shouldn't be cached and the last filter present in the query should only be executed on the documents that match other filters. In order to do this, we need to modify our query, so it should look as follows:

```
q=solr+cookbook&fq=category:books&fq={!frange l=10 u=100
cache=false cost=50}log(sum(sqrt(popularity),100))&fq={!frange l=0
u=10 cache=false cost=150}if(exists(price_promotion),sum(0,price_
promotion),sum(0,price))
```

As you can see, we've added another two attributes, `cache=false` and `cost` with two values `50` and `150`. Let's see what they mean.

How it works...

As you can see in the first query, we search for the words `solr cookbook` and we want the result set to be narrowed to the `books` category. This part of the query is not heavy when it comes to execution. We also want the documents to be narrowed to the `documents` category to only those that have the value of the `log(sum(sqrt(popularity),100))` function between `10` and `100`. And in addition to that, the last filter query specifies that we want our documents to be filtered to only those that have the `price_promotion` field (or the `price` field if the `price_promotion` field isn't filled) value between `0` and `10`.

Our requirements were such that the second filter query (the one with the `log` function query) should be executed after the `fq=category:books` filter query and the last filter should be executed at the end, only on the documents that were matched by other filters. So basically, the last filter should be executed on a subset of the whole results set. We wanted to do this because the last filter is heavy when it comes to execution and we want to limit the number of documents it needs to process.

To match the requirements, we set these two filters to not be cached (`cache=false`) and introduced the `cost` parameter. The `cost` parameter in filter queries specifies the order in which noncached filter queries are executed—the higher the `cost` value, the later the filter query will be executed.

So our second filter (the one with `cost=50`) should be executed after the `fq=category:books` filter query and the last filter query (the one with `cost=150`) will be executed as the last one.

In addition to this, because the cost of the second noncached filter query is higher or equal to `100`, that filter will be only executed on the documents that matched the main query and all the other filters.

Remember that the `cost` attribute only works when the filter query is not cached.

Configuring numerical fields for high-performance sorting and range queries

Let's assume we have Apache Solr deployment where we use range queries. Some of those are run against string fields, while others are run against numerical fields. We identified that our numerical range queries are executing slower than we would like them to run. The usual question arises—is there something that we can do? Of course there is, and this recipe will show you what.

How to do it...

1. Let's begin with the definition of a field that we use to run our numerical range queries (we add it to the `schema.xml` file):

   ```
   <field name="price" type="float" indexed="true" stored="true"/>
   ```

2. The second step is to define the `float` field type (again, we add this to the `schema.xml` file):

   ```
   <fieldType name="float" class="solr.TrieFloatField"
   precisionStep="8" />
   ```

3. And now the usual query that is run against the preceding field:

   ```
   q=*:*&fq=price:[10.0+TO+59.00]&facet=true&facet.field=price
   ```

4. In order to have your numerical range queries' performance improved, there is just a single thing you need to do—decrease the `precisionStep` attribute of the `float` field type; for example, from `8` to `4`. Our field type definition will look as follows:

   ```
   <fieldType name="float" class="solr.TrieFloatField"
   precisionStep="4" positionIncrementGap="0"/>
   ```

After the preceding change, you will have to reindex your data and you will see that your numerical queries are running faster. How much faster—that depends on your setup. Now let's take a look at how it works.

How it works...

As you can see in the preceding example, we use a simple `float` based field to run numerical range queries. Before the changes, we set `precisionStep` on our field type as `8`. This attribute (specified in bits) tells Lucene (which Solr is built on top of) how many tokens should be indexed for a single value in such a field. Smaller `precisionStep` values (when `precisionStep` is greater than `0`) will lead to more tokens generated by a single value and thus making range queries faster. Because of this, when we decreased our `precisionStep` value from `8` to `4`, we saw the performance increase.

However, remember that decreasing the `precisionStep` value will lead to slightly larger indices. Also setting the `precisionStep` value to `0` turns off indexing of multiple tokens per value, so don't use that value if you want your range queries to perform faster.

See also

- If you would like to read more about how exactly precision step works, refer to the numeric range query Javadoc available at `http://lucene.apache.org/core/4_10_0/core/org/apache/lucene/search/NumericRangeQuery.html`

7
In the Cloud

In this chapter, we will cover the following topics:

- Creating a new SolrCloud cluster
- Setting up multiple collections on a single cluster
- Splitting shards
- Having more than a single shard from a collection on a node
- Creating a collection on defined nodes
- Adding replicas after collection creation
- Removing replicas
- Moving shards between nodes
- Using aliasing
- Using routing

Introduction

With the release of Apache Solr 4.0, we were given a new, powerful mode Solr could work in—SolrCloud. What we got is out-of-the-box distributed indexing and searching at a full scale. We can distribute our collection along multiple machines without having to think about doing it in our application. We can have multiple logical collections defined, running, and managed automatically. In this chapter, we'll see how to manage your SolrCloud instances, how to increase the number of replicas, and have multiple collections inside the same cluster.

This chapter covers both Solr 4.x and Solr 5 when it comes to the creation of SolrCloud clusters and handling collections.

Creating a new SolrCloud cluster

Imagine a situation where one day you have to set up a distributed cluster with the use of Solr. The amount of data is just too much for a single server to handle. Of course, you can just set up a second server or go for another master server with another set of data. But before Solr 4.0, you would have to take care of the data distribution yourself. In addition to this, you would also have to take care of setting up replication, data duplication, and so on. With SolrCloud, you don't have to do this—you can just set up a new cluster, and this recipe will show you how to do that.

Getting ready

Before continuing further, I advise you to read the *Installing ZooKeeper for SolrCloud* recipe from *Chapter 1, Apache Solr Configuration*. It shows you how to set up a Zookeeper cluster in order to be ready for production use. However, if you already have Zookeeper running, you can skip this recipe.

How to do it...

Let's assume that we want to create a cluster that will have four Solr servers. We also would like to have our data divided between the four Solr servers in such a way that we have the original data on two machines, and in addition to this, we would also have a copy of each shard available in case something happens with one of the Solr instances. I also assume that we already have our Zookeeper cluster set up, ready, and available at the address `192.168.1.10` on the `9983` port. For this recipe, we will set up four SolrCloud nodes on the same physical machine:

1. We will start by running an empty Solr server (without any configuration) on port `8983`. We do this by running the following command (for Solr 4.x):

   ```
   java -DzkHost=192.168.1.10:9983 -jar start.jar
   ```

2. For Solr 5, we will run the following command:

   ```
   bin/solr -c -z 192.168.1.10:9983
   ```

3. Now we start another three nodes, each on a different port (note that different Solr instances can run on the same port, but they should be installed on different machines). We do this by running one command for each installed Solr server (for Solr 4.x):

   ```
   java -Djetty.port=6983 -DzkHost=192.168.1.10:9983 -jar start.jar
   java -Djetty.port=4983 -DzkHost=192.168.1.10:9983 -jar start.jar
   java -Djetty.port=2983 -DzkHost=192.168.1.10:9983 -jar start.jar
   ```

4. For Solr 5, the commands will be as follows:

```
bin/solr -c -p 6983 -z 192.168.1.10:9983
bin/solr -c -p 4983 -z 192.168.1.10:9983
bin/solr -c -p 2983 -z 192.168.1.10:9983
```

5. Now we need to upload our collection configuration to ZooKeeper. Assuming that we have our configuration in `/home/conf/solrconfiguration/conf`, we will run the following command from the `home` directory of the Solr server that runs first (the `zkcli.sh` script can be found in the Solr deployment example in the `scripts/cloud-scripts` directory):

```
./zkcli.sh -cmd upconfig -zkhost 192.168.1.10:9983 -confdir /home/conf/solrconfiguration/conf/ -confname collection1
```

6. Now we can create our collection using the following command:

```
curl 'localhost:8983/solr/admin/collections?action=CREATE&name=firstCollection&numShards=2&replicationFactor=2&collection.configName=collection1'
```

7. If we now go to `http://localhost:8983/solr/#/~cloud`, we will see the following cluster view:

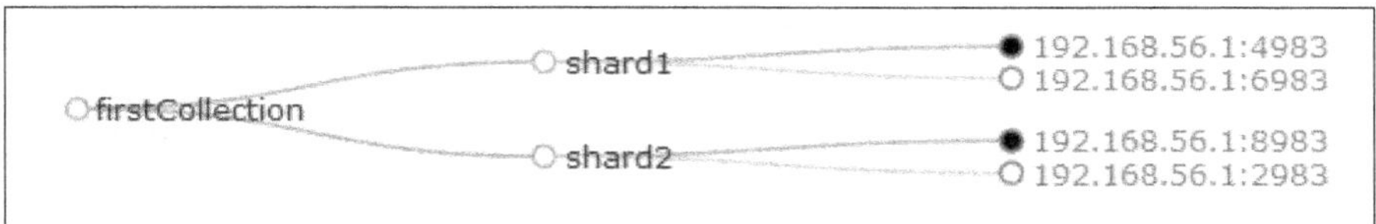

As we can see, Solr has created a new collection with a proper deployment. Let's now see how it works.

How it works...

We assume that we already have ZooKeeper installed—it is empty and doesn't have information about any collection, because we didn't create them.

For Solr 4.x, we started by running Solr and telling it that we want it to run in SolrCloud mode. We did that by specifying the `-DzkHost` property and setting its value to the IP address of our ZooKeeper instance. Of course, in the production environment, you would point Solr to a cluster of ZooKeeper nodes—this is done using the same property, but the IP addresses are separated using the comma character.

For Solr 5, we used the `solr` script provided in the `bin` directory. By adding the `-c` switch, we told Solr that we want it to run in the SolrCloud mode. The `-z` switch works exactly the same as the `-DzkHost` property for Solr 4.x—it allows you to specify the ZooKeeper host that should be used.

Of course, the other three Solr nodes run exactly in the same manner. For Solr 4.x, we add the `-DzkHost` property that points Solr to our ZooKeeper. Because we are running all four nodes on the same physical machine, we needed to specify the `-Djetty.port` property, because we can run only a single Solr server on a single port. For Solr 5, we use the `-z` property of the `bin/solr` script and we use the `-p` property to specify the port on which Solr should start.

The next step is to upload the collection configuration to ZooKeeper. We do this because Solr will fetch this configuration from ZooKeeper when you request the collection creation. To upload the configuration, we use the `zkcli.sh` script provided with the Solr distribution. We use the `upconfig` command (the `-cmd` switch), which means that we want to upload the configuration. We specify the ZooKeeper host using the `-zkHost` property. After that, we can say which directory our configuration is stored (the `-confdir` switch). The directory should contain all the needed configuration files such as `schema.xml`, `solrconfig.xml`, and so on. Finally, we specify the name under which we want to store our configuration using the `-confname` switch.

After we have our configuration in ZooKeeper, we can create the collection. We do this by running a command to the Collections API that is available at the `/admin/collections` endpoint. First, we tell Solr that we want to create the collection (`action=CREATE`) and that we want our collection to be named `firstCollection` (`name=firstCollection`). Remember that the collection names are case sensitive, so `firstCollection` and `firstcollection` are two different collections. We specify that we want our collection to be built of two primary shards (`numShards=2`) and we want each shard to be present in two copies (`replicationFactor=2`). This means that we will have a primary shard and a single replica. Finally, we specify which configuration should be used to create the collection by specifying the `collection.configName` property.

As we can see in the cloud, a view of our cluster has been created and spread across all the nodes.

There's more...

There are a few things that I would like to mention—the possibility of running a Zookeeper server embedded into Apache Solr and specifying the Solr server name.

Starting an embedded ZooKeeper server

You can also start an embedded Zookeeper server shipped with Solr for your test environment. In order to do this, you should pass the `-DzkRun` parameter instead of `-DzkHost=192.168.0.10:9983`, but only in the command that sends our configuration to the Zookeeper cluster. So the final command for Solr 4.x should look similar to this:

```
java -DzkRun -jar start.jar
```

In Solr 5.0, the same command will be as follows:

```
bin/solr start -c
```

By default, ZooKeeper will start on the port higher by 1,000 to the one Solr is started at. So if you are running your Solr instance on `8983`, ZooKeeper will be available at `9983`.

The thing to remember is that the embedded ZooKeeper should only be used for development purposes and only one node should start it.

Specifying the Solr server name

Solr needs each instance of SolrCloud to have a name. By default, that name is set using the IP address or the hostname appended with the port the Solr instance is running on and the `_solr` postfix. For example, if our node is running on `192.168.56.1` and port `8983`, it will be called `192.168.56.1:8983_solr`. Of course, Solr allows you to change that behavior by specifying the hostname. To do this, start using the `-Dhost` property or add the host property to `solr.xml`.

For example, if we would like one of our nodes to have the name of `server1`, we can run the following command to start Solr:

```
java -DzkHost=192.168.1.10:9983 -Dhost=server1 -jar start.jar
```

In Solr 5.0, the same command would be:

```
bin/solr start -c -h server1
```

Setting up multiple collections on a single cluster

Having a single collection inside the cluster is nice, but there are multiple use cases when we want to have more than a single collection running on the same cluster. For example, we might want users and books in different collections or logs from each day to be only stored inside a single collection. This recipe will show you how to create multiple collections on the same cluster.

Getting ready

Before reading further, I advise you to read the *Creating a new SolrCloud cluster* recipe of this chapter. This recipe will show you how to create a new SolrCloud cluster. We also assume that ZooKeeper is running on `192.168.1.10` and is listening on port `2181` and that we already have four SolrCloud nodes running as a cluster.

How to do it...

As we already have all the prerequisites, such as ZooKeeper and Solr up and running, we need to upload our configuration files to ZooKeeper to be able to create collections:

1. Assuming that we have our configurations in `/home/conf/firstcollection/conf` and `/home/conf/secondcollection/conf`, we will run the following commands from the `home` directory of the first run Solr server to upload the configuration to ZooKeeper (the `zkcli.sh` script can be found in the Solr deployment example in the `scripts/cloud-scripts` directory):

```
./zkcli.sh -cmd upconfig -zkhost localhost:2181 -confdir /home/conf/firstcollection/conf/ -confname firstcollection
./zkcli.sh -cmd upconfig -zkhost localhost:2181 -confdir /home/conf/secondcollection/conf/ -confname secondcollection
```

2. We have pushed our configurations into Zookeeper, so now we can create the collections we want. In order to do this, we use the following commands:

```
curl 'localhost:8983/solr/admin/collections?action=CREATE&name=firstCollection&numShards=2&replicationFactor=2&collection.configName=firstcollection'
curl 'localhost:8983/solr/admin/collections?action=CREATE&name=secondcollection&numShards=4&replicationFactor=1&collection.configName=secondcollection'
```

3. Now, just to test whether everything went well, we will go to `http://localhost:8983/solr/#/~cloud`. As the result, we will see the following cluster topology:

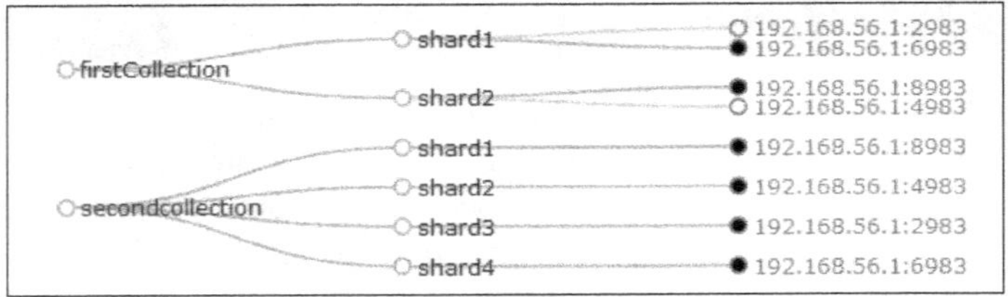

As we can see, both the collections were created the way we wanted. Now let's see how that happened.

How it works...

We assume that we already have ZooKeeper installed—it is empty and doesn't have information about any collections, because we didn't create them. We also assumed that we have our SolrCloud cluster configured and started.

To create collections, we start by uploading the configuration to ZooKeeper. This is what we already discussed in the *Creating a new SolrCloud cluster* recipe of this chapter. We start by uploading two configurations to ZooKeeper, one called `firstcollection` and the other called `secondcollection`. After that, we are ready to create our collections.

We start by creating the collection named `firstCollection` that is built of two primary shards and one replica. The second collection, called `secondcollection`, is built of four primary shards and it doesn't have any replicas. We can see that easily in the cloud view of the deployment. The `firstCollection` collection has two shards—`shard1` and `shard2`. Each of the shards has two physical copies—one green (which means active) and one with a black dot, which is the primary shard. The `secondcollection` collection is built of four physical shards—each shard has a black dot near its name, which means that they are primary shards.

Splitting shards

Imagine a situation where you reach a limit of your current deployment—the number of shards is just not enough. For example, the indexing throughput is lower and lower, because the disks are not able to keep up. Of course, one of the possible solutions is to spread the index across more shards; however, you already have a collection and you want to keep the data and reindexing is not an option, because you don't have the original data. Solr can help you with such situations by allowing splitting shards of already created collections. This recipe will show you how to do it.

Getting ready

Before reading further, I would suggest you all to read the *Creating a new SolrCloud cluster* recipe of this chapter. This recipe will show you how to create a new SolrCloud cluster. We also assume that ZooKeeper is running on `192.168.1.10` and is listening on port `2181` and that we already have four SolrCloud nodes running as a cluster.

How to do it...

Let's assume that we already have a SolrCloud cluster up and running and it has one collection called `books`. So our cloud view (which is available at `http://localhost:8983/solr/#/~cloud`) looks as follows:

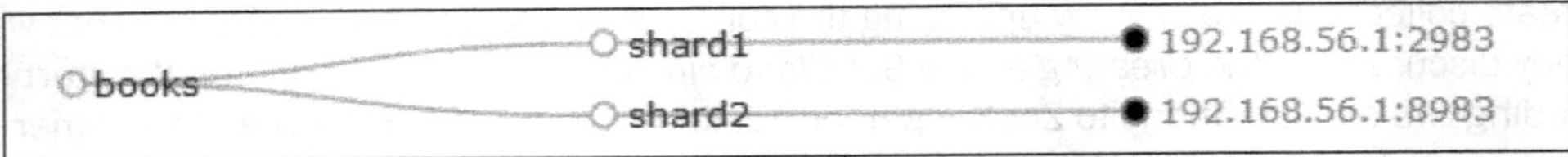

We have four nodes and we don't utilize them fully. We can say that these two nodes in which we have our shards are almost fully utilized. What we can do is create a new collection and reindex the data or we can split shards of the already created collection. Let's go with the second option:

1. We start by splitting the first shard. It is as easy as running the following command:

```
curl 'http://localhost:8983/solr/admin/collections?action=SPLITSHA
RD&collection=books&shard=shard1'
```

2. After this, we can split the second shard by running a similar command to the one we just used:

```
curl 'http://localhost:8983/solr/admin/collections?action=SPLITSHA
RD&collection=books&shard=shard2'
```

3. Let's take a look at the cluster cloud view now (which is available at `http://localhost:8983/solr/#/~cloud`):

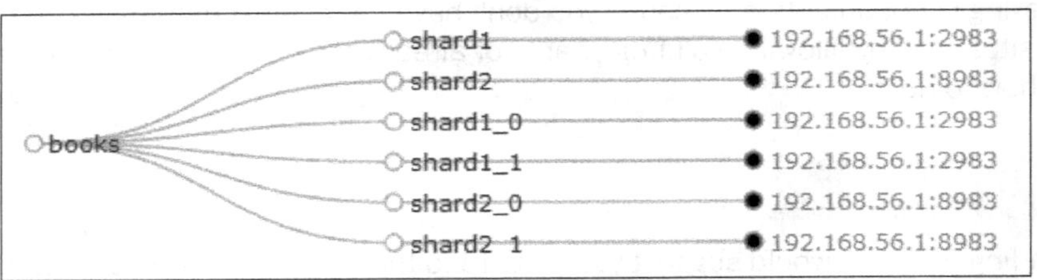

As we can see, both shards were split—`shard1` was divided into `shard1_0` and `shard1_1` and `shard2` was divided into `shard2_0` and `shard2_1`. Of course, the data was copied as well, so everything is ready.

However, the last step should be to delete the original shards. Solr doesn't delete them, because sometimes applications use shard names to connect to a given shard. However, in our case, we can delete them by running the following commands:

```
curl 'http://localhost:8983/solr/admin/collections?action=DELETESHARD&collection=books&shard=shard1'
```

```
curl 'http://localhost:8983/solr/admin/collections?action=DELETESHARD&collection=books&shard=shard2'
```

Now if we would again look at the cloud view of the cluster, we will see the following:

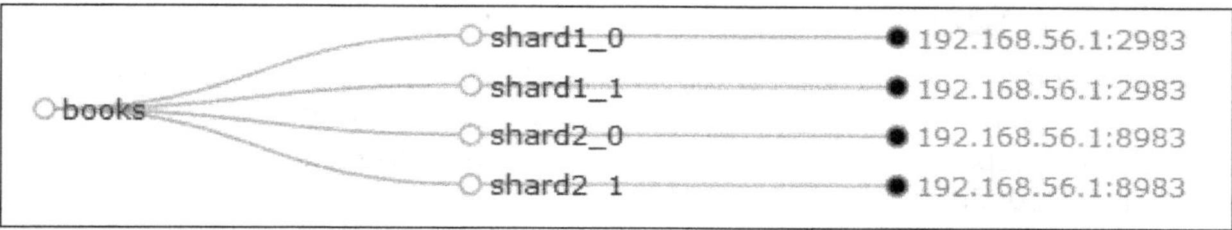

How it works...

We start with a simple collection called `books` that is built of two primary shards and no replicas. This is the collection which shards we will try to divide it without stopping Solr.

Splitting shards is very easy. We just need to run a simple command in the Collections API (the `/admin/collections` endpoint) and specify that we want to split a shard (`action=SPLITSHARD`). We also need to provide additional information such as which collection we are interested in (the `collection` parameter) and which shard we want to split (the `shard` parameter). You can see the name of the shard by looking at the cloud view or by reading the cluster state from ZooKeeper. After sending the command, Solr might force us to wait for a substantial amount of time—shard splitting takes time, especially on large collections. Of course, we can run the same command for the second shard as well.

Finally, we end up with six shards—four new and two old ones. The original shard will still contain data, but it will start to re-route requests to newly created shards. The data was split evenly between the new shards. The old shards were left although they are marked as inactive and they won't have any more data indexed to them. Because we don't need them, we can just delete them using the `action=DELETESHARD` command sent to the same Collections API. Similar to the `split shard` command, we need to specify the collection name, which shard we want to delete, and the name of the shard. After we delete the initial shards, we now see that our cluster view shows only four shards, which is what we were aiming at.

We can now spread the shards across the cluster, and we do this in the *Moving shards between nodes* recipe later in this chapter.

Having more than a single shard from a collection on a node

Let's assume that we have a cluster of four nodes, but we are sure that we will have eight nodes in the near future. We want to be prepared for this, so when the new nodes are installed, we don't need to split collection shards or reindex the data. By default, Solr won't allow you to do that, but this recipe will show you how to achieve such a setup.

Getting ready

Before reading further, I would suggest you all to read the *Creating a new SolrCloud cluster* recipe in this chapter. This recipe will show you how to create a new SolrCloud cluster. We also assume that ZooKeeper is running on `192.168.1.10` and is listening on port `2181` and that we already have four SolrCloud nodes running as a cluster.

How to do it...

Let's assume that we already have a cluster with four nodes and the configuration uploaded to ZooKeeper (if you don't know how to do it, take a look at the *Creating a new SolrCloud cluster* recipe in this chapter). Our collection configuration is called `firstcollection`.

As we said, we have four nodes, but we would like to create a collection that has eight shards. We want to be prepared for cluster growth, which will happen in the future, and we don't want to use shard splitting, because we know it will take time and that operation is resource intensive. What we need to do is force Solr to put more than a single shard of the collection on a node and create a collection that is built of eight shards:

1. Let's try to create a new collection by running the following command:

   ```
   curl 'localhost:8983/solr/admin/collections?action=CREATE&name
   =firstTryCollection&numShards=8&replicationFactor=1&collection.
   configName=firstcollection'
   ```

   After running this command, we will see the following response from Solr:

   ```
   <?xml version="1.0" encoding="UTF-8"?>
   <response>
   <lst name="responseHeader"><int name="status">400</int><int
   name="QTime">74</int></lst><str name="Operation createcollection
   caused exception:">org.apache.solr.common.SolrException:org.
   apache.solr.common.SolrException: Cannot create collection
   firstTryCollection. Value of maxShardsPerNode
   ```

```
is 1, and the number of live nodes is 4. This allows a maximum
of 4 to be created. Value of numShards is 8 and value of
replicationFactor is 1. This requires 8 shards to be created
(higher than the allowed number)</str><lst name="exception"><str
name="msg">Cannot create collection firstTryCollection. Value
of maxShardsPerNode is 1, and the number of live nodes is 4.
This allows a maximum of 4 to be created. Value of numShards
is 8 and value of replicationFactor is 1. This requires 8
shards to be created (higher than the allowed number)</
str><int name="rspCode">400</int></lst><lst name="error"><str
name="msg">Cannot create collection firstTryCollection. Value of
maxShardsPerNode is 1, and the number of live nodes is
4. This allows a maximum of 4 to be created. Value of numShards
is 8 and value of replicationFactor is 1. This requires 8
shards to be created (higher than the allowed number)</str><int
name="code">400</int></lst>
</response>
```

This means that Solr won't create the collection, because there are not enough Solr nodes.

2. Let's now add `maxShardsPerNode=2` to our command so that it looks as follows:

```
curl 'localhost:8983/solr/admin/collections?action=CREATE&name=sec
ondTryCollection&numShards=8&replicationFactor=1&collection.config
Name=firstcollection&maxShardsPerNode=2'
```

3. If we now take a look at `http://localhost:8983/solr/#/~cloud`, we will see the following:

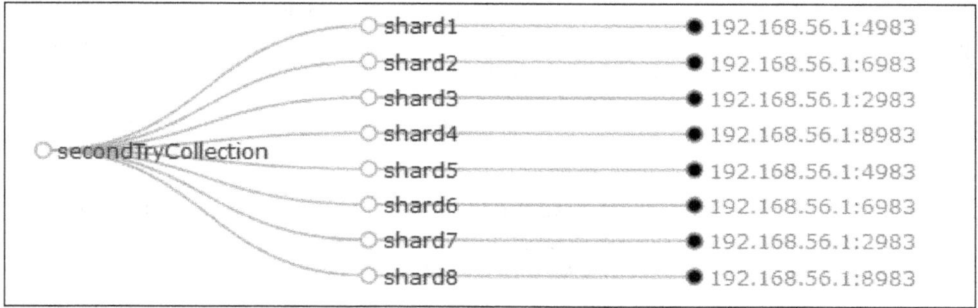

As we can see, it worked. Let's now see why.

How it works...

Of course, we assume that we have our four nodes up and running and we have a collection configuration stored in ZooKeeper under the name `firstcollection`.

When we run the first command, we tell Solr that we want our `firstTryCollection` collection to be created with eight shards (`numShards=8`) and with only a single physical copy of each shard (`replicationFactor=1`), so no replicas. However, Solr returned with an error telling us that we can't do that. That is because, by default, Solr allows only a single shard of the same collection to be present on a given node. The default behavior is good, but it is not what we want in some use cases.

Because of this, we introduced the `maxShardsPerNode` property and we set it to `2`. The default value for that property is `1`, but in our case, we have four nodes and we create a collection built of eight shards, which means that we need at least two shards of the same collection on a single node. As we can see, after introducing this parameter and sending the command to create a collection, we ended up with a collection created.

Now, after our new nodes arrive, we will be able to spread the shards across the cluster. You will learn how to do this in the *Moving shards between nodes* recipe later in this chapter.

Creating a collection on defined nodes

There are use cases where we want to create a collection only on some of the nodes. For example, we would like to have one collection created on other better machines, because we know that this collection will be heavier in terms of indexing and querying. The other collections can live on the smaller and worse performing nodes. In such cases, we still have all the collections in a single cluster, but we know that they will be placed on hardware we want them to be placed. This recipe will show you how to do this.

Getting ready

Before reading further, I advise you to read the *Creating a new SolrCloud cluster* and *Having more than a single shard from a collection on a node* recipes of this chapter. These recipes will show you how to create a new SolrCloud cluster. We also assume that ZooKeeper is running on `192.168.1.10` and is listening on port `2181` and that we already have four SolrCloud nodes running as a cluster. We also assume that we have a configuration called `firstCollection` stored in ZooKeeper.

How to do it...

Let's assume that we have a cluster of four SolrCloud nodes and, as we wrote, we would like the primary shards to only be present on the better machines—in our case, these are the nodes called `192.168.56.1:8983_solr` and `192.168.56.1:7983_solr`:

1. If we run a standard collection creation command and specify that we will allow two shards of that collection per node, we will use the following command:

   ```
   curl 'localhost:8983/solr/admin/collections?action=CREATE&name=firstTry&numShards=2&replicationFactor=1&collection.configName=firstcollection&maxShardsPerNode=2'
   ```

   It might happen that our collection has been created the way we wanted, but let's check this by taking a look at `http://localhost:8983/solr/#/~cloud`. This is what we see:

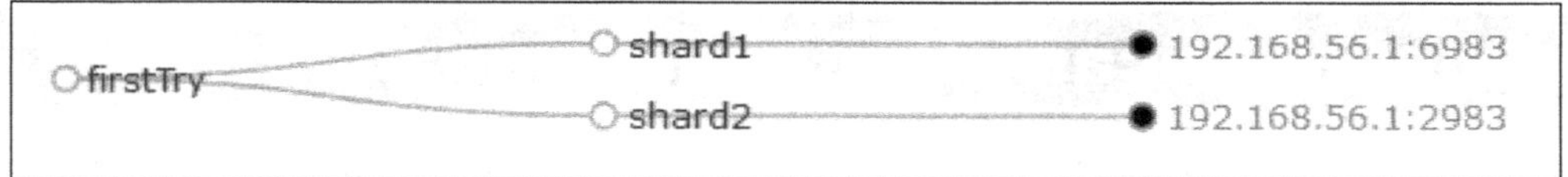

   As you can see, it is not exactly what we wanted.

2. So let's try specifying the nodes we want our collection to be created at by adding the `createNodeSet` property. Our new command looks as follows:

   ```
   curl 'localhost:8983/solr/admin/collections?action=CREATE&name=secondTry&numShards=2&replicationFactor=1&collection.configName=firstcollection&maxShardsPerNode=2&createNodeSet=192.168.56.1:8983_solr,192.168.56.1:6983_solr'
   ```

3. If we now again take a look at `http://localhost:8983/solr/#/~cloud`, we will see the following cluster view:

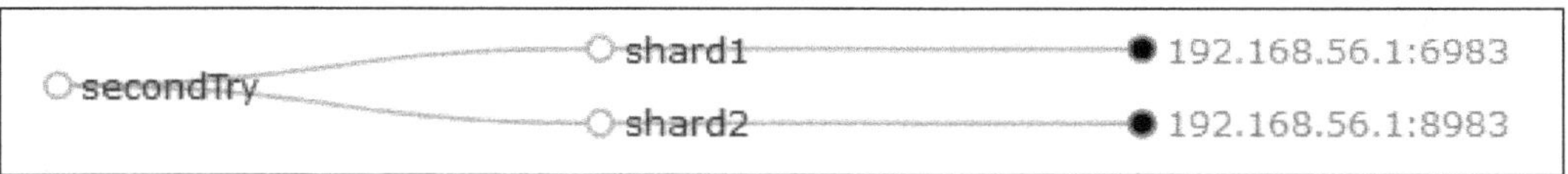

As we can see, everything worked as we wanted. Let's now see why that happened.

How it works...

We assume that the better nodes are the ones that have the names of `192.168.56.1:8983_solr` and `192.168.56.1:6983_solr`. When we run our standard collection creation command, we can end up with collections created on those nodes; however, we can't count on that. In fact, in our example, we ended up with collections created on nodes `192.168.56.1:2983_solr` and `192.168.56.1:6983_solr`. This is not what we wanted.

To achieve what we want, we need to add the `createNodeSet` property. The value of this property should be a comma-separated list of SolrCloud node names, which should be taken into consideration when creating collections. In our case, the value of the `createNodeSet` property should be `192.168.56.1:8983_solr,192.168.56.1:6983_solr`. As we can see, after we added this property, our collection named `secondTry` was properly created only on the nodes we were interested in.

Adding replicas after collection creation

Replicas are copies of the primary shard. They are very useful when it comes to handing performance issues—for example, if your current cluster can't keep up with queries, you can add new nodes and increase the number of replicas. This way, more Solr servers can serve queries and each of them will have fewer queries to process. In this recipe, we will learn how to add new shards to already created collections.

Getting ready

Before reading further, I advise you to read the *Creating a new SolrCloud cluster* and *Having more than a single shard from a collection on a node* recipes of this chapter. These recipes will show you how to create a new SolrCloud cluster and a collection. We also assume that ZooKeeper is running on `192.168.1.10` and is listening on port `2181`. We already have the configuration called `firstcollection` stored in ZooKeeper and we already have four SolrCloud nodes running as a cluster.

How to do it...

1. Let's start by creating a sample collection with two shards and no replicas. We do this by running the following command:

```
curl 'localhost:8983/solr/admin/collections?action=CREATE&nam
e=collAddReplicas&numShards=2&replicationFactor=1&collection.
configName=firstcollection'
```

After running the preceding command, our cluster view should look as follows:

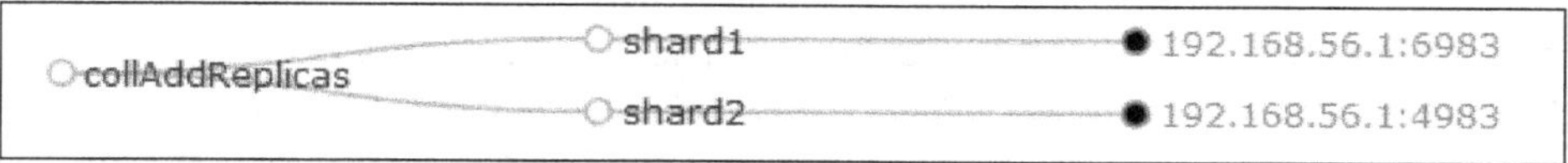

2. Now, let's add a replica of `shard1` and let's place it on a node called `192.168.56.1:8983_solr`. To do this, we will run the following command:

```
curl 'http://localhost:8983/solr/admin/collections?action=ADDREPLI
CA&shard=shard1&collection=collAddReplicas&node=192.168.56.1:8983_
solr'
```

   After Solr is done working, our cluster view should look similar to the following screenshot:

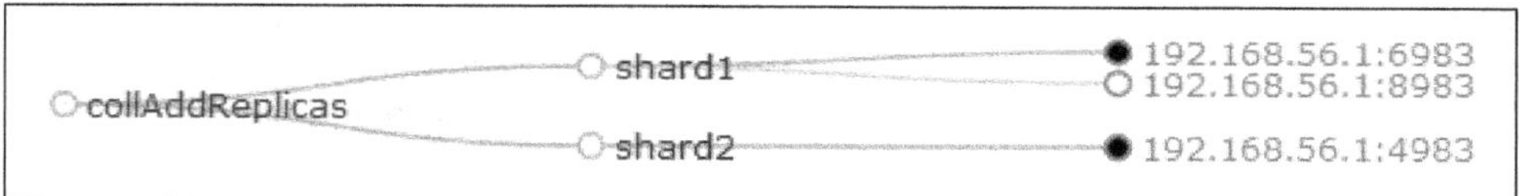

3. Now, let's add a replica of `shard2` and let's place it on a node called `192.168.56.1:2983_solr`. To do this, we will run the following command:

```
curl 'http://localhost:8983/solr/admin/collections?action=ADDREPLI
CA&shard=shard2&collection=collAddReplicas&node=192.168.56.1:2983_
solr'
```

4. If we now again look at the cluster view, we will be able to see something similar to this:

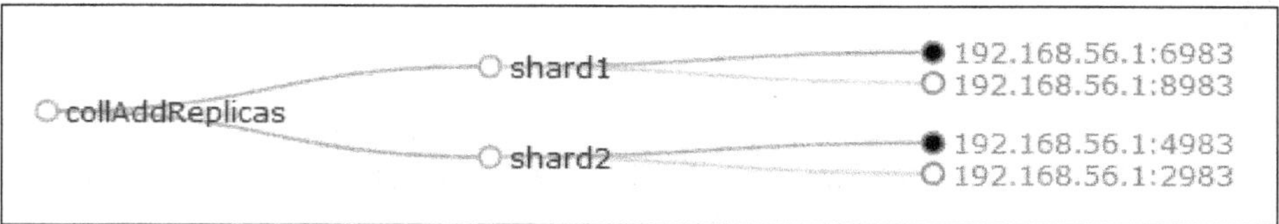

As we can see, everything works as it should.

How it works...

We started by creating a new collection called `collAddReplicas`. Of course, we have our SolrCloud cluster up and running, ZooKeeper installed and running, and the `firstcollection` configuration stored in it. Our collection is created with two shards (`numShards=2`) and with only primary shards (`replicationFactor=1`).

As we said, after some time, we added new nodes to our cluster because our initial cluster was heavily used and the queries started to be slow. Because of that, we decided to add more replicas.

We started by creating a replica for `shard1`. To do this, we need to call the Collections API `ADDREPLICA` command (`action=ADDREPLICA`) and specify the shard we want to create the replica for (`shard=shard1` in our case), the collection that this command should modify (`collection=collAddReplicas`), and the node name on which the replica should be created (`node=192.168.56.1:8983_solr`). After receiving this command, Solr will create that replica and start replication. After replication has ended, Solr will automatically start using that replica. We do the same for `shard2`—although we put the replica on a different node.

As we can see, after adding two replicas, we now have four shards in our collection, two for each shard, and Solr successfully initiated our new shards.

Removing replicas

Sometimes, there is a need of removing one or more replicas from your Solr cluster. Either because you want to get rid of some nodes and you want your cluster state to become clean or you want to move some shard to another node and delete the original shard. No matter what the case is, there might come a time where you need to delete a shard. This recipe will show you how to do it.

Getting ready

Before reading further, I advise you to read the *Creating a new SolrCloud cluster* and *Having more than a single shard from a collection on a node* recipes in this chapter. These recipes will show you how to create a new SolrCloud cluster and create a collection. We also assume that ZooKeeper is running on `192.168.1.10` and is listening on port `2181`. We already have the configuration called `firstcollection` stored in ZooKeeper and we already have four SolrCloud nodes running as a cluster.

How to do it...

1. To show you how to delete replicas from the already existing collection, we will create a new collection that is built of two shards and have a replica of each of the shards. To do this, we will run the following command:

   ```
   curl 'localhost:8983/solr/admin/collections?action=CREATE&nam
   e=testCollection&numShards=2&replicationFactor=2&collection.
   configName=firstcollection'
   ```

   After the collection is created, we should see the following cluster view when we take a look at `http://localhost:8983/solr/#/~cloud`:

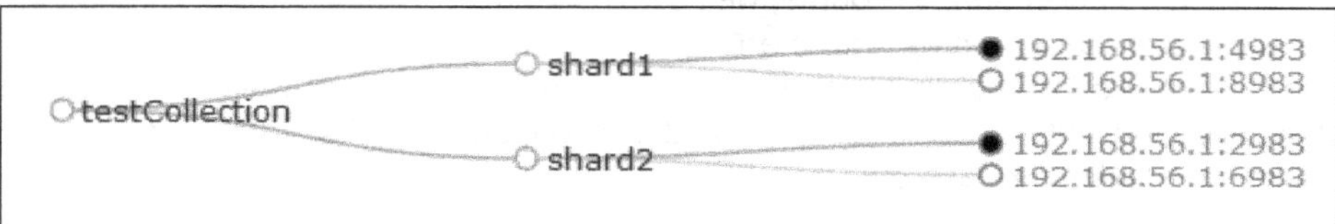

   Now, let's assume that we want to get rid of two servers in our cluster, `192.168.56.1:8983` and `192.168.56.1:6983`. And we don't want to leave any traces in the cluster state. To do this, we need to remove the replicas that are placed on those nodes.

2. We start by removing the `192.168.56.1:8983_solr` replica by running the following command:

   ```
   curl 'http://localhost:8983/solr/admin/collections?action=DELETERE
   PLICA&collection=testCollection&shard=shard1&replica=core_node2'
   ```

3. After the command is executed, we can see the following cluster view:

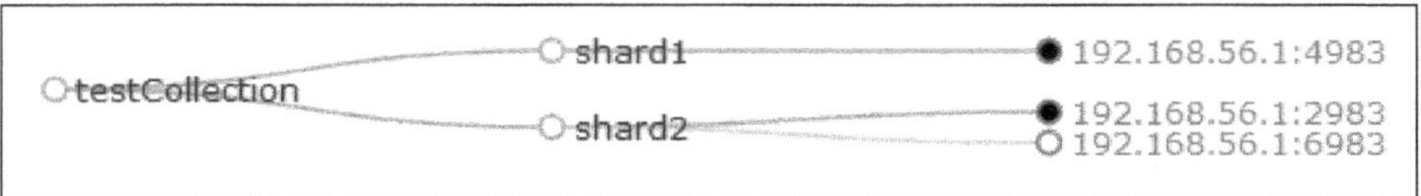

4. We can now remove the replica of the second shard by running the following command:

   ```
   curl 'http://localhost:8983/solr/admin/collections?action=DELETERE
   PLICA&collection=testCollection&shard=shard2&replica=core_node4'
   ```

And again let's take a look at the cluster view:

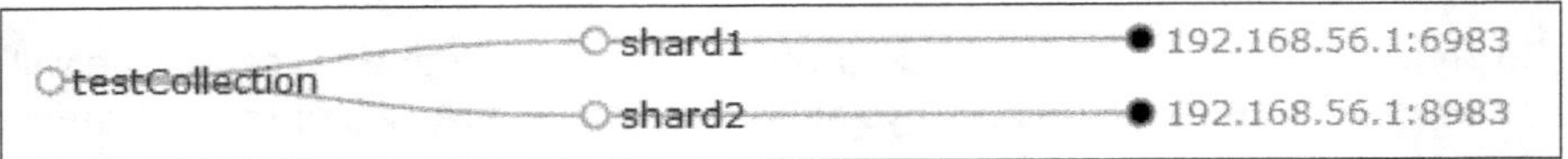

As we can see, everything worked.

How it works...

We start by creating a collection that we will use to demonstrate how to remove replicas from the already created collection. Of course, we have our SolrCloud cluster up and running, ZooKeeper installed and running, and the `firstcollection` configuration stored in it. The `collection creation` command was already mentioned a few times—in our case, we created a collection called `testCollection` that is built of four physical shards—two primary shards and one replica for each of them.

What we try to do is delete the replicas of the primary shards, because we want to remove the server on which they are running and throw the hardware away. To do this, we start by removing the replica that is stored on the node running on port `8983`. The thing is that this time we don't specify the node name like during replica creation, but we need to specify the actual shard name that Solr uses internally. We can do this by taking a look at `clusterstate.json` in the Solr admin panel (you can do that by going to `http://localhost:8983/solr/#/~cloud?view=tree` with your web browser and choosing the mentioned file). In our case, that file looks as follows:

```
{"testCollection":{
    "shards":{
      "shard1":{
        "range":"80000000-ffffffff",
        "state":"active",
        "replicas":{
          "core_node1":{
            "state":"active",
            "core":"testCollection_shard1_replica1",
            "node_name":"192.168.56.1:4983_solr",
            "base_url":"http://192.168.56.1:4983/solr",
            "leader":"true"},
          "core_node2":{
            "state":"active",
            "core":"testCollection_shard1_replica2",
            "node_name":"192.168.56.1:8983_solr",
            "base_url":"http://192.168.56.1:8983/solr"}}},
      "shard2":{
```

```
        "range":"0-7fffffff",
        "state":"active",
        "replicas":{
          "core_node3":{
            "state":"active",
            "core":"testCollection_shard2_replica1",
            "node_name":"192.168.56.1:2983_solr",
            "base_url":"http://192.168.56.1:2983/solr",
            "leader":"true"},
          "core_node4":{
            "state":"active",
            "core":"testCollection_shard2_replica2",
            "node_name":"192.168.56.1:6983_solr",
            "base_url":"http://192.168.56.1:6983/solr"}}}},
    "maxShardsPerNode":"1",
    "router":{"name":"compositeId"},
    "replicationFactor":"2",
    "autoAddReplicas":"false"}}
```

For example, for `shard1`, we have two replicas, one named `core_node1` and the second one named `core_node2`. The first one is the primary shard (`leader=true`). For `shard2`, we also have two replicas, one named `core_node3` and the second one named `core_node4`. In this case, the first is also the primary shard.

To delete a shard, we need to send an appropriate request to the Collections API (`/admin/collections`) and specify the delete action (`action=DELETEREPLICA`), collection (`collection=testCollection`), the shard (`shard=shard1`), and the name of the replica (`replica=core_node2`). In our case, we want to remove the replica from nodes running on port `8983` for `shard1` (which means that we remove `core_node4`) and on port `6983` for `shard2` (which means we remove `core_node4`).

As we can see, after both the commands were executed, we are now left with a collection that has only primary shards. If we look at the cluster state now, we will see that there are no trace of the replicas, which means that Solr removed them properly.

Moving shards between nodes

There are moments where we want to move shards between nodes in SolrCloud cluster. Until now, the Solr Collections API doesn't have a command telling Solr to move a single shard to another node. We need to do such an operation manually. For example, let's assume that we want to exchange one of the nodes in our cluster with a new server, but we don't want any downtime or interruptions to our service. This recipe will show you how to do that.

Getting ready

Before reading further, I would suggest you all to read the *Creating a new SolrCloud cluster*, *Adding replicas after collection creation*, and *Removing replicas* recipes of this chapter. These recipes will show you how to create a new SolrCloud cluster and create a collection. We also assume that ZooKeeper is running on `192.168.1.10` and is listening on port `2181`. We already have the configuration called `firstcollection` stored in ZooKeeper and we already have four SolrCloud nodes running as a cluster.

How to do it...

1. To keep things simple, we will start by creating a collection that is built of two shards and no replicas. We do this by running the following command:

   ```
   curl 'localhost:8983/solr/admin/collections?action=CREATE&nam
   e=testCollection&numShards=2&replicationFactor=1&collection.
   configName=firstcollection'
   ```

   Our cluster view will look as follows:

   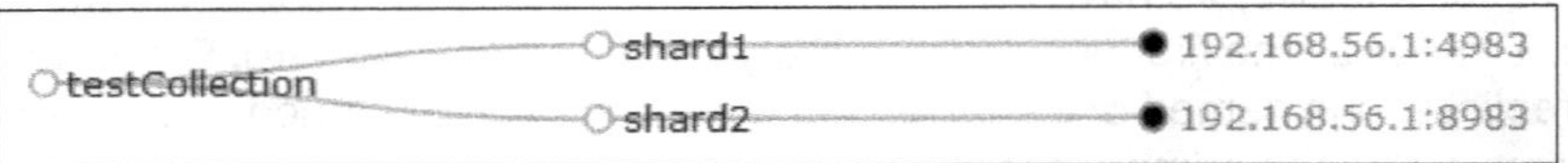

2. Now, let's try to move `shard1` from `192.168.56.1:4983` to `192.168.56.1:6983` (of course, we assume that we have that node in the cluster). We do this because we want to replace the server identified by Solr as `192.168.56.1:4983` with the one identified as `192.168.56.1:6983`.
3. To do this, we need to create a new replica on the `192.168.56.1:6983` node; we do that by running the following command:

   ```
   curl 'http://localhost:8983/solr/admin/collections?action=ADDREPLI
   CA&shard=shard1&collection=testCollection&node=192.168.56.1:6983_
   solr'
   ```

   After the command is completed and Solr synchronizes the replica, the cluster view should look as follows:

   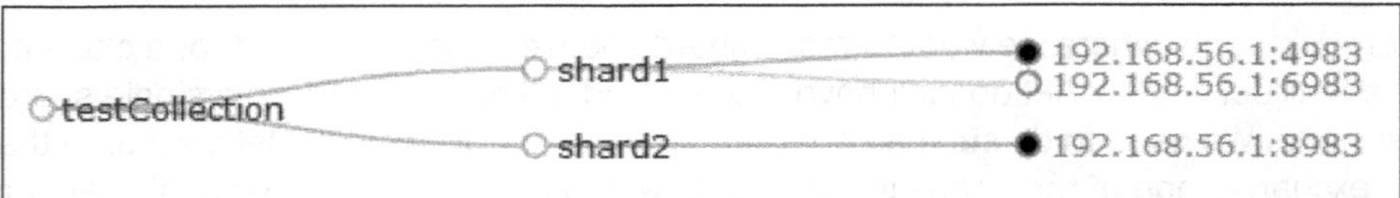

4. Now we need to remove the primary shard of `shard1`—the one on `192.168.561:8983`. We do this by running the following command:

```
curl 'http://localhost:8983/solr/admin/collections?action=DELETERE
PLICA&collection=testCollection&shard=shard1&replica=core_node2'
```

5. After the command succeeds, we can see the following cluster view:

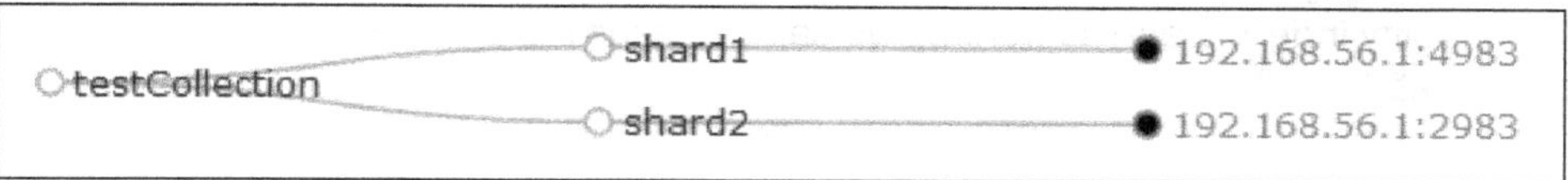

As we can see, the primary shard of `shard1` is now located on the node `192.168.56.1:6983`, which is what we wanted.

How it works...

We start by creating a collection that we will use to demonstrate the migration of a shard from one node to another. Of course, we have our SolrCloud cluster and ZooKeeper installed and running and also have the `irstcollection` configuration stored in it. The `collection creation` command was already mentioned a few times—in our case, we created a collection called `testCollection` that is built of four physical shards—two primary shards and one replica for each of them.

As we said, we want to move `shard1` from the node `192.168.56.1:4983` to node `192.168.56.1:6983`. To do this, we need to create a new shard first—a replica of the shard we want to migrate on the node we want our shard to be migrated. In our case, we created a replica of `shard1` on the `192.168.56.1:6983` node by running an `ADDREPLICA` command using the Collections API (if you are not familiar with the `add replica` command, refer to the *Adding replicas after collection creation* recipe in this chapter).

After Solr created the replica and finished replicating the data, we are now ready to delete the original shard. In some cases, it would be good to stop indexing and wait for the data in the primary shard to be in the same state as the data on the replica. This will ensure us that no data loss will happen. After we know Solr is ready, we can just run the `DELETEREPLICA` command and remove the primary shard (if you are not familiar with the `delete replica` command, refer to the *Removing replicas* recipe in this chapter). After the delete command succeeds, we end up with collection built of two primary shards, one left intact and the second one moved to a new node. We can now turn off the old node and still have the cluster state clean. Of course, we should wait for the replication to finish (we can check the status in the Solr administration UI).

Using aliasing

Aliasing is the functionality of giving your collections more than a single name. It might seem not very useful, but in fact this is very useful—for example, when dealing with time series data. Imagine that you have data that stores logfiles and as the data is so large, you create a new collection every day. In addition to this, you usually search for the latest or one week worth of data. To simplify indexing and searching, we can use aliasing, and this recipe will show you how to do that.

Getting ready

Before reading further, I would advise you all to read the *Creating a new SolrCloud cluster* recipe of this chapter. This recipe will show you how to create a new SolrCloud cluster and create a collection. We also assume that ZooKeeper is running on `192.168.1.10` and is listening on port `2181`. We already have the configuration called `firstcollection` stored in ZooKeeper and we already have four SolrCloud nodes running as a cluster.

How to do it...

1. When we created our cluster, we started with a single collection that was created using the following command:

   ```
   curl 'localhost:8983/solr/admin/collections?action=CREATE&name=logs_2014-09-01&numShards=2&replicationFactor=1&collection.configName=firstcollection'
   ```

2. We then created our daily collection and now we need to add two aliases—one for indexing and searching today's data (called `today`) and one for searching last week's data (called `lastWeek`). We do this by running the following commands:

   ```
   curl 'localhost:8983/solr/admin/collections?action=CREATEALIAS&name=today&collections=logs_2014-09-01'
   curl 'localhost:8983/solr/admin/collections?action=CREATEALIAS&name=lastWeek&collections=logs_2014-09-01'
   ```

   If we take a look at the tree view in the Solr admin panel and the `aliases.json` file, we will see the following (you can do this by going to `http://localhost:8983/solr/#/~cloud?view=tree` with your web browser and choosing the mentioned file):

   ```
   {"collection":{
       "lastWeek":"logs_2014-09-01",
       "today":"logs_2014-09-01"}}
   ```

3. After the day has ended, we create a new daily collection by running the following command:

```
curl 'localhost:8983/solr/admin/collections?action=CREATE&nam
e=logs_2014-09-02&numShards=2&replicationFactor=1&collection.
configName=firstcollection'
```

4. Once done, we need to modify our aliases. We also need the `today` alias to point the newly created collection and the `lastWeek` alias to cover two collections. We do this by running the following commands:

```
curl 'localhost:8983/solr/admin/collections?action=CREATEALIAS&nam
e=today&collections=logs_2014-09-02'
```

```
curl 'localhost:8983/solr/admin/collections?action=CREATEALIAS&nam
e=lastWeek&collections=logs_2014-09-02,logs_2014-09-01'
```

5. If we again look at the `aliases.json` file, we will see the following:

```
{"collection":{
    "lastWeek":"logs_2014-09-02,logs_2014-09-01",
    "today":"logs_2014-09-02"}}
```

Of course, everything worked as it should and we can easily run queries and indexing requests. For example, to take a look at the data from last week, we will run the following command:

```
curl 'localhost:8983/solr/lastWeek/select?q=*:*'
```

Now we can repeat the same steps daily and can continue using aliases, which will help you to change a script or application every day.

How it works...

We started off by creating our first daily collection called `logs_2014-09-01`. This will be used to index logs from September 1. Because we don't want our application to be forced to roll the indices, we create aliases. The alias called `today` will be used for indexing and searching the newest data; the second alias called `lastWeek` will be only used for searching. One thing to remember is that we can use aliases for indexing only if an alias points to a single index—which is true for our `today` alias.

However, let's get back to the commands used to create the aliases. Of course, we call the Collections API (`/admin/collections`) and we tell Solr that we want an alias to be created (`action=CREATEALIAS`). We specify the name of the alias using the `name` property and finally we specify the name of collections (using the `collections` parameter) separated by the comma character that will be covered by that alias. After the command execution ends, you are allowed to use both the alias and the collection name.

When the day ended, we changed the aliases. The one called `today` was changed to the new collection—the `logs_2014-09-02` one—and the second one called `lastWeek` was also changed to include the newest collection. Note that Solr will overwrite the previously created alias if we request to create an alias with a name already present.

Using routing

Routing is the ability to point queries and index it to a single shard of the collection. Let's assume that we have a single collection and store data of hundreds of clients in that collection. We can have a single collection per customer, but there are just too many of them, so such a solution is not scalable at all. Instead we go with one collection and we keep the data of a single customer in a single shard, so when querying we don't have to query all the shards. This allows you to save resources when querying. This recipe will show you how to do it.

Getting ready

Before reading further, I advise you to read the *Creating a new SolrCloud cluster* recipe of this chapter. This recipe will show you how to create a new SolrCloud cluster and create a collection. We also assume that ZooKeeper is running on `192.168.1.10` and is listening on port `2181` and we already have four SolrCloud nodes running as a cluster.

How to do it...

1. For the purpose of this recipe, we will use the following index structure (we need to add the following section to our `schema.xml` file):

```
<field name="id" type="string" indexed="true" stored="true"
required="true" />
<field name="title" type="text_general" indexed="true"
stored="true" />
<field name="customer" type="string" indexed="true" stored="true"
/>
```

2. For a customer named as `customer_1`, we have the following data (stored in a file called `data_customer_1.xml`):

```
<add>
 <doc>
  <field name="id">customer_1!1</field>
  <field name="title">Customer document 1</field>
  <field name="customer">customer_1</field>
 </doc>
 <doc>
```

```
    <field name="id">customer_1!2</field>
    <field name="title">Customer document 2</field>
    <field name="customer">customer_1</field>
  </doc>
</add>
```

3. For a customer named as `customer_2`, we have the following data (stored in a file called `data_customer_2.xml`):

```
<add>
  <doc>
    <field name="id">customer_2!3</field>
    <field name="title">Customer document</field>
    <field name="customer">customer_2</field>
  </doc>
</add>
```

4. We start by uploading our collection configuration to ZooKeeper. Assuming that we have our configuration in `/home/configuration/customers/conf`, we run the following command from the `home` directory of the first run Solr server (the `zkcli.sh` script can be found in the example Solr deployment in the `scripts/cloud-scripts` directory):

```
./zkcli.sh -cmd upconfig -zkhost 192.168.1.10:9983 -confdir /home/configuration/customers/conf/ -confname customersConfig
```

5. After this, we can create our collection by running the following command:

```
curl 'localhost:8983/solr/admin/collections?action=CREATE&name=customers&collection.configName=customersConfig&numShards=4&replicationfactor=1'
```

6. Now we can start indexing our data—we do this in the same way that we would index the data without routing. For example, to index the two files, we will use the following commands:

```
curl 'http://localhost:8983/solr/customers/update' --data-binary @data_customer_1.xml -H 'Content-type:application/xml'

curl 'http://localhost:8983/solr/customers/update' --data-binary @data_customer_2.xml -H 'Content-type:application/xml'

curl 'http://localhost:8983/solr/customers/update' --data-binary '<commit/>' -H 'Content-type:application/xml'
```

7. Now let's try to query the data. For example, if we would like to only get data for a customer named as `customer_2`, we will run a standard query with the `_route_` property set to the routing value for that customer. We also need a proper filter query. So for a customer named as `customer_2`, the following command will be used:

 ```
 curl 'localhost:8983/solr/customers/select?q=*:*&fq=customer:custo
 mer_2&_route_=customer_2!'
 ```

 The response returned by Solr will be as follows:

 ```
 <?xml version="1.0" encoding="UTF-8"?>
 <response>
  <lst name="responseHeader">
   <int name="status">0</int>
   <int name="QTime">13</int>
   <lst name="params">
    <str name="q">*:*</str>
    <str name="fq">customer:customer_2</str>
    <str name="_route_">customer_2!</str>
   </lst>
  </lst>
  <result name="response" numFound="1" start="0" maxScore="1.0">
   <doc>
    <str name="id">customer_2!3</str>
    <str name="title">Customer document</str>
    <str name="customer">customer_2</str>
    <long name="_version_">1478847760611409920</long>
   </doc>
  </result>
 </response>
 ```

As we can see, everything worked as it should.

How it works...

Our index structure is very simple. Each of the documents have three fields—one for the document identifier (the `id` field), one for the title of the document (the `title` field), and the customer field that will be used for filtering. What we have to look at is the data itself. Take a closer look at the identifiers of documents. Each identifier is prefixed with the customer name followed by the `!` character. When using composite routing (when no router is specified during collection creation), we can prefix the document identifier with a value and the `!` character after that, for example, `cookbook1234!1`. This means that Solr will use the `cookbook1234` value to determine in which shard the document will be indexed (by default, Solr uses the document identifier to determine that). The thing is that Solr will put the documents with the same routing value in the same shard. This means that data for a single customer will be put in the same shard in our case.

There is one additional thing to remember though—you usually end up with more routing values than what you have shards. In our case, we have four shards, but we might have hundreds of clients. Because of this, we need to remember about filtering during querying.

Next, we uploaded the configuration to ZooKeeper and finished creating the collection and then indexed our data. As you can see, there is nothing new in the indexation command. That's because nothing additional is needed while indexing apart from prefixing document identifiers with the routing value.

Finally, while querying, we need two things—the filter that will limit the data to only that customer (because we might have more than a single customer data in a single shard) and the second thing is the routing value. The routing value is the same as we used for prefixing document identifiers with the `!` character. We do this by adding the `_route_` property to our query. So for example, if we want to point our query to a shard where data for `customer_2` was indexed, we should add `_route_=customer_2!` to our query.

Also note that while using a composite router, Solr supports up to two levels of nesting, for example, `_route_=customer_2!USA!1` is allowed.

8
Using Additional Functionalities

In this chapter, we will cover the following topics:

- Finding similar documents
- Highlighting fragments found in documents
- Efficient highlighting
- Using versioning
- Retrieving information about the index structure
- Altering the index structure on a live collection
- Grouping documents by the field value
- Grouping documents by the query value
- Grouping documents by the function value
- Efficient documents grouping using the post filter

Introduction

There are many features of Solr that we don't use every day. Highlighting words, word ignoring, or statistics computation might not be useful in day-to-day activities, but they can come in handy in many situations. In this chapter, I'll try to show you how to overcome some typical problems that can be fixed using some of the Solr functionalities. In addition to this, we will see how to use the Solr grouping mechanism in order to get documents that have some fields in common.

Finding similar documents

Imagine a situation where you want to show documents similar to those that were returned by Solr. For example, let's assume that we have an e-commerce library, and we want to show users similar books to the ones that they found while using your application. Of course, we can use machine learning and one of the collaborative filtering algorithms, but we can also use Solr for that. This recipe will show you how to do this.

How to do it...

1. Let's start with the following index structure (just add this to your `schema.xml` file):

   ```
   <field name="id" type="string" indexed="true" stored="true"
   required="true" />
   <field name="name" type="text_general" indexed="true"
   stored="true" termVectors="true" />
   ```

2. Next, let's index the following test data:

   ```
   <add>
    <doc>
     <field name="id">1</field>
     <field name="name">Solr Cookbook first edition</field>
    </doc>
    <doc>
     <field name="id">2</field>
     <field name="name">Solr Cookbook second edition</field>
    </doc>
    <doc>
     <field name="id">3</field>
     <field name="name">Solr by example first edition</field>
    </doc>
    <doc>
     <field name="id">4</field>
     <field name="name">My book second edition</field>
    </doc>
   </add>
   ```

3. Now let's assume that our hypothetical user wants to find books that have `cookbook` and `second` in their names. However, in addition to the results for the user query, we would also like to show books that are similar to the query. To do this, we will send the following query:

   ```
   http://localhost:8983/solr/cookbook/select?q=cookbook+second&mm=
   2&qf=name&defType=edismax&mlt=true&mlt.fl=name&mlt.mintf=1&mlt.
   mindf=1
   ```

The results returned by Solr for the preceding query are as follows:

```
<?xml version="1.0" encoding="UTF-8"?>
<response>
 <lst name="responseHeader">
  <int name="status">0</int>
  <int name="QTime">3</int>
  <lst name="params">
   <str name="mm">2</str>
   <str name="q">cookbook second</str>
   <str name="defType">edismax</str>
   <str name="mlt">true</str>
   <str name="qf">name</str>
   <str name="mlt.fl">name</str>
   <str name="mlt.mintf">1</str>
   <str name="mlt.mindf">1</str>
  </lst>
 </lst>
 <result name="response" numFound="1" start="0">
  <doc>
   <str name="id">2</str>
   <str name="name">Solr Cookbook second edition</str>
   <long name="_version_">1481427182978859008</long></doc>
 </result>
 <lst name="moreLikeThis">
  <result name="2" numFound="3" start="0">
   <doc>
    <str name="id">1</str>
    <str name="name">Solr Cookbook first edition</str>
    <long name="_version_">1481427182903361536</long></doc>
   <doc>
    <str name="id">4</str>
    <str name="name">My book second edition</str>
    <long name="_version_">1481427182979907585</long></doc>
   <doc>
    <str name="id">3</str>
    <str name="name">Solr by example first edition</str>
    <long name="_version_">1481427182979907584</long></doc>
  </result>
 </lst>
</response>
```

Now let's see how it works.

How it works...

As you can see, the index structure and data are really simple. One thing that we need to notice is the `termVectors` attribute, which is set to `true` in the `name` field definition. To achieve the best results with this component, we should always enable term vectors for fields which we plan to use more, such as this functionality. It enables more detailed computation of similarity between documents and will show more similar results. If term vectors are not present, Solr will use data from the stored fields.

Now let's take a look at the query. As you can see, we have added some additional parameters besides the standard `q` one (and the ones such as `mm` and `defType`, which specify how our query should be handled). The `mlt=true` parameter tells you that we want to add the `MoreLikeThis` component to the result processing. The `mlt.fl` parameter specifies which fields we want to use with the `MoreLikeThis` component. In our case, we will use the `name` field. The `mlt.mintf` parameter tells Solr to ignore terms from the source document (the ones from the original result list) with the term frequency below the given value. In our case, we don't want to include the terms that will have the frequency lower than `1`. The last parameter, `mlt.mindf`, tells Solr that words that appear in less than the value of the parameter documents should be ignored. In our case, we want to consider words that appear in at least one document.

The last thing is the search results. As you can see, there is an additional section (`<lst name="moreLikeThis">`), which is responsible for showing us the `MoreLikeThis` component results. For each document in the results, there is one more similar to this section added to the response. In our case, Solr added a section for the document with the unique identifier `2` (`<result name="2" numFound="3" start="0">`) and there were three similar documents found. The value of the `id` attribute is assigned the value of the unique identifier of the document that the similar documents are calculated for.

Highlighting fragments found in documents

Imagine a situation where you want show your users the words that were matching from the document, which were shown in the results list. For example, you want to show which words in the book name were matched and displayed to the user. Do you have to store the documents and do the matching on the application side? The answer is no—we can force Solr to do this for us, and this recipe will show you how to do this.

How to do it...

1. We will begin with creating the following index structure (just add the following fields to your `schema.xml` file):

```
<field name="id" type="string" indexed="true" stored="true"
required="true" />
<field name="name" type="text_general" indexed="true"
stored="true" />
```

2. For the purpose of this recipe, we will use the following test data:

```
<add>
 <doc>
  <field name="id">1</field>
  <field name="name">Solr Cookbook first edition</field>
 </doc>
 <doc>
  <field name="id">2</field>
  <field name="name">Solr Cookbook second edition</field>
 </doc>
 <doc>
  <field name="id">3</field>
  <field name="name">Solr by example first edition</field>
 </doc>
 <doc>
  <field name="id">4</field>
  <field name="name">My book second edition</field>
 </doc>
</add>
```

3. Let's assume that our user is searching for the word `book`. To tell Solr that we want to highlight the matches, we will send the following query:

```
http://localhost:8983/solr/cookbook/select?q=name:book&hl.
fl=name&hl=true
```

The response from Solr should be similar to this:

```
<?xml version="1.0" encoding="UTF-8"?>
<response>
 <lst name="responseHeader">
  <int name="status">0</int>
  <int name="QTime">9</int>
  <lst name="params">
```

```
    <str name="q">name:book</str>
    <str name="hl">true</str>
    <str name="hl.fl">name</str>
   </lst>
  </lst>
  <result name="response" numFound="1" start="0">
   <doc>
    <str name="id">4</str>
    <str name="name">My book second edition</str>
    <long name="_version_">1481428771125854209</long></doc>
  </result>
  <lst name="highlighting">
   <lst name="4">
    <arr name="name">
     <str>My &lt;em&gt;book&lt;/em&gt; second edition</str>
    </arr>
   </lst>
  </lst>
</response>
```

As you can see, besides the normal results list, we got the highlighting results (the highlighting results are grouped by the `<lst name="highlighting">` XML tag). The word `book` is surrounded with the `<em>` and `</em>` HTML tags (of course, they escaped because the result is in the XML format). So everything is working as intended. Now let's see how it works.

How it works...

As you can see, the index structure and the data are really simple, so I'll skip those parts. Note that in order to use the highlighting mechanism, your fields should be stored and should not analyzed by aggressive filters (such as stemming). Otherwise, the highlighting results can be misleading. The example of such a behavior can be simple—imagine the user types the word `bought` in the search but Solr highlighted the word `buy` because of the stemming algorithm.

The query is also not complicated. We can see the standard `q` parameter that passes the query to Solr. However, there is also one additional parameter, `hl` set to `true`. This parameter tells Solr to include the highlighting component results to the results list. In addition to this, we included the `hl.fl` parameter, and we set it to `name`. This parameter specifies which field Solr should use for highlighting. We can also include more fields in this parameter—each should be separated by a comma character.

As you can see in the results list, in addition to the standard results, there is a new section—`<lst name="highlighting">`, which contains the highlighting results. For every document, in our case the only one found (`<lst name="4">` means that the highlighting result is presented for the document with the unique identifier value of `4`), there is a list of fields that contain the sample data with the matched word (or words) highlighted. By highlighted, I mean surrounded with the HTML tag, in this case the `<em>` tag.

There's more...

There are a few things that can be useful while using the highlighting mechanism.

Changing the default HTML tags that surround the matched content

There are situations where you would like to change the default `<em>` and `</em>` HTML tags to the ones of your choice. To do this, you should add the `hl.simple.pre` parameter and the `hl.simple.post` parameter. The first one specifies the prefix that will be added in front of the matched word, and the second one specifies the postfix that will be added after the matched word. For example, if you would like to surround the matched word with the `<b>` and `</b>` HTML tags, the query will look similar to this:

```
http://localhost:8983/solr/cookbook/select?q=name:book&hl=true&hl.
fl=name&hl.simple.pre=<b>&hl.simple.post=</b>
```

Efficient highlighting

In certain situations, the standard highlighting mechanism might not be performing as you would like it to be. For example, you might have long text fields and want the highlighting mechanism to work with them. In such cases, there is a need of another, more efficient highlighter. Thankfully, there is a highlighter that is very efficient, and this recipe will show you how to use it.

How to do it...

1. We begin with the index structure configuration, which looks as follows (just add the following section to your `schema.xml` file):

```
<field name="id" type="string" indexed="true" stored="true"
required="true" />
<field name="name" type="text_general" indexed="true"
stored="true"  termVectors="true" termPositions="true"
termOffsets="true" />
```

2. The next step is to index the data. We will use the following test data for the purpose of this recipe:

```
<add>
 <doc>
  <field name="id">1</field>
  <field name="name">Solr Cookbook first edition</field>
 </doc>
 <doc>
```

```
    <field name="id">2</field>
    <field name="name">Solr Cookbook second edition</field>
   </doc>
   <doc>
    <field name="id">3</field>
    <field name="name">Solr by example first edition</field>
   </doc>
   <doc>
    <field name="id">4</field>
    <field name="name">My book second edition</field>
   </doc>
  </add>
```

3. Let's assume that our user is searching for the word `book`. To tell Solr that we want to highlight the matches, we will send the following query:

```
http://localhost:8983/solr/cookbook/select?q=name:book&hl=true&hl.
fl=name&hl.useFastVectorHighlighter=true
```

The response from Solr should be similar to this:

```
<?xml version="1.0" encoding="UTF-8"?>
<response>
 <lst name="responseHeader">
  <int name="status">0</int>
  <int name="QTime">2</int>
  <lst name="params">
   <str name="q">name:book</str>
   <str name="hl.useFastVectorHighlighter">true</str>
   <str name="hl">true</str>
   <str name="hl.fl">name</str>
  </lst>
 </lst>
 <result name="response" numFound="1" start="0">
  <doc>
   <str name="id">4</str>
   <str name="name">My book second edition</str>
   <long name="_version_">1481429570147057665</long></doc>
 </result>
 <lst name="highlighting">
  <lst name="4">
   <arr name="name">
    <str>My &lt;em&gt;book&lt;/em&gt; second edition</str>
   </arr>
  </lst>
 </lst>
</response>
```

As you can see, everything is working as intended. Now let's see how it works.

How it works...

As you can see, the index structure and the data are really simple, but there is a difference between using the standard highlighter and the new `FastVectorHighlighting` highlighter. To use the new highlighting mechanism, you need to store the information about term vectors, terms positions, and offsets. This is done by adding the following attributes to the field definition or to the type definition: `termVectors="true"`, `termPositions="true"`, and `termOffsets="true"`.

Note that in order to use the highlighting mechanism, your fields should be stored and should not analyzed by aggressive filters (such as stemming). Otherwise, the highlighting results can be a misleading. The example of such a behavior can be simple—imagine the user types the word `bought` in the search but Solr highlighted the word `buy` because of the stemming algorithm.

The query is also not complicated. We can see the standard `q` parameter that passes the query to Solr. But there is also one additional parameter, `hl` set to `true`. This parameter tells Solr to include the highlighting component results to the results list. We have also included the `hl.fl` parameter that informs Solr about the field that the highlighting should be performed on. We set this parameter to `name`, so the highlighting is done on the `name` field. We can also pass multiple field names to that parameter—they should be concatenated by a comma character. In addition to this, we add the parameter to tell Solr to use `FastVectorHighlighting`—`hl.useFastVectorHighlighter=true`.

As you can see in the results list, in addition to the standard results, there is a new section—`<lst name="highlighting">`, which contains the highlighting results. For every document, in our case, the only one found (`<lst name="4">` means that the highlighting result is presented for the document with the unique identifier value of `4`), there is a list of fields that contain the sample data with the matched word (or words) highlighted. By highlighted, I mean surrounded with the HTML tag, in this case the `<em>` tag.

Using versioning

When working with NoSQL solutions such as Solr, we usually don't have the notion of transaction and we can't predict the sequence in which documents will be received by Solr and indexed especially when indexing is done from multiple threads and machines. However, in certain cases, such a functionality is needed at least to some degree. For example, we don't want to run an update on a document that was updated between the time period we read the document and sent the update. This recipe will show you how to avoid such situations.

Getting ready

This recipe uses the functionality discussed in the *Updating document fields* recipe from *Chapter 2, Indexing Your Data*. Read this recipe before proceeding.

How to do it...

For the purpose of this recipe, we assume that we have an e-commerce library. When updating prices of the books, we need to read the document to get the current price, update it in the UI, and index the document. However, it can happen that the same book is being updated by different people and we should reject concurrent updates.

1. We will start with the index structure. For the purpose of this recipe, we assume that we have the following fields in the `schema.xml` file:

```
<field name="id" type="string" indexed="true" stored="true"
required="true" />
<field name="name" type="text_general" indexed="true"
stored="true" />
<field name="price" type="tfloat" indexed="true" stored="true" />
<field name="_version_" type="long" indexed="true" stored="true"/>
```

2. The next step is to index the test data, which looks as follows:

```
<add>
 <doc>
  <field name="id">1</field>
  <field name="name">Solr cookbook</field>
  <field name="price">39.99</field>
 </doc>
 <doc>
  <field name="id">2</field>
  <field name="name">Mechanics cookbook</field>
  <field name="price">19.99</field>
 </doc>
 <doc>
  <field name="id">3</field>
  <field name="name">ElasticSearch book</field>
  <field name="price">49.99</field>
 </doc>
</add>
```

3. Now if we would like to get our books and update them, we will just run a simple search similar to this:

   `http://localhost:8983/solr/cookbook/select?q=*:*`

   The response to the preceding query will look as follows:

```
<?xml version="1.0" encoding="UTF-8"?>
<response>
 <lst name="responseHeader">
  <int name="status">0</int>
  <int name="QTime">0</int>
  <lst name="params">
   <str name="q">*:*</str>
  </lst>
 </lst>
 <result name="response" numFound="3" start="0">
  <doc>
   <str name="id">1</str>
   <str name="name">Solr cookbook</str>
   <float name="price">39.99</float>
   <long name="_version_">1481498739861356544</long></doc>
  <doc>
   <str name="id">2</str>
   <str name="name">Mechanics cookbook</str>
   <float name="price">19.99</float>
   <long name="_version_">1481498739931611136</long></doc>
  <doc>
   <str name="id">3</str>
   <str name="name">ElasticSearch book</str>
   <float name="price">49.99</float>
   <long name="_version_">1481498739932659712</long></doc>
 </result>
</response>
```

4. Now let's update the book called `Solr cookbook`, the one with the `id` field equal to `1`. To do this, we will run the following command (note that the values of the `_version_` field will be different if you run the example on your Solr, so adjust it accordingly):

```
curl 'localhost:8983/solr/cookbook/update?commit=true&_
version_=1481498739861356544' -H 'Content-type:application/json'
-d '[{"id":"1","price":{"set":29.99}}]'
```

If everything goes well, our book will be updated and we should see the following response returned by Solr:

```
{"responseHeader":{"status":0,"QTime":79}}
```

However, if someone has already modified the document, we will see a response similar to the following one:

```
{"responseHeader":{"status":409,"QTime":4},"error":{"msg":"version conflict for 1 expected=1481498739861356544 actual=148149982428816 9984","code":409}}
```

As we can see, the optimistic locking works. Let's now see how it works.

How it works...

To keep the recipe as simple as I can, I decided to keep the index structure simple. It consist of three fields—one responsible for document identifier (the `id` field), one used to hold the name of the book (the `name` field), and the last one used to hold the price of the book (the `price` field). Of course, we also have `_version_`, which is an internal field used by Solr for versioning, and it is required for SolrCloud deployments. Our example data is also very simple, so I'll skip discussing it.

As you can see in the response along with the stored fields in the results, Solr returns the `_version_` field with a generated value. We use this value during the update request that we send to Solr. We set the `_version_` field value in the request to the same value that we got in the search results. By doing this, we tell Solr that we expect it to update the document with a certain version.

The logic behind the `_version_` field is as follows:

- If the `_version_` parameter is set to a value greater than 1 during the update, Solr will require the document to have the same version as the value of the parameter. If the versions don't match, the update will be rejected.
- If the `_version_` parameter is set to `1` during the update, Solr requires the updated document to exist and doesn't care about a specific version. If the document doesn't exist, the update will be rejected.
- If the `_version_` parameter is set to `0` during the update, Solr doesn't put any constrains on the document in the index. If the document exists, it will be updated; if the document doesn't exist, it will be created.
- If the `_version_` parameter is set to a value lower than `0` during the update, Solr will require the document not to exist in the index as no such document will be created. If the document exists, the update will be rejected.

As you can see, the second update that we made using the same `_version_` value was not successful. This is because the document has already been updated and its version is already different. This is exactly what we are aiming for.

Retrieving information about the index structure

Until Solr 4.2, we had to look at the `schema.xml` file to see the full structure of the document. With the release of Solr 4.2, we got the ability to use the so-called Schema API to read the schema of collections that are running inside the cluster or on a node. In this recipe, we will take a look at the possibilities of reading the Solr schema.

How to do it...

The actual `schema.xml` file that we will use for reading doesn't really matter, as we will not focus on the actual index structure, but the API and how to get the particular information from Solr.

We assume that we are using a collection named `cookbook`.

1. We will start with retrieving all the fields defined in our `schema.xml` file. To do this, we will run the following query:

   http://localhost:8983/solr/cookbook/schema/fields

   The response to the preceding command will be as follows:

```
{
  "responseHeader":{
    "status":0,
    "QTime":2},
  "fields":[{
      "name":"_version_",
      "type":"long",
      "indexed":true,
      "stored":true},
    {
      "name":"id",
      "type":"string",
      "indexed":true,
      "required":true,
      "stored":true,
      "uniqueKey":true},
    {
```

```
      "name":"name",
      "type":"text_general",
      "indexed":true,
      "stored":true},
    {
      "name":"price",
      "type":"tfloat",
      "indexed":true,
      "stored":true}]}
```


2. If we would like to get the data for a single field, we can do that. For example, to get the configuration for the `price` field, we only need to append `/price` to the previous command. So the final command will look as follows:

   http://localhost:8983/solr/cookbook/schema/fields/price

3. Next, let's take a look at how to get the information about field types defined in our schema. If we would like to get information about all the field types defined, we will run the following request:

   http://localhost:8983/solr/cookbook/schema/fieldtypes

   The response to this request will be as follows:


```
{
  "responseHeader":{
    "status":0,
    "QTime":5},
  "fieldTypes":[{
      "name":"binary",
      "class":"solr.BinaryField",
      "fields":[],
      "dynamicFields":[]},
    {
      "name":"boolean",
      "class":"solr.BoolField",
      "sortMissingLast":true,
      "fields":[],
      "dynamicFields":[]},
    {
      "name":"date",
      "class":"solr.TrieDateField",
      "positionIncrementGap":"0",
      "precisionStep":"0",
```

```
        "fields":[],
        "dynamicFields":[]},
      {
        "name":"double",
        "class":"solr.TrieDoubleField",
        "positionIncrementGap":"0",
        "precisionStep":"0",
        "fields":[],
        "dynamicFields":[]},
   {
        "name":"float",
        "class":"solr.TrieFloatField",
        "positionIncrementGap":"0",
        "precisionStep":"4",
        "fields":[],
        "dynamicFields":[]},
      {
        "name":"int",
        "class":"solr.TrieIntField",
        "positionIncrementGap":"0",
        "precisionStep":"0",
        "fields":[],
        "dynamicFields":[]},
      {
        "name":"long",
        "class":"solr.TrieLongField",
        "positionIncrementGap":"0",
        "precisionStep":"0",
        "fields":["_version_"],
      "dynamicFields":[]},
      {
        "name":"random",
        "class":"solr.RandomSortField",
        "indexed":true,
        "fields":[],
        "dynamicFields":[]},
      {
        "name":"string",
        "class":"solr.StrField",
        "sortMissingLast":true,
  "fields":["id"],
```

```
  "dynamicFields":[]},
{
  "name":"tdate",
  "class":"solr.TrieDateField",
  "positionIncrementGap":"0",
  "precisionStep":"6",
  "fields":[],
  "dynamicFields":[]},
{
  "name":"tdouble",
  "class":"solr.TrieDoubleField",
  "positionIncrementGap":"0",
  "precisionStep":"8",
  "fields":[],
  "dynamicFields":[]},
{
  "name":"text_general",
  "class":"solr.TextField",
  "positionIncrementGap":"100",
  "indexAnalyzer":{
    "tokenizer":{
      "class":"solr.StandardTokenizerFactory"},
    "filters":[{
        "class":"solr.LowerCaseFilterFactory"}]},
  "queryAnalyzer":{
    "tokenizer":{
      "class":"solr.StandardTokenizerFactory"},
    "filters":[{
        "class":"solr.LowerCaseFilterFactory"}]},
  "fields":["name"],
  "dynamicFields":[]},
{
  "name":"tfloat",
  "class":"solr.TrieFloatField",
  "positionIncrementGap":"0",
  "precisionStep":"8",
  "fields":["price"],
  "dynamicFields":[]},
{
```

```
        "name":"tint",
        "class":"solr.TrieIntField",
        "positionIncrementGap":"0",
        "precisionStep":"8",
        "fields":[],
        "dynamicFields":[]},
      {
        "name":"tlong",
        "class":"solr.TrieLongField",
        "positionIncrementGap":"0",
        "precisionStep":"8",
        "fields":[],
        "dynamicFields":[]}]}
```

4. We can also get information about a single field type, which is similar to how we got information about a single field. To do this, we just append the name of the type we are interested in to the preceding command. So, if we would like to get information about the `tint` field, we will run the following command:

   http://localhost:8983/solr/cookbook/schema/fieldtypes/tint

As we can see, we can get all of the information related to fields and their types. In addition to this, we can get information about:

- Schema name by running `http://localhost:8983/solr/cookbook/schema/name`
- Schema version by running `http://localhost:8983/solr/cookbook/schema/version`
- Defined unique key by running `http://localhost:8983/solr/cookbook/schema/uniquekey`
- Defined similarity by running `http://localhost:8983/solr/cookbook/schema/similarity`
- Default operator by running `http://localhost:8983/solr/cookbook/schema/solrqueryparser/defaultoperator`

Finally, if we would like to retrieve the information about the whole schema, we can run the following command:

http://localhost:8983/solr/cookbook/schema

Now let's see how it works.

How it works...

We start with the command that retrieves information about the fields defined in the `schema.xml` file. It is very simple as it is only a GET HTTP request to the `/schema/fields` endpoint. We are also required to specify which collection we are interested in—in our case, this is `collection1`. The results returned by Solr contain a standard header and an array of fields. Each field contains the standard information such as the name of the field (the `name` property), type (the `type` property), whether the field is indexed (the `indexed` property), whether the field is required (the `required` property), whether the field is stored (the `stored` property), and whether the field is defined as the unique key (the `uniqueKey` property). If a property is set to `false`, Solr will not return it. The same information is returned when we request information about a single field—of course, a single field related information is returned instead of an array of fields.

When it comes to retrieving the information about field types, the situation is similar to how we request information about fields. We run a GET HTTP request to `/schema/fieldtypes` and we need to specify the collection as well. The returned information differs for different field types. Usually, we will get the name of the type (the `name` property), the class implementing the type (the `class` property), position increment gap (the `positionIncrementGap` property), precision step for numeric fields (the `precisionStep` property), array of fields using that type (the `fields` property), and an array of dynamic fields using that type (the `dynamicFields` property).

In addition to the preceding properties, for the more complex types, we will get information about the analyzer used during indexation (the `indexAnalyzer` property) and the analyzer used during querying (the `queryAnalyzer` property). Each of the analyzers will be characterized by tokenizer (the `tokenizer` property) and an array of filters (the `filters` property)—char filters can also be present. In addition to this, each tokenizer, filter, and char filer can include their own properties, but we will skip these. The same information is returned when we request information about a single field type, of course, only about the requested type.

The rest of the Schema API calls are pretty easy to understand, so I'll skip discussing them.

There's more...

There is one more thing that I would like to mention.

Retrieving the index structure information in XML

As we can see, by default, Solr returns the data about the index structure in JSON. We can force Solr to return the XML format instead of JSON. We do this by adding the `wt=xml` parameter to our requests; for example:

```
http://localhost:8983/solr/cookbook/schema/fields?wt=xml
```

Retrieving information about dynamic fields

In addition to retrieving fields-related information, we can also retrieve information about dynamic fields defined in the `schema.xml` file in the same way as we retrieve data for standard fields. To do this, we will run the following command:

```
http://localhost:8983/solr/cookbook/schema/dynamicfields
```

Retrieving information about copy fields

In addition to retrieving information related to fields and dynamic fields, we can also retrieve information about copy fields defined in the `schema.xml` file in the same way as we retrieve data for standard fields. To do this, we will run the following command:

```
http://localhost:8983/solr/cookbook/schema/copyfields
```

See also

- The full information about the Schema API in Solr can be found in the official Solr documentation available at `https://cwiki.apache.org/confluence/display/solr/Schema+API`

Altering the index structure on a live collection

The ability to push a new index structure definition (the `schema.xml` file) to ZooKeeper is nice, but it requires the collection to be reloaded. The same goes for Solr, when it works in noncloud mode, we need to reload a core for Solr to see the changes. This is also not super convenient when you would like to change the index structure from outside Solr. That is why with the release of Solr 4.3, the Schema API allows you to alter the index structure using simple HTTP-based requests. In this recipe, we will take a look at how to use the Schema API to alter our index structure.

Getting ready

Before continuing with the recipe, read the *Retrieving information about the index structure* recipe discussed earlier in this chapter, as it provides information on how to read index structure information using Solr Schema API.

How to do it...

For the purpose of this recipe, let's assume that we have a very basic index structure that we want to add a field to and a copy field to.

We assume that we are using a collection named cookbook.

1. We will start with the following index structure (just add the following to your schema.xml file):

```
<field name="id" type="string" indexed="true" stored="true"
required="true" />
<field name="name" type="text_general" indexed="true"
stored="true" />
```

2. In addition to this, we need the following entry in the solrconfig.xml file:

```
<schemaFactory class="ManagedIndexSchemaFactory">
 <bool name="mutable">true</bool>
 <str name="managedSchemaResourceName">managed-schema</str>
</schemaFactory>
```

3. Now, let's try to add a copy of the name field that we will use for sorting, so let's call it name_sort. To do this, we need to use the following command (note the usage of POST HTTP method):

```
curl -XPOST 'localhost:8983/solr/cookbook/schema/fields' -H
'Content-type:application/json' -d '[
 {
  "name" : "name_sort",
  "type" : "string",
  "stored" : "false",
  "indexed" : "true",
  "docValues" : "false",
  "default" : "",
  "copyFields" : []
 }
]'
```

If everything goes well, you should see a response as follows:

```
{
  "responseHeader":{
    "status":0,
    "QTime":14}}
```

4. Now let's try adding a new copy field definition so that the content of the `name` field is automatically copied to `name_sort`. To do this, we need to run the following command:

```
curl -XPOST 'localhost:8983/solr/cookbook/schema/copyfields' -H
'Content-type:application/json' -d '[
 {
  "source" : "name",
  "dest" : [
   "name_sort"
  ]
 }
]'
```

   If everything goes well, Solr should respond with something similar to this:

```
{
  "responseHeader":{
    "status":0,
    "QTime":14}}
```

5. Let's now run the following command to retrieve our field's definition so that we can check what was done. We do this by running the following command:

```
curl http://localhost:8983/solr/cookbook/schema/fields
```

   The response should look as follows:

```
{
  "responseHeader":{
    "status":0,
    "QTime":2},
  "fields":[{
      "name":"_version_",
      "type":"long",
      "indexed":true,
   "stored":true},
    {
      "name":"id",
      "type":"string",
      "indexed":true,
      "required":true,
      "stored":true,
      "uniqueKey":true},
    {
```

```
        "name":"name",
        "type":"text_general",
        "indexed":true,
        "stored":true},
      {
        "name":"name_sort",
        "type":"string",
        "indexed":true,
        "default":"",
        "docValues":false,
        "stored":false}]}
```

6. Now let's take a look at the copy field's definition by running the following command:

   curl http://localhost:8983/solr/cookbook/schema/copyfields

   The Solr response should look as follows:

```
{
  "responseHeader":{
    "status":0,
    "QTime":1},
  "copyFields":[{
      "source":"name",
      "dest":"name_sort"}]}
```

As we can see, everything is working as it should. Now let's check what Solr does to make it work.

Also remember that the already indexed documents won't be modified until you reindex the data.

How it works...

The index structure is very simple as it only contains two fields. The first field is the unique identifier of the document (the `id` field) and the second field is the name of the document (the `name` field).

To use the Schema API to update the index structure definition, Solr requires you to use the so-called managed schema. What Solr does is that it reads the schema definition that the collection was created with, changes its name on the local filesystem, and starts taking care of that schema. One thing that you need to remember is that you shouldn't try to change the managed schema manually because that might lead to problems such as losing changes done to the schema.

To configure the managed schema, we need to add or alter the `schemaFactory` section of the `solrconfig.xml` file. We have to specify two properties there. The `mutable` property set to `true` means that the `schema.xml` file will be managed by Solr. The second property, `managedSchemaResourceName` specifies the name of the resource that Solr will use to load the index structure instead of the `schema.xml` file. This property can be set to whatever value we want, but it can't take the value of `schema.xml`. If the resource specified by the `managedSchemaResourceName` property does not exist, Solr will load the data from the `schema.xml` and rename the `schema.xml` file to `schema.xml.bak`. We are now ready to use the Schema API to change our index structure definition.

The first thing that we tried is to add a new field to our managed schema. To do this, we send an HTTP POST request to the `/schema/fields` REST endpoint of our collection (which is `collection1` in our case). During the writing of the book, the request body that contains the fields definition had to be JSON, and because of this, we specify the content type as `Content-type:application/json`. This is required. The request body contains information about fields that we want to add—we provide an array of field definitions. In our case, it contains a single field definition, but you can provide multiple if you want. Each field definition can take the following properties:

- `name`: This is the name of the field we want to create
- `type`: This is the type of the field we want to create
- `stored`: This specifies whether the field should be stored or not and can take the value of `true` or `false`
- `indexed`: This specifies whether the fields should be indexed or not and can take the value of `true` or `false`
- `docValues`: This specifies whether the field should be using doc values and can take the value of `true` or `false`
- `default`: This is the default value for the field
- `copyFields`: This is an array of names of fields we want our field to be copied to

So we created a new field called `name_sort` that is of type `string`, which is not stored, is indexed and doesn't use `doc` values. As we can see, Solr responded with a proper response, which means that everything went well.

Adding a `copy` field is very similar to adding a field, but simpler. We need to run a POST HTTP request to the `/schema/copyfields` REST endpoint of our collection (which is `collection1` in our case). We also need to provide proper content type, which is again JSON (so `Content-type:application/json` needs to be present in the request header). The request body is again an array of `copy` field definitions and again, we only need to define a single `copy` field, although we are allowed to create multiples of them. Each `copy` field definition requires a source field specified by the `source` property. This is the field from which data will be copied.

The second required property is the `dest` one, which is an array of field names, that the field defined in the `source` property will be copied to. So in our case, the contents of the `name` field will be copied to the `name_sort` field. Again, after running the command, we need to cross-check that everything went well.

Finally, we checked the index structure using the read abilities of Schema API, but we already discussed that in the *Retrieving information about the index structure* recipe earlier in this chapter, so if you haven't read that, do read it.

See also

- Solr allows you to use PUT HTTP method to add a single field to our index structure, but using PUT requires a bit different request body. Refer to the official Apache Solr documentation available at `https://cwiki.apache.org/confluence/display/solr/Schema+API` if you are interested.

Grouping documents by the field value

Imagine a situation where your dataset is divided into different categories, subcategories, price ranges, and things like that. What if you would like to not only get information about counts in such groups (with the use of faceting), but you would only like to show the most relevant document in each of the groups. In such cases, a Solr grouping mechanism comes in handy. This recipe will show you how to group your documents on the basis of the value of the field.

How to do it...

1. Let's start with the index structure. Let's assume that we have the following fields in our index (just add the following section to the `schema.xml` file):

```
<field name="id" type="string" indexed="true" stored="true"
required="true" />
<field name="name" type="text_general" indexed="true"
stored="true" />
<field name="category" type="string" indexed="true" stored="true"
/>
<field name="price" type="tfloat" indexed="true" stored="true" />
```

2. The example data, which we are going to index, looks as follows:

```
<add>
 <doc>
  <field name="id">1</field>
  <field name="name">Solr cookbook</field>
  <field name="category">it</field>
  <field name="price">39.99</field>
```

```
 </doc>
 <doc>
  <field name="id">2</field>
  <field name="name">Mechanics cookbook</field>
  <field name="category">mechanics</field>
  <field name="price">19.99</field>
 </doc>
 <doc>
  <field name="id">3</field>
  <field name="name">ElasticSearch book</field>
  <field name="category">it</field>
  <field name="price">49.99</field>
 </doc>
</add>
```

3. Let's assume that we would like to get our data divided into groups on the basis of their category. In order to do this, we will send the following query to Solr:

```
http://localhost:8983/solr/cookbook/select?q=*:*&group=true&group.
field=category
```

The results returned by the preceding query are as follows:

```
<?xml version="1.0" encoding="UTF-8"?>
<response>
 <lst name="responseHeader">
  <int name="status">0</int>
  <int name="QTime">1</int>
  <lst name="params">
   <str name="q">*:*</str>
   <str name="group.field">category</str>
   <str name="group">true</str>
  </lst>
 </lst>
 <lst name="grouped">
  <lst name="category">
   <int name="matches">3</int>
   <arr name="groups">
    <lst>
     <str name="groupValue">it</str>
     <result name="doclist" numFound="2" start="0">
      <doc>
       <str name="id">1</str>
       <str name="name">Solr cookbook</str>
       <str name="category">it</str>
```

```
            <float name="price">39.99</float>
            <long name="_version_">1481430286414643200</long></doc>
          </result>
        </lst>
        <lst>
          <str name="groupValue">mechanics</str>
          <result name="doclist" numFound="1" start="0">
            <doc>
              <str name="id">2</str>
              <str name="name">Mechanics cookbook</str>
              <str name="category">mechanics</str>
              <float name="price">19.99</float>
              <long name="_version_">1481430286497480704</long></doc>
          </result>
        </lst>
      </arr>
    </lst>
  </lst>
</response>
```

As you can see, the grouped results are different from the ones returned during usual search, but as you can see we got a single document per group—it worked. So let's see how it works.

How it works...

Our index structure is very simple. It consist of four fields—one responsible for document identifier (the `id` field), one used to hold the name of the book (the `name` field), its category (the `category` field), and the last one used to hold the price of the book (the `price` field). Our example data is also very simple, but notice that the first and third book belongs to the same `it` category and the second book belongs to the `mechanics` category.

Let's take a look at our query now. We said that we want to have our documents divided on the basis of contents of the `category` field. In order to do this, we added a new parameter called `group` set to `true`. This tells Solr that we want to enable the grouping functionality. Similar to faceting, we added a second parameter and we are not familiar with the `group.field` parameter, which is set to the name of the field, that holds the `books` category. That's all we need. Of course, we can have more than a single field that Solr will use for grouping—we just need to add multiple `group.field` parameters to our query.

If we take a look at the results returned by Solr, they are a bit different than the usual results. You can see the usual response header; however, the resulting groups are returned in the `<lst name="grouped">` tag. The `<lst name="category">` tag is generated for each `group.field` parameter passed in the query—this time it tells you that the following results will be for the `category` field. The `<int name="matches">3</int>` tag informs you how many documents were found for our query—this is the same as `numFound` during our usual query.

Next, we have the `groups` array that holds the information about the groups that were created by Solr in the results. Each group is described by its value, that is, the `<str name="groupValue">it</str>` section for the first group means that all documents in that group have the `it` value in the field used for grouping (which is `category` in our case). In the `result` tag, we can see the documents returned for the group. By default, Solr will return the most relevant document for each group. I'll skip commenting on the `result` tag because it is almost identical to the results Solr return for a nongrouped query, and we are familiar with those, right?

There's more...

There are two things more about grouping on the basis of field values I would like to write about.

Having more than a single document in a group

Sometimes, you might need to return more than a single document in a group. In order to do this, you need to add the `group.limit` parameter and set it to the maximum number of documents you want to have. For example, if we would like to have `10` documents per group of results, we can send the following query:

```
http://localhost:8983/solr/cookbook/select?q=*:*&group=true&group.
field=category&group.limit=10
```

Modifying the number of returned groups

Sometimes, you might need to return more or less groups than the default 10. Solr allows you to do this and it is very simple actually. What we need to do is add the `rows` parameter to our query with the desired maximum number of groups in the response. For example, if we would like to have maximum two groups, we can use the following query:

```
http://localhost:8983/solr/cookbook/select?q=*:*&group=true&group.
field=category&rows=2
```

Grouping documents by the query value

Sometimes, grouping results on the basis of field values is not enough. For example, imagine that we would like to group documents in some kind of price brackets—show the most relevant document for documents with the price range of 1.0 to 19.99, a document for documents with the price range of 20.00 to 50.0, and so on. Solr allows you to group results on the basis of queries results. This recipe will show you how to do that.

Getting ready

In this chapter, we will use the same index structure and test data as we used in the *Grouping documents by the field value* recipe in this chapter. Read it before we continue.

How to do it...

1. Because we are reusing the data and index structure from the *Grouping documents by the field value* recipe, we can start with the query. In order to group our documents on the basis of query results, we can send the following query:

```
http://localhost:8983/solr/cookbook/select?q=*:*&group=true&group.
query=price:[20.0+TO+50.0]&group.query=price:[1.0+TO+19.99]
```

2. The results of the preceding query looks as follows:

```
<?xml version="1.0" encoding="UTF-8"?>
<response>
 <lst name="responseHeader">
  <int name="status">0</int>
  <int name="QTime">0</int>
  <lst name="params">
   <str name="q">*:*</str>
   <arr name="group.query">
    <str>price:[20.0 TO 50.0]</str>
    <str>price:[1.0 TO 19.99]</str>
   </arr>
   <str name="group">true</str>
  </lst>
 </lst>
 <lst name="grouped">
  <lst name="price:[20.0 TO 50.0]">
   <int name="matches">3</int>
   <result name="doclist" numFound="2" start="0">
    <doc>
     <str name="id">1</str>
     <str name="name">Solr cookbook</str>
     <str name="category">it</str>
     <float name="price">39.99</float>
     <long name="_version_">1481430286414643200</long></doc>
   </result>
  </lst>
  <lst name="price:[1.0 TO 19.99]">
   <int name="matches">3</int>
```

```
        <result name="doclist" numFound="1" start="0">
         <doc>
          <str name="id">2</str>
          <str name="name">Mechanics cookbook</str>
          <str name="category">mechanics</str>
          <float name="price">19.99</float>
          <long name="_version_">1481430286497480704</long></doc>
        </result>
       </lst>
      </lst>
     </response>
```

So now let's take a look how it works.

How it works...

As you can see, in the query, we tell Solr that we want to use the grouping functionality using the `group=true` parameter. In addition to this, we specified that we want to have two groups calculated on the basis of queries. The first group should contain documents that match the following range query `price=[20.0+TO+50.00]` (the `group.query=price:[20.0+TO+50.00]` parameter) and the second group should contain documents that match the following range query `price=[1.0+TO+19.99]` (the `group.query=price:[1.0+TO+19.99]` parameter).

If you look at the results, they are very similar to the ones for grouping on the basis of field values. The only difference is in the name of groups. When using the field values for grouping, groups were named after the used field names. However, when using queries to group documents, groups are named as our grouping queries. So in our case, we have two groups—one named `price:[20.0 TO 50.0]` (the `<lst name="price:[20.0 TO 50.0]">` tag) and the second one called `price:[1.0+TO+19.99]` (the `<lst name="price:[1.0 TO 19.99]">` tag).

Grouping documents by the function value

Imagine that you would like to group results not by using queries or field contents, but instead you would like to use a value returned by a function query. An example use case can be grouping documents on the basis of their distance from a point. Sounds nice right? Solr allows that and in this recipe, we will see how we can use a simple function query to group results.

Getting ready

In this recipe, we will use the knowledge that we've gained in the *Grouping documents by the field value* recipe in this chapter. Read the mentioned recipe before we continue.

How to do it...

1. Let's start with the following index structure (just add the following fields definition to your `schema.xml` file):

```
<field name="id" type="string" indexed="true" stored="true"
required="true" />
<field name="name" type="text_general" indexed="true"
stored="true" />
<field name="geo" type="location" indexed="true" stored="true" />
<dynamicField name="*_coordinate"  type="tdouble" indexed="true"
stored="false" />
```

2. Our test data that we want to index looks similar to this:

```
<add>
 <doc>
  <field name="id">1</field>
  <field name="name">Company one</field>
  <field name="geo">10.1,10.1</field>
 </doc>
 <doc>
  <field name="id">2</field>
  <field name="name">Company two</field>
  <field name="geo">11.1,11.1</field>
 </doc>
 <doc>
  <field name="id">3</field>
  <field name="name">Company three</field>
  <field name="geo">12.2,12.2</field>
 </doc>
</add>
```

   In addition to this, we also need to define the following field type in the `schema.xml` file:

```
<fieldType name="location" class="solr.LatLonType"
subFieldSuffix="_coordinate"/>
```

3. I assume that we would like to have our documents grouped on the basis of the distance from a given point (in real life, we would probably like to have some kind of brackets calculated, but let's skip that for now). For the purpose of this recipe, we will assume that we want to use the North Pole as our geographical point. In order to achieve what we want, we will send the following query:

```
http://localhost:8983/solr/cookbook/select?q=*:*&group=true&group.
func=geodist(geo,0.0,0.0)
```

4. The following results were returned by Solr after running the preceding query:

```
<?xml version="1.0" encoding="UTF-8"?>
<response>
 <lst name="responseHeader">
  <int name="status">0</int>
  <int name="QTime">0</int>
  <lst name="params">
   <str name="q">*:*</str>
   <str name="group.func">geodist(geo,0.0,0.0)</str>
   <str name="group">true</str>
  </lst>
 </lst>
 <lst name="grouped">
  <lst name="geodist(geo,0.0,0.0)">
   <int name="matches">3</int>
   <arr name="groups">
    <lst>
     <double name="groupValue">1584.126028923632</double>
     <result name="doclist" numFound="1" start="0">
      <doc>
       <str name="id">1</str>
       <str name="name">Company one</str>
       <str name="geo">10.1,10.1</str>
       <long name="_version_">1481432265913270272</long></doc>
     </result>
    </lst>
    <lst>
     <double name="groupValue">1740.0195023531824</double>
     <result name="doclist" numFound="1" start="0">
      <doc>
       <str name="id">2</str>
       <str name="name">Company two</str>
       <str name="geo">11.1,11.1</str>
       <long name="_version_">1481432265990864896</long></doc>
     </result>
    </lst>
    <lst>
     <double name="groupValue">1911.187477467305</double>
     <result name="doclist" numFound="1" start="0">
      <doc>
       <str name="id">3</str>
```

```
        <str name="name">Company three</str>
        <str name="geo">12.2,12.2</str>
        <long name="_version_">1481432265991913472</long></doc>
      </result>
    </lst>
  </arr>
 </lst>
</lst>
</response>
```

Everything worked as it should, so now let's see how that works.

How it works...

Let's start from the index structure. We have four fields in our index—one that holds the unique identifier (the `id` field), one that holds the name of the company (the `name` field), one field for the geographical location of the company (the `geo` one). The last field, the dynamic one, is needed in order for the location type to work. The data is pretty simple, so let's just skip discussing that.

As you can see, the query is very similar to the one we used while grouping our documents on the basis of field values. So, we again pass the `group=true` parameter to enable grouping, but this time in addition to this, we pass the `group.func` parameter with the value that is our function query on which results Solr should group our documents.

If you take a look at the results, they are again very similar to the ones that we had seen while grouping on the basis of field values. The only difference is the group names. When using the field values for grouping, groups are named after the used field names. However, when using function queries to group documents, groups are named by the result of function query. So in our case, we have three groups because our function query returned three different results:

- A group named `1584.126028923632` (the `<double name="groupValue">1584.126028923632</double>` tag)
- A group named `1740.0195023531824` (the `<double name="groupValue">1740.0195023531824</double>` tag)
- A group named `1911.187477467305` (the `<double name="groupValue">1911.187477467305</double>` tag)

Of course, in real life you would like to use a more complicated function query example that would give you buckets of distances—such as 5, 10, and 100 kilometers. However, we will skip discussing that as this is not the main purpose of this recipe.

Efficient documents grouping using the post filter

Sometimes, the standard field collapsing provided by Solr is not enough when it comes to performance. This is especially true when we want to perform field collapsing on fields that will result in large number of unique groups in the results, so mostly, for high cardinality fields. For such use cases, Solr provides an efficient post filter approach of field collapsing, and this recipe will show you how to use that approach.

Getting ready

In this chapter, we will use the same index structure and test data as we used in the *Grouping documents by the field value* recipe of this chapter. Read it before we continue.

How to do it...

1. Let's start with the index structure. Let's assume that we have the following fields in our index (just add the following section to the `schema.xml` files):

```
<field name="id" type="string" indexed="true" stored="true"
required="true" />
<field name="name" type="text_general" indexed="true"
stored="true" />
<field name="category" type="string" indexed="true" stored="true"
/>
<field name="price" type="tfloat" indexed="true" stored="true" />
```

2. The example data, which we are going to index, looks as follows:

```
<add>
 <doc>
  <field name="id">1</field>
  <field name="name">Solr cookbook</field>
  <field name="category">it</field>
  <field name="price">39.99</field>
 </doc>
 <doc>
  <field name="id">2</field>
  <field name="name">Mechanics cookbook</field>
  <field name="category">mechanics</field>
  <field name="price">19.99</field>
 </doc>
 <doc>
```

```
    <field name="id">3</field>
    <field name="name">ElasticSearch book</field>
    <field name="category">it</field>
    <field name="price">49.99</field>
  </doc>
  <doc>
    <field name="id">4</field>
    <field name="name">Mechanics for dummies</field>
    <field name="category">mechanics</field>
    <field name="price">29.99</field>
  </doc>
</add>
```

3. Let's assume that we would like to get our data divided into groups on the basis of their category, but we know that our `category` field has hundreds of thousands categories. So to achieve optimal performance, instead of the standard field collapsing, we can run the following query:

```
http://localhost:8983/solr/cookbook/select?q=*:*&fq={!collapse
field=category}
```

The results returned by the preceding query are as follows:

```
<?xml version="1.0" encoding="UTF-8"?>
<response>
 <lst name="responseHeader">
  <int name="status">0</int>
  <int name="QTime">0</int>
  <lst name="params">
   <str name="q">*:*</str>
   <str name="fq">{!collapse field=category}</str>
  </lst>
 </lst>
 <result name="response" numFound="2" start="0">
  <doc>
   <str name="id">1</str>
   <str name="name">Solr cookbook</str>
   <str name="category">it</str>
   <float name="price">39.99</float>
   <long name="_version_">1481493621619294208</long></doc>
  <doc>
   <str name="id">2</str>
   <str name="name">Mechanics cookbook</str>
   <str name="category">mechanics</str>
   <float name="price">19.99</float>
   <long name="_version_">1481493621691645952</long></doc>
 </result>
</response>
```

As you can see, the grouped results are almost the same to the ones that were returned during usual search, but as you can see, we got a single document per group, so the collapsing worked. So let's see how it works.

How it works...

Our index structure is very simple. It consist of four fields—one responsible for document identifier (the `id` field), one used to hold the name of the book (the `name` field), its category (the `category` field), and the last one used to hold the price of the book (the `price` field). Our example data is also very simple, but notice that the first and third book belongs to the same `it` category, and the second and fourth book also belongs to the same `mechanics` category.

Let's take a look at our query now. We have already said that we want to have our documents divided on the basis of the contents of the `category` field. Because we know that our `category` field is a high cardinality one, we are using the post filter collapsing approach. To tell Solr to use that post filter, we add the `fq={!collapse field=category}` parameter. It tells Solr to use `CollapsingQParserPlugin` and to collapse the results on the basis of the values in the `category` field.

As you can see, the results are the same as standard search results returned by Solr. Each document in the returned results represents the top-scored document in each group, so this is where the difference is and you should remember about this.

There's more...

There is one more thing that I would like to share about group collapsing.

Expanding collapsed groups

Similar to the standard field collapsing approach, we have the ability to expand groups that were collapsed. To do this, we need to add the `expand` parameter to our query and set it to `true`:

```
http://localhost:8983/solr/cookbook/select?q=*:*&fq={!collapse
field=category}&expand=true
```

The results of such a query would be as follows:

```
<?xml version="1.0" encoding="UTF-8"?>
<response>
 <lst name="responseHeader">
  <int name="status">0</int>
  <int name="QTime">1</int>
  <lst name="params">
   <str name="q">*:*</str>
```

```
      <str name="expand">true</str>
      <str name="fq">{!collapse field=category}</str>
    </lst>
  </lst>
  <result name="response" numFound="2" start="0">
    <doc>
      <str name="id">1</str>
      <str name="name">Solr cookbook</str>
      <str name="category">it</str>
      <float name="price">39.99</float>
      <long name="_version_">1481494160166879232</long></doc>
    <doc>
      <str name="id">2</str>
      <str name="name">Mechanics cookbook</str>
      <str name="category">mechanics</str>
      <float name="price">19.99</float>
      <long name="_version_">1481494160168976384</long></doc>
  </result>
  <lst name="expanded">
    <result name="mechanics" numFound="1" start="0">
      <doc>
        <str name="id">4</str>
        <str name="name">Mechanics for dummies</str>
        <str name="category">mechanics</str>
        <float name="price">29.99</float>
        <long name="_version_">1481494160171073536</long></doc>
    </result>
    <result name="it" numFound="1" start="0">
      <doc>
        <str name="id">3</str>
        <str name="name">ElasticSearch book</str>
        <str name="category">it</str>
        <float name="price">49.99</float>
        <long name="_version_">1481494160170024960</long></doc>
    </result>
  </lst>
</response>
```

As we can see, Solr has included expanded groups in the additional list called `expanded`. We can also specify the number of documents for each group by adding the `expand.rows` parameter (by default, it is set to `5`) and determine the sort order of the documents in the expanded groups by adding the `expand.sort` parameter (by default, it is set to `score desc`).

9
Dealing with Problems

In this chapter, we will cover the following topics:

- Dealing with the too many opened files exception
- Diagnosing and dealing with memory problems
- Configuring sorting for non-English languages
- Migrating data to another collection
- SolrCloud read-side fault tolerance
- Using the check index functionality
- Adjusting the Jetty configuration to avoid deadlocks
- Tuning segment merging
- Avoiding swapping

Introduction

Solr is a great piece of software; it is mature and stable, but even in some situations, things can break. We can run into memory issues limited to the number of files to be handled that Solr can use or hardware can fail leading to index corruption. That's normal and we need to be prepared for such situations or at least know how to deal with them.

In this chapter, we will take a look at some common problems that you might encounter during your everyday work with Solr and I will try to show you a quick win—simple ways to handle such situations.

Dealing with the too many opened files exception

Sometimes, you might encounter a strange error—something that lays on the edge between Lucene and the operating system—the too many opened files exception. Such an error means that the user that Solr is running with is not allowed to use more file descriptors (`http://en.wikipedia.org/wiki/File_descriptor`). This results in Solr not being able to open new files, so indexing documents, merging segments, and many similar activities are not possible. Is there something we can do about it? Yes, we can, and this recipe will show you.

How to do it...

For the purpose of this recipe, let's assume that the header of the exception thrown by Solr looks as follows:

```
java.io.FileNotFoundException: /use/share/solr/data/index/_1.fdx (Too
many open files)
```

1. What can you do instead of trying to pull your hair out of your head? First of all, this probably happened on a Unix/Linux-based operating system. So, let's start with setting the opened files limit higher. To do this, you need to edit the `limits.conf` file of your operating system (in the case of Ubuntu, this file is placed in `/etc/security/`) and set the following (I assume that Solr is running as a `solr` user):

   ```
   solr soft nofile 32000
   solr hard nofile 32000
   ```

2. Now let's try running the following command (you need to log out and log in again if you are logged in as a `solr` user):

   ```
   sudo -u solr -s "ulimit -Sn"
   ```

   The response to this command should look more or less as follows:

   ```
   32000
   ```

3. If this is still not the case, we need to run the following command (the following example is from Ubuntu and can be different for different distributions):

   ```
   egrep -r pam_limits /etc/pam.d/
   ```

   The response from the operating system should be similar to the following one:

   ```
   /etc/pam.d/lightdm-greeter:session required        pam_limits.so
   /etc/pam.d/lightdm:session required                pam_limits.so
   ```

```
/etc/pam.d/cron:session    required                    pam_limits.so
/etc/pam.d/login:session    required                   pam_limits.so
/etc/pam.d/su:# session    required                    pam_limits.so
/etc/pam.d/lightdm-autologin:session required          pam_limits.so
```

If we see any of the `pam_limits.so` entries commented out, such as the line next to the last in the preceding example, we need to comment that out. After this, we should be more than ready. Now let's see what the options mean.

How it works...

We haven't discussed the operating system's internals in this book, but this time we will make an exception. The mentioned `limits.conf` file in the `/etc/security` directory lets you specify the number of opened files limit for the users of your system. In the example shown earlier, we set the two necessary limits to `32000` for the user `solr`, so if you had problems with the number of opened files with the default setup, you should see the difference after restarting Solr. However, remember that if you are working as the user, you can change the limits as you might need to log out and log in again to see those changes.

However, sometimes changing the `limits.conf` file is not enough. This is usually the case when some of the `pam_limits.so` entries are commented out. Not to get into too many details—these entries are responsible for the PAM module used to limit resources. Because of this we need to uncomment those.

Note that saying how to set the limit and giving the exact amount is just not possible. Usually, you want to set it to a large enough value and just monitor how many file descriptors are used.

Diagnosing and dealing with memory problems

As with every application, written in Java or not, sometimes there are memory problems. When dealing with Solr, these problems are usually related to the amount of data you have and your queries. These problems usually happen when the heap size is too low or your data is very large and not spread enough. This recipe will show you how to quickly deal with these problems and what to do to avoid them.

How to do it...

So, what do you do when you see an exception as follows:

```
SEVERE: java.lang.OutOfMemoryError: Java heap space
```

First of all, you can do something to make your day a bit easier—you can add more memory that Java virtual machine can use, of course, if you have some free physical memory available in your system. To do this, you need to add the `Xmx` and `Xms` parameters to the startup script of your servlet container (Apache Tomcat or Jetty). This is how it is done for the Solr 4.x deployment:

```
java -Xmx2g -Xms2g -jar start.jar
```

Don't give more than 50 to 60 percent of the total memory available to the operating system for the JVM. In addition to this, you should consider not giving JVM more than 31 GB of memory (because of the compressed option and how Java addresses memory).

The long term activities you can do in order to reduce the amount of memory used are as follows:

- Take a look at your queries and how they are built. Try optimizing them.
- How you use the faceting mechanism and so on (the `facet.method=fc` parameter tends to use less memory when the field has many unique terms in the index).
- Remember that fetching too many documents at one time might cause Solr to run out of heap memory (for example, when setting a large value for the query result window). If you need a large amount of data to be fetched, use a cursor.
- Reduce the number of calculated faceting results (the `facet.limit` parameter).
- Check the memory usage of your caches—this can also be one of the reasons of the problems with memory.
- Use doc values for fields that you facet or sort on.
- Reduce the amount of data on each Solr node by introducing more nodes and dividing your collections into more shards.
- If you don't need to use a normalization factor for text fields, you can set the `omitNorms="true"` parameter for such fields and save some additional memory too.
- Remember that the grouping mechanism requires memory for big result sets and for many numbers of groups a vast amount of memory might be needed.

Also, add monitoring to your Solr instances so that it will allow you to diagnose when the problems happen and before they do. You can do this using dedicated commercial solutions such as Sematext SPM (`http://sematext.com/spm/`), open source solution such as Ganglia (`http://ganglia.sourceforge.net/`), or Graphite (`http://graphite.wikidot.com/`).

How it works...

So what do the `Xmx` and `Xms` Java virtual machine parameters do? The `Xms` parameter specifies how much heap memory should be assigned by the virtual machine at the start and thus, this is the minimal size of heap memory that will be assigned by the virtual machine. The `Xmx` parameter specifies the maximum size of the heap. The Java virtual machine will not be able to assign more memory for the heap than the `Xmx` parameter.

You should remember one thing—sometimes, it's good to set the `Xmx` and `Xms` parameters to the same values. This will ensure that the virtual machine won't be resizing the heap size during the application execution and thus lose precious time for heap resizing.

Be careful when setting the heap size to be too big. It is usually not advised to give the heap size more than 50 to 60 percent of your total memory available in the system. This is because your operating system I/O cache will suffer, especially when your indices are large. It is wise to leave a lot of memory for the operating system I/O cache so that Lucene and the operating system can share the same cache and use it in a better way. What's more, having a large heap size will put a lot of pressure on the garbage collector and can result in worse performance.

There's more...

There is one more thing that I would like to discuss when it comes to memory issues.

Seeing heap when out of memory error occurs

If the out of memory errors pop up even after taking the necessary actions, then you should start monitoring your heap. One of the easiest ways to do this is by adding the appropriate Java virtual machine parameters. The parameters are `XX:+HeapDumpOnOutOfMemoryError` and `XX:HeapDumpPath`. These two parameters tell the virtual machine to dump the heap on out of memory error and write it to a file created in the specified directory. So the default Solr deployment `start` command will look as follows (again, shown for Solr 4.x):

```
java -jar -XX:+HeapDumpOnOutOfMemoryError -XX:HeapDumpPath=/var/log/dump/
start.jar
```

The heap dump can be analyzed using various tools such as jhat (`http://docs.oracle.com/javase/7/docs/technotes/tools/share/jhat.html`).

Configuring sorting for non-English languages

As you might already know that Solr supports UTF-8 encoding and thus can handle data in many languages. However, if you ever needed to sort some languages that have characters specific to them, you probably know that it doesn't work well on the standard Solr `string` type. This recipe will show you how to deal with sorting and Solr.

How to do it...

1. For the purpose of this recipe, I assumed that we will have to sort text that contains Polish characters. To show good and bad sorting behavior, we need to create the following index structure (add this to your `schema.xml` file):

```
<field name="id" type="string" indexed="true" stored="true"
required="true" />
<field name="name" type="text_general" indexed="true"
stored="true" />
<field name="name_sort_bad" type="string" indexed="true"
stored="true" />
<field name="name_sort_good" type="text_sort" indexed="true"
stored="true" />
```

2. Now let's define some copy fields to automatically fill the `name_sort_bad` and `name_sort_good` fields. Here is how they are defined (again, we only need to add the following section to the `schema.xml` file):

```
<copyField source="name" dest="name_sort_bad" />
<copyField source="name" dest="name_sort_good" />
```

3. The last thing about the `schema.xml` file is the new type. So, the `text_sort` definition looks as follows:

```
<fieldType name="text_sort" class="solr.CollationField"
language="pl" country="PL" strength="primary" />
```

4. The test that needs to be indexed looks as follows (note that the file with the following data needs to be encoded with UTF-8):

```
<add>
 <doc>
  <field name="id">1</field>
  <field name="name">Łąka</field>
 </doc>
 <doc>
```

```
    <field name="id">2</field>
    <field name="name">Lalka</field>
  </doc>
  <doc>
    <field name="id">3</field>
    <field name="name">Ząb</field>
  </doc>
</add>
```

5. First, let's take a look at how the incorrect sorting order looks like. To do this, we will send the following query to Solr:

   ```
   http://localhost:8983/solr/cookbook/select?q=*:*&sort=name_sort_
   bad+asc
   ```

   And now the response that was returned for the preceding query looks as follows:

   ```
   <?xml version="1.0" encoding="UTF-8"?>
   <response>
    <lst name="responseHeader">
     <int name="status">0</int>
     <int name="QTime">1</int>
     <lst name="params">
      <str name="q">*:*</str>
      <str name="sort">name_sort_bad asc</str>
     </lst>
    </lst>
    <result name="response" numFound="3" start="0">
     <doc>
      <str name="id">2</str>
      <str name="name">Lalka</str>
      <str name="name_sort_bad">Lalka</str>
      <str name="name_sort_good">Lalka</str>
      <long name="_version_">1481928342372352000</long></doc>
     <doc>
      <str name="id">3</str>
      <str name="name">Ząb</str>
      <str name="name_sort_bad">Ząb</str>
      <str name="name_sort_good">Ząb</str>
      <long name="_version_">1481928342372352001</long></doc>
     <doc>
      <str name="id">1</str>
      <str name="name">Łąka</str>
      <str name="name_sort_bad">Łąka</str>
   ```

```
    <str name="name_sort_good">Łąka</str>
    <long name="_version_">1481928342282174464</long></doc>
  </result>
</response>
```

6. Now let's send the query that should return the documents sorted in the correct order. The query looks similar to this:

   ```
   http://localhost:8983/solr/cookbook/select?q=*:*&sort=name_sort_
   good+asc
   ```

   The results returned by Solr are as follows:

   ```
   <?xml version="1.0" encoding="UTF-8"?>
   <response>
    <lst name="responseHeader">
     <int name="status">0</int>
     <int name="QTime">1</int>
     <lst name="params">
      <str name="q">*:*</str>
      <str name="sort">name_sort_good asc</str>
     </lst>
    </lst>
    <result name="response" numFound="3" start="0">
     <doc>
      <str name="id">2</str>
      <str name="name">Lalka</str>
      <str name="name_sort_bad">Lalka</str>
      <str name="name_sort_good">Lalka</str>
      <long name="_version_">1481928342372352000</long></doc>
     <doc>
      <str name="id">1</str>
      <str name="name">Łąka</str>
      <str name="name_sort_bad">Łąka</str>
      <str name="name_sort_good">Łąka</str>
      <long name="_version_">1481928342282174464</long></doc>
     <doc>
      <str name="id">3</str>
      <str name="name">Ząb</str>
      <str name="name_sort_bad">Ząb</str>
      <str name="name_sort_good">Ząb</str>
      <long name="_version_">1481928342372352001</long></doc>
    </result>
   </response>
   ```

As you can see, the order is different and believe me, it's correct. Now let's see how it works.

How it works...

Every document in the index is built of four fields. The `id` field is responsible for holding the unique identifier of the document. The `name` field is responsible for holding the name of the document. The last two fields are used for sorting.

The `name_sort_bad` field is nothing new—it's just a `string` based field that is used to perform sorting. The `name_sort_good` field is based on a new type—the `text_sort` field type. The field is based on the `solr.CollationField` type. The field allows Solr to sort the defined language correctly. We used three attributes while defining the field. First, the `language` attribute tells Solr about the language of the field. The second attribute is `country`, which tells Solr about the country variant (this can be skipped if necessary). The `strength` attribute informs Solr about the collation strength used. More information about these parameters can be found in the JDK documentation. One thing that is crucial is you need to create an appropriate field and set the appropriate attributes value for every non-English language you want to sort.

The two queries that you can see in the examples have one difference—the field used for sorting. The first query uses the `string` based field `name_sort_bad`. When sorting on this field, the document order will be incorrect when there will be non-English characters present. However, when sorting on the `name_sort_good` field, everything will be in the correct order, as shown in the preceding example.

Migrating data to another collection

There are times when migrating data from one collection to another is a good option, for example, if you have data of multiple clients in different shards. Some of the clients are paying for faster searches and more indexing throughput, and you would like to migrate the data of those clients to another collection so that it can be moved to new, more powerful nodes. If we use routing during indexation, Solr has a nice feature for us—the Collections API and its `migrate` command. This recipe will show you how to use it.

Getting ready

Before continuing, you should read the *Using routing* recipe in *Chapter 7, In the Cloud*. It provides a description on how to use routing, which is essential to fully understand this recipe. We also assume that we have two collections—one called `customers` that will hold our data and the second, empty one called `important_customers`. Both the collections were created using the same configuration shown in this recipe. If you want to know more about how to create a new SolrCloud cluster, refer to the *Creating a new SolrCloud cluster* recipe in *Chapter 7, In the Cloud*. This recipe will show you how to create a new SolrCloud cluster and create a collection.

How to do it...

For the purpose of this recipe, we will use the following index structure (we need to add the following section to our `schema.xml` file):

```
<field name="id" type="string" indexed="true" stored="true"
required="true" />
<field name="title" type="text_general" indexed="true" stored="true"
/>
<field name="customer" type="string" indexed="true" stored="true" />
```

For a customer with the name `customer_1`, we have the following data (stored in a file called `data_customer_1.xml`):

```
<add>
 <doc>
  <field name="id">customer_1!1</field>
  <field name="title">Customer document 1</field>
  <field name="customer">customer_1</field>
 </doc>
 <doc>
  <field name="id">customer_1!2</field>
  <field name="title">Customer document 2</field>
  <field name="customer">customer_1</field>
 </doc>
</add>
```

For a customer with the name `customer_2`, we have the following data (stored in a file called `data_customer_2.xml`):

```
<add>
 <doc>
  <field name="id">customer_2!3</field>
  <field name="title">Customer document 3</field>
  <field name="customer">customer_2</field>
 </doc>
 <doc>
  <field name="id">customer_2!4</field>
  <field name="title">Customer document 4</field>
  <field name="customer">customer_2</field>
 </doc>
</add>
```

We assume that we have the data indexed into the collection called `customers`:

1. Let's now try moving the data of the `customer_2` collection to another collection called `important_customers` that we already created and that is empty. To do this, we will run the following command:

   ```
   curl 'localhost:8983/solr/admin/collections?action=MIGRATE&col
   lection=customers&target.collection=important_customers&split.
   key=customer_2!&forward.timeout=60'
   ```

2. After the command was executed, we run the `commit` command to force the reload of index reader. We will do this using the following command:

   ```
   curl 'http://localhost:8983/solr/important_customers/update'
   --data-binary '<commit/>' -H 'Content-type:application/xml'
   ```

3. We can now check the contents of the new collection by running the following query:

   ```
   http://localhost:8983/solr/important_customers/select?q=*:*
   ```

   The response should be as follows:

   ```
   <?xml version="1.0" encoding="UTF-8"?>
   <response>
    <lst name="responseHeader">
     <int name="status">0</int>
     <int name="QTime">1</int>
     <lst name="params">
      <str name="q">*:*</str>
     </lst>
    </lst>
    <result name="response" numFound="2" start="0">
     <doc>
      <str name="id">customer_2!3</str>
      <str name="title">Customer document 3</str>
      <str name="customer">customer_2</str>
      <long name="_version_">1481976223112364032</long></doc>
     <doc>
      <str name="id">customer_2!4</str>
      <str name="title">Customer document 4</str>
      <str name="customer">customer_2</str>
      <long name="_version_">1481976223113412608</long></doc>
    </result>
   </response>
   ```

As we can see in the new collection, we have only the data for the customer we wanted. We can now remove this data from the original collection because Solr doesn't do that by default.

Let's now see how it works.

How it works...

Our index structure is very simple. Each of the documents has three fields—one for the document identifier (the `id` field), one for the title of the document (the `title` field), and the field `called` customer that will be used for filtering. Each identifier is prefixed with the customer name followed by the `!` character. We talked about this already in *Chapter 7, In the Cloud*; when using the composite routing, we can prefix the document identifier with a value and the `!` character after that. This means that Solr will use the `cookbook1234` value to determine in which shard the document will be indexed.

We assumed that we have the data indexed and we want to migrate the data of the second customer to another collection that we created upfront. We do this by running the `MIGRATE` command to the Collections API (`action=MIGRATE` sent to the `/solr/admin/collections` REST endpoint). We provide the source collection, which is in our case the `customers` collection (the `collection=customers` parameter), and we provide the target collection to where the data should be migrated to (the `target.collection=important_customers` parameter). In addition to this, we need the routing key, which we used during indexation, which for our second customer is `customer_2!` (the `split.key` parameter). Finally, we define the `forward.timeout` parameter that controls for how long Solr will re-route the write request from the source collection to the target one. It is the user's responsibility to switch read and write operations to the target collection after the migration has been done. Note that the source collection will not be modified by the migrate request. The migration of documents is a synchronous operation and it is advised to keep the timeout on the client side high, although even with that the `HTTP` command might timeout during execution when a large number of documents need to be migrated. This doesn't mean that the operation will not be successful—Solr will continue the migration in the background and you should check the logs if errors occur.

There are a few things that we need to remember when migrating data between collections:

- The migration can be performed on multiple shards at once if the `shard.key` parameter value spans multiple shards. Solr will do this automatically.
- Because the migration is a synchronous operation, it can take a long time on large collections.
- Multiple temporary collections can be created during execution of the `migrate` command although they should be removed once the command finishes executing.
- The command only works with collections that use the `CompositeId` router.
- The collection that is a target shouldn't receive any updates during the migration process because it might lead to data loss.
- Duplication is not done as a part of the migration process, so if the target collection contains data with the same identifiers as the ones in the source collection, you might end up with duplicates.

Finally, after the command was successful, we send the `commit` command to refresh the index reader so that the data is visible. As we can see in the response, everything went well and we can now remove data from the original collection.

SolrCloud read-side fault tolerance

When a single shard from your collection fails to respond to the query, Solr will fail the whole request. This is good for most use cases, but not for all. Sometimes, you might like to show partial results so that your users can see at least some portion of the results. By default, this is not possible, but luckily Solr allows you to adapt to its behavior when it comes to such situations on per request basis. This recipe will show you how to force Solr to return even partial results.

Getting ready

We assume that we already have a running SolrCloud cluster with two nodes and a collection created with two leader shards and no replica. If you don't know how to do this, refer to the *Creating a new SolrCloud cluster* recipe in *Chapter 7, In the Cloud*. This recipe will show you how to create a new SolrCloud cluster and create a collection.

How to do it...

We indexed four sample documents to our Solr cluster. Two documents are placed in one shard and the other two documents are placed in the second shard. Let's now assume that one of the shards failed and Solr is not responding to any calls:

1. First, we try to run a simple query to Solr in such a situation:

   ```
   http://localhost:8983/solr/testcollection/select?q=*:*&rows=0
   ```

   The results would be as follows:

   ```
   <?xml version="1.0" encoding="UTF-8"?>
   <response>
    <lst name="responseHeader">
     <int name="status">503</int>
     <int name="QTime">2</int>
     <lst name="params">
      <str name="q">*:*</str>
      <str name="rows">0</str>
     </lst>
    </lst>
    <lst name="error">
     <str name="msg">no servers hosting shard: </str>
     <int name="code">503</int>
    </lst>
   </response>
   ```

2. Now, if we would like to force Solr to return partial results, we would have to provide the `shards.tolerant` parameter and set it to `true` so that our query looks as follows:

```
http://localhost:8983/solr/testcollection/select?q=*:*&shards.
tolerant=true
```

The response returned by Solr will be as follows:

```
<?xml version="1.0" encoding="UTF-8"?>
<response>
 <lst name="responseHeader">
  <bool name="partialResults">true</bool>
  <int name="status">0</int>
  <int name="QTime">5</int>
  <lst name="params">
   <str name="q">*:*</str>
   <str name="shards.tolerant">true</str>
   <str name="rows">0</str>
  </lst>
 </lst>
 <result name="response" numFound="2" start="0" maxScore="1.0">
 </result>
</response>
```

As we can see, even though one of the shards fail, Solr returned partial results. Let's now see how it works.

How it works...

As we can see, the first request failed. This is because, by default, Solr will fail a search request if it can't execute a search on full results set. Solr tries to execute the search request on all the shards that build the collection and fails to do that, which results in a failed search request. As we said, we are not interested in such a behavior, because we are good with even partial results.

To achieve this, we introduced the `shards.tolerant` parameter to our query and we set it to `true` (by default, it is `false`). By doing this, we tell Solr that we want to have partial results of the query, which means that even if only a single shard of our collection is working, Solr will still return the data to us. To notify us that the results are not full, but partial, Solr included the `partialResults` property in the `response` header and set it to `true`. If all the shards return the data, that property would be set to `false`.

There's more...

Of course, search time fault tolerance (being able to operate even in case of partial system failure) is not everything—Solr also supports indexing time fault tolerance.

Defining the achieved replication factor

Similar to what we just discussed, Solr allows you to specify the `min_rf` property on update requests. The value passed to this property should be set to the desired replication factor. For example, if we want Solr to only ensure that the update was processed by the leader shard, we should set it to `1`; if we want one leader and one replica, we should set it to `2`, and so on. For example, if we set the `min_rf` property to `1` and only the leader shard should successfully index the document, but all the replicas fail, Solr will return the `rf` property in the results and set it to `1`. This means that only the leader successfully indexed the document and the replicas will have to sync with the leader once they recover. Such an update is still considered successful, but we can force Solr to return such information as the update request response.

Using the check index functionality

It's night; the phone is ringing, you answer it and hear: "We've got a problem—the index is corrupted, nothing works, the apocalypse is coming". What can we do? Is there anything besides the full indexation or restoring from backup? There is something that we can do and this recipe will show you.

How to do it...

For the purpose of this recipe, let's suppose that we have a corrupted index that we want to check and fix. To use the `CheckIndex` class that we will use, we will need to point it to the index we want to fix. We will need to run a command similar to the following one:

```
java -cp LUCENE_JAR_LOCATION -ea:org.apache.lucene... org.apache.lucene.
index.CheckIndex INDEX_PATH -fix
```

Here, `INDEX_PATH` is the path to the index, for example, `/usr/share/solr/data/index` and `LUCENE_JAR_LOCATION` is the path to the Lucene core JAR library (which is provided with the Solr distribution). So, with the given index location, the command will look as follows:

```
java -cp lucene-core-4.10.0.jar -ea:org.apache.lucene... org.apache.
lucene.index.CheckIndex /usr/share/solr/data/index -fix
```

After running the preceding command, you should see a series of information about the process of index repair, which in my case looked as follows:

```
Opening index @ /usr/share/solr/data/index

Segments file=segments_2 numSegments=1 version=4.10.0 format= userData
={commitTimeMSec=1395237413525}
  1 of 1: name=_0 docCount=11
    version=4.7.0
    codec=Lucene46
    compound=false
    numFiles=10
    size (MB)=0.002
    diagnostics = {os=Windows 8.1, java.vendor=Oracle Corporation,
java.version=1.8.0, lucene.version=4.10.0 1570806 - simon - 2014-
12-22 08:25:23, os.arch=amd64, source=flush, os.version=6.3,
timestamp=1395237413563}
    no deletions
    test: open reader.........FAILED
    WARNING: fixIndex() would remove reference to this segment; full
exception:
java.io.IOException: Invalid vInt detected (too many bits)
        at org.apache.lucene.store.DataInput.readVInt(DataInput.
java:138)
        at org.apache.lucene.store.DataInput.readString(DataInput.
java:232)
        at org.apache.lucene.store.DataInput.
readStringStringMap(DataInput.java:263)
    at org.apache.lucene.codecs.lucene46.Lucene46FieldInfosReader.
read(Lucene46FieldInfosReader.java:93)
        at org.apache.lucene.index.SegmentReader.
readFieldInfos(SegmentReader.java:289)
        at org.apache.lucene.index.SegmentReader.<init>(SegmentReader.
java:107)
        at org.apache.lucene.index.CheckIndex.checkIndex(CheckIndex.
java:583)
        at org.apache.lucene.index.CheckIndex.main(CheckIndex.
java:2096)

WARNING: 1 broken segments (containing 11 documents) detected
WARNING: 11 documents will be lost
```

```
NOTE: will write new segments file in 5 seconds; this will remove 11
docs from the index. THIS IS YOUR LAST CHANCE TO CTRL+C!
  5...
  4...
  3...
  2...
  1...
Writing...
OK
Wrote new segments file "segments_3"
```

And that's all. After this, you should have the index processed and depending on the case, you can have your index repaired. Now, let's see how it works.

How it works...

As you see, the command-line instruction runs the `CheckIndex` class from the `org.apache.lucene.index` package. We also provided the absolute path to the directory that contains the index files, the library that contains the necessary classes, and the `-fix` parameter, which tells the `CheckIndex` tool to try to repair any errors found in the index structure. In addition to this, we provided the `ea` parameter to enable the assertions. We did this to make the test more accurate. Let's take a look at the response that the `CheckIndex` tool provided. As you can see, we have information about the segments, the number of documents, and the version of Lucene used to build the index. We can also see the number of files that the index consists of, the operating system, and so on. This information might be useful but it is not crucial. The most interesting thing for us is the following information:

```
WARNING: 1 broken segments (containing 11 documents) detected
WARNING: 11 documents will be lost
```

This information tells us that the `CheckIndex` tool found one broken segment, which contains 11 documents and that all the 11 documents will be lost in the repair process. This is not always the case, but it can happen and you should be aware of that.

The next lines of the `CheckIndex` tool response tells us about the process of writing the new segment files that will be repaired. And that's actually all. Of course, when dealing with larger indexes, the response generated by the `CheckIndex` tool will be much larger and will contain information about all the segments of the index. The preceding example is simple but it should illustrate how the tool works.

Note that you should turn off Solr and not have any process accessing the index at the same time `CheckIndex` tool is working.

When using the `CheckIndex` tool, you need to be very careful. There are many situations where the index files can't be repaired and the `CheckIndex` tool will result in the deletion of all the documents in the index. That's not always the case, but you should be aware of that and be extra careful—for example, a good practice is to make a backup of the existing index before running the `CheckIndex` tool.

There's more...

There is one more thing worth noticing when talking about the `CheckIndex` tool.

Checking the index without the repair procedure

If you only want to check the index for any errors without the need to repair it, you can run the `CheckIndex` tool in the repair mode. To do this, run the command-line fragment shown in the recipe without the `-fix` part. For example:

```
java -ea:org.apache.lucene... org.apache.lucene.index.CheckIndex /usr/
share/solr/data/index
```

Adjusting the Jetty configuration to avoid deadlocks

Adjusting Jetty to properly handle all the requests sent to Solr and SolrCloud is very important. The request that the application sends to Solr is one, but it is also important to allow Solr to process the internal requests sent between nodes and shards. Because of this we need to prepare our container to handle a higher number of requests than usual. This recipe will show and discuss how to properly set up Jetty to handle traffic to and between Solr nodes.

Getting ready

If you are not familiar with how to set up Jetty, please refer to *Running Solr on a standalone Jetty* recipe in *Chapter 1, Apache Solr Configuration*, before proceeding. I also assume that we are using Jetty 8.1.10 and Solr 4.x, which was distributed as a WAR file.

How to do it...

I assume that each of the Solr instances will run on its own Jetty container. Each of the Jetty servers has the `jetty.xml` file that we will need to alter (this file should be present in the `$JETTY_HOME/etc` directory). By default, Jetty contains the following configuration:

```
<Set name="ThreadPool">
 <New class="org.eclipse.jetty.util.thread.QueuedThreadPool">
  <Set name="minThreads">10</Set>
```

```
    <Set name="maxThreads">200</Set>
    <Set name="detailedDump">false</Set>
  </New>
</Set>
```

We need to alter this configuration so that it looks as follows:

```
<Set name="ThreadPool">
  <New class="org.eclipse.jetty.util.thread.QueuedThreadPool">
    <Set name="minThreads">10</Set>
    <Set name="maxThreads">10000</Set>
    <Set name="detailedDump">false</Set>
  </New>
</Set>
```

After this change, you will no longer have Solr vulnerable to the deadlock state, at least for most cases. Now let's see what we did.

How it works...

The default Jetty configuration is not sufficient, especially when it comes to SolrCloud. When you run a large number of indexing requests and large number of queries per second, your cluster can hang in a state called deadlock. In such a state, Solr will stop responding to new requests and old requests will be hanging. To avoid this, we need to increase the number of threads that are allowed to be running at the same time. By default, this is only `200`, which is very low if you are running SolrCloud with a large number of nodes.

What we did is we increased the number of threads that are allowed to run in parallel to `10000` (by changing the `maxThreads` property), which should be more than enough for any deployment. However, if you see deadlock problems in your deployment, try increasing the value even higher.

Tuning segment merging

As you might know, a Lucene index is built of one or more segments. In general, a segment is a write-once, read-many data structure, which means that once written it won't be updated (only some parts of it will be, such as information about a deleted document). Segment merging is a process of combining multiple segments to a new one to reduce the overall number of segments the index is built of. The reason Lucene does this is because of performance—the smaller the number of segments, the better the search performance is. On the other hand, segment merge is a resource-intensive process as it requires you to read the old segments and write the new ones. Because of all this, it is good to know how to tune segment merging for our own purposes and this recipe will show you how to do that.

How to do it...

1. For the purpose of this recipe, I assume that we are starting with the basic Solr configuration, which looks as follows when it comes to segment merging (we modify the `solrconfig.xml` file):

```
<mergePolicy class="org.apache.lucene.index.TieredMergePolicy">
 <int name="maxMergeAtOnce">10</int>
 <int name="segmentsPerTier">10</int>
</mergePolicy>
```

2. Let's assume that the default configuration produced too many segments for our use case—we have fast disks and we would like to have a lower number of segments to speed up our searches.

   Actually, if we take a look at the number of segments after indexing a few thousands of documents, we would see the following:

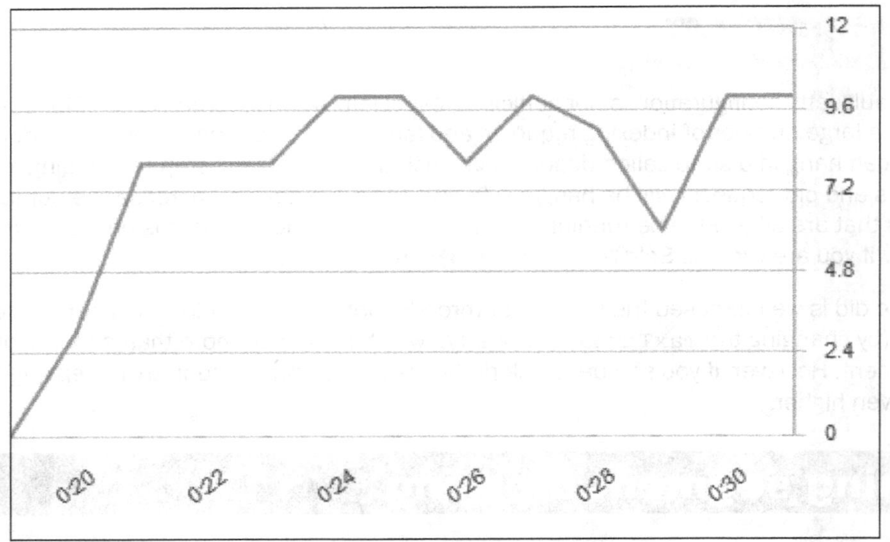

3. To lower down the number of segments that are produced during our normal indexing procedure, we will alter the merge policy configuration so that it looks as follows:

```
<mergePolicy class="org.apache.lucene.index.TieredMergePolicy">
 <int name="maxMergeAtOnce">2</int>
 <int name="segmentsPerTier">2</int>
</mergePolicy>
```

If we now index the same number of documents and take a look at the merging visualization, we would see the following:

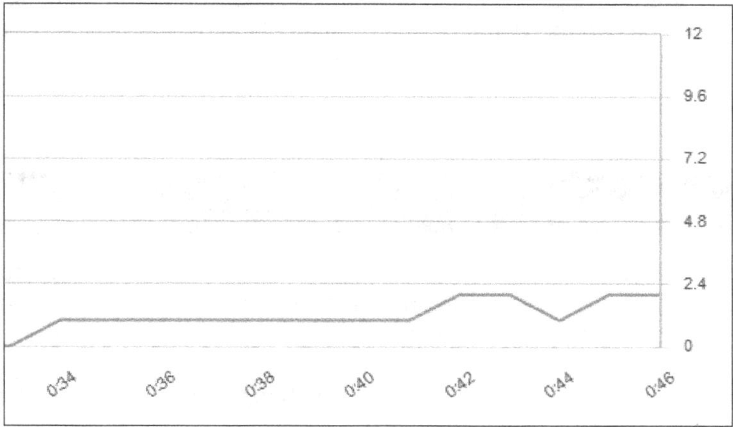

Now let's see how it works.

How it works...

To control the behavior of segment merging process, Solr allows you to specify the class implementing the merge policy. We do this by including the `mergePolicy` section in the `solrconfig.xml` file and specifying its `class` property. The default merge policy since Solr 3.3 is `org.apache.lucene.index.TieredMergePolicy` that classifies index segments into tiers and merges those segments inside the tiers.

We are allowed to specify many different properties (take a look at the official Javadoc of the merge policy to learn about them all available at `http://lucene.apache.org/core/4_10_0/core/org/apache/lucene/index/TieredMergePolicy.html`); however, we are interested in two of them—`maxMergeAtOnce` and `segmentsPerTier`. The first property specifies how many segments can be merged at once and the second property specifies how many segments will be put into each tier.

By default, the `maxMergeAtOnce` and `segmentsPerTier` properties are set to `10`. If we lower this value, then we should get a lower number of segments compared to the default value at the cost of indexing speed. This should speed up searches as fewer segments will be used in the index. If we set these properties to higher values, we will get more segments compared to the default value. This will result in faster indexing, but will lower the query performance as more segments will be present.

In our example, we can clearly see that with the default configuration, we had about 10 segments on average. After the change, we had about one or two segments on average, which means that our change made a difference in the direction we wanted.

See also

- There is a great blog post by Mike McCandless about segment merges, merge policies, and the visualization of segments merging in Lucene available at `http://blog.mikemccandless.com/2011/02/visualizing-lucenes-segment-merges.html`. If you are interested in this topic, I strongly advise that you read it.

Avoiding swapping

One of the crucial things when running your Solr instances in production is performance. What you want is to give your clients relevant results in the blink of an eye. If your clients have to wait for their results for too long, some of them might choose other vendors or sites that provide similar services. One of the things when running Java application such as Apache Solr is to ensure that the operating system won't write the heap to disk, to ensure that the part of the memory used by Solr won't be swapped at all. This recipe will show you how to achieve this on a Linux operating system.

Getting ready

Note that the following recipe is only valid when you are running Apache Solr on a Linux operating system. In addition to this, be advised that turning off swapping should only be done when you have enough memory to handle all the necessary applications in your system and you want to be sure that there won't be any swapping.

How to do it...

1. Before turning off swapping, let's take a look at the amount of swap memory used by our operating system. In order to do this, let's take a look at the main page of the Solr administration panel:

2. As you can see, some swap memory is being used. In order to demonstrate how to turn off swap usage, I freed some memory on the virtual machine that I was using for tests and after that I ran the following commands:

```
sudo sysctl -w vm.swappiness=0
sudo /sbin/swapoff -a
```

3. After the second command is done running, I refreshed the main page of our Solr admin instance and this is what it showed:

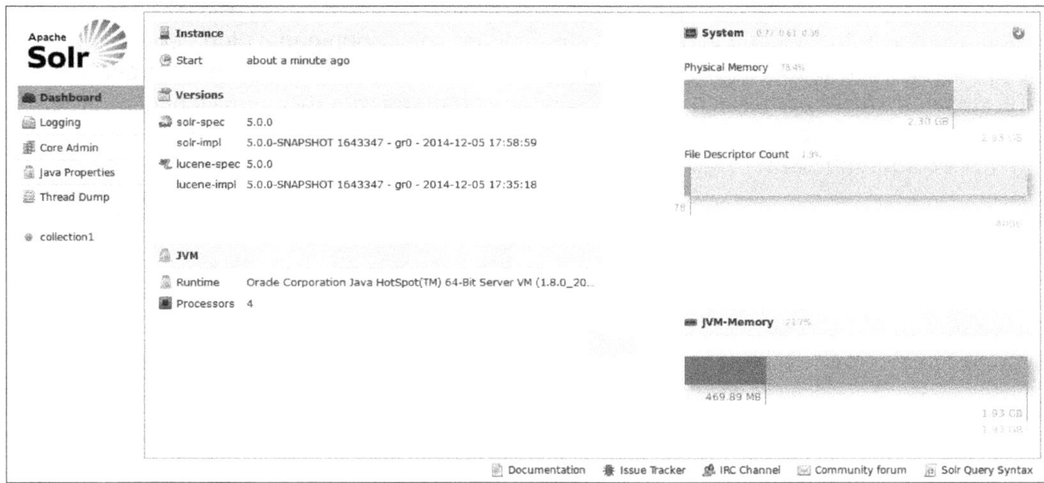

4. It seems that it is working, but in order to be sure, I will run the following command:

   ```
   free -m
   ```

   The response was as follows:

   ```
                    total      used      free    shared  buffers      cached
   Mem:              3001      2326       675         0        3          97
   -/+ buffers/cache:          2226       775
   Swap:                0         0         0
   0        0         0
   ```

And again, we can see that there is no swap usage. Now let's see how that works.

How it works...

In the first provided screenshot, you can see that there is a bit more than 183 MB of swap memory being used. This is not good—in a production environment, you want to avoid swapping, of course, if you have the needed amount of memory. Swapping will write the contents of the memory onto the hard disk drive and thus make your operating system and applications execution slower. This can also affect Solr.

So, in order to turn off swapping in a Linux operating system, we will run two commands. The first one sets the `vm.swappiness` operating system property to `0`, which means that we want to avoid swapping. We need to use `sudo`, because in order to set this property with the use of the `sysctl` command, we need administration privileges. The second command (the `/sbin/swapoff -a` one) disables swapping on all known devices.

As you can see in the second screenshot, the Solr administration panel didn't even include the swapping information, so we can suspect that it was turned off. However, in order to be sure, we used another Linux command, the `free` command with the `-m` switch in order to see the memory usage on our system. As you can see, the `Swap` section shows `0`, so we can now be sure that swapping was turned off.

10
Real-life Situations

In this chapter, we will cover the following topics:

- Implementing the autocomplete functionality for products
- Implementing the autocomplete functionality for categories
- Handling time-sliced data using aliases
- Boosting words closer to each other
- Using the Solr spellchecking functionality
- Using the Solr administration panel for monitoring
- Automatically expiring Solr documents
- Exporting whole query results

Introduction

During the previous nine chapters, we discussed the different Apache Solr functionalities and how to overcome some common problems and situations. However, there are some real-life situations that were not yet described and I decided that it would be nice to have them shown to you in a dedicated chapter. All of the problems described in this chapter were raised during our work with clients or appeared in on the Apache Solr mailing list. This chapter is dedicated to describing how to handle such situations and I hope that you'll find it useful.

Implementing the autocomplete functionality for products

Recently, the autocomplete functionality has gained popularity. You can find it in on Google, Bing, and many more similar e-commerce sites. It enables your users or clients to find what they want and do it fast. In most cases, the autocomplete functionality also increases the relevance of your search by pointing to the right author, title, and so on right away without looking at the search results. What's more, sites that use autocomplete reported higher revenue after deploying such a functionality compared to the situation before implementing it. It is a win-win situation both for you and your clients. So let's take a look at how to implement the product autocomplete functionality in Solr.

How to do it...

Let's assume that we want to show you the full product name whenever our users enter part of the word that the product name is built of. In addition to this, we want to show you the number of documents with the same names.

1. Let's start with the example data that is going to be indexed:

```
<add>
 <doc>
  <field name="id">1</field>
  <field name="name">First Solr Cookbook</field>
 </doc>
 <doc>
  <field name="id">2</field>
  <field name="name">Second Solr Cookbook</field>
 </doc>
 <doc>
  <field name="id">3</field>
  <field name="name">Elasticsearch book</field>
 </doc>
</add>
```

2. We will need two main fields in the index—one for the document identifier and one for the name; and we will need two additional fields—one for autocomplete and one for faceting that we will use. So our index structure will look as follows (we should put it into the `schema.xml` section):

```
<field name="id" type="string" indexed="true" stored="true"
required="true" />
<field name="name" type="text_general" indexed="true"
stored="true" />
```

```
<field name="name_autocomplete" type="text_autocomplete"
indexed="true" stored="false" />
<field name="name_show" type="string" indexed="true"
stored="false" />
```

3. In addition to this, we want Solr to automatically copy data from the `name` field to the `name_autocomplete` and `name_show` fields. So we will add the following to the `schema.xml` file:

```
<copyField source="name" dest="name_autocomplete"/>
<copyField source="name" dest="name_show"/>
```

4. Now the final thing about the `schema.xml` file—the `text_autocomplete` field type, which will look as follows (place it into the `schema.xml` file):

```
<fieldType name="text_autocomplete" class="solr.TextField"
positionIncrementGap="100">
 <analyzer type="index">
  <tokenizer class="solr.WhitespaceTokenizerFactory"/>
  <filter class="solr.LowerCaseFilterFactory"/>
  <filter class="solr.EdgeNGramFilterFactory" minGramSize="1"
maxGramSize="25" />
 </analyzer>
 <analyzer type="query">
  <tokenizer class="solr.WhitespaceTokenizerFactory"/>
  <filter class="solr.LowerCaseFilterFactory"/>
 </analyzer>
</fieldType>
```

5. That's all! Now, if we would like to show our users all the products that start with the `sol` word, we will send the following query:

```
curl 'http://localhost:8983/solr/cookbook/select?q=name_
autocomplete:sol&q.op=AND&rows=0&&facet=true&facet.field=name_
show&facet.mincount=1&facet.limit=5'
```

The response returned by Solr will be as follows:

```
<?xml version="1.0" encoding="UTF-8"?>
<response>
<lst name="responseHeader">
  <int name="status">0</int>
```

```
    <int name="QTime">1</int>
    <lst name="params">
      <str name="q">name_autocomplete:sol</str>
      <str name="facet.limit">5</str>
      <str name="facet.field">name_show</str>
      <str name="q.op">AND</str>
      <str name="facet.mincount">1</str>
      <str name="rows">0</str>
      <str name="facet">true</str>
    </lst>
  </lst>
  <result name="response" numFound="2" start="0">
  </result>
  <lst name="facet_counts">
    <lst name="facet_queries"/>
    <lst name="facet_fields">
      <lst name="name_show">
        <int name="First Solr Cookbook">1</int>
        <int name="Second Solr Cookbook">1</int>
      </lst>
    </lst>
    <lst name="facet_dates"/>
    <lst name="facet_ranges"/>
    <lst name="facet_intervals"/>
  </lst>
  </response>
```

As you can see, the faceting results returned by Solr are exactly what we were looking for. So now, let's see how it works.

How it works...

Our example documents are pretty simple—they are only built of an identifier and the name that we will use to make autocomplete happen. The index structure is where things will get interesting. The first two fields are the ones you would have expected—they are used to hold the identifier of the document and its name. However, we have two additional fields available—the `name_autocomplete` field, which will be used for querying and the `name_show` field, which will be used for faceting. The `name_show` field is based on the string type, because we want to have a single token per name when we use faceting.

With the use of the copy field sections, we can let Solr automatically copy values of fields defined by the `source` attribute to the field defined by the `dest` field. The copying is done before any analysis. Solr will copy the values that were originally sent to it.

The `name_autocomplete` field is based on the `text_autocomplete` field type, which is defined differently for indexing and querying. During the query time, we divide the entered query on the basis of whitespace characters using `solr.WhitespaceTokenizerFactory` and we lowercase the tokens with the use of `solr.LowerCaseFilterFactory`. For query time it's what we want, because we don't want any more processing. For index time, we use the same tokenizer and filter, but we also use `solr.NGramFilterFactory`. We use it, because we want to allow our users to efficiently search for prefixes, so when someone enters the `sol` word, we would like to show all the products that have a word starting with that prefix and `solr.NGramFilterFactory` allows you to doing that. For the `solr` word, it will produce the tokens `s`, `so`, `sol`, and `solr`, as shown on the **Analysis** page:

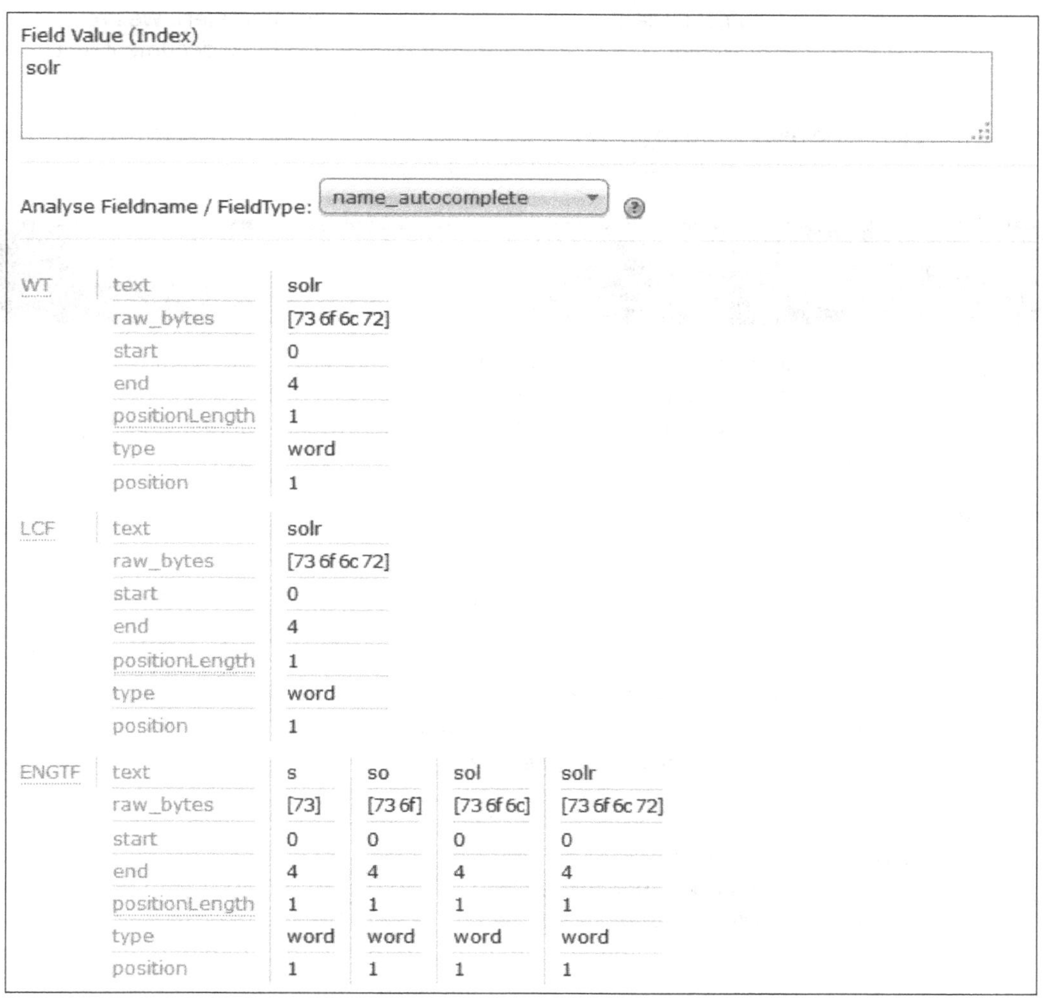

We also said that we are interested in grams starting from a single character (the `minGramsSize` property) and the maximum size of grams allowed is 25 (the `maxGramSize` property).

Now let's take a look at the query. As you can see, we sent the prefix of the word that users have entered to the `name_autocomplete` field (`q=name_autocomplete:sol`). In addition to this, we also said that we want words in our query to be connected with the `AND` logical operator (the `q.op` parameter) and that we are not interested in the search results (the `rows=0` parameter). As we said, we will use faceting for our autocomplete functionality because we need the information about the amount of documents with the same titles. So we turned on faceting (the `facet=true` parameter) and said that we want to calculate the faceting on our `name_show` field (the `facet.field=name_show` parameter). We are also only interested in faceting calculation for the values that have at least one document in it (`facet.mincount=1`) and we want the top five results (`facet.limit=5`).

As you can see in the results, we've got two distinct values in the faceting results both with a single document with the same title, which matches our sample data.

Implementing the autocomplete functionality for categories

Sometimes, we are interested not in our product's name for autocomplete, but in something else. Imagine that we want to show the category of our products in the autocomplete box along with the number of products in each category. Let's see how we can use faceting to achieve such functionality.

How to do it...

1. Let's start with the example data, which is going to be indexed and looks as follows:

```
<add>
 <doc>
  <field name="id">1</field>
  <field name="name">First Solr Cookbook</field>
  <field name="category">Books</field>
 </doc>
 <doc>
  <field name="id">2</field>
  <field name="name">Second Solr Cookbook</field>
  <field name="category">Books And Tutorials</field>
 </doc>
 <doc>
```

```
    <field name="id">3</field>
    <field name="name">Elasticsearch Server</field>
    <field name="category">Books And Tutorials</field>
  </doc>
</add>
```

2. Our `schema.xml` configuration file that can handle the preceding data will look as follows:

```
<field name="id" type="string" indexed="true" stored="true"
required="true" />
<field name="name" type="text_general" indexed="true"
stored="true" />
<field name="category" type="text_lowercase" indexed="true"
stored="true" />
```

3. One final thing is the `text_lowercase` type definition, which will be also placed in the `schema.xml` file, and it will look as follows:

```
<fieldType name="text_lowercase" class="solr.TextField"
positionIncrementGap="100">
 <analyzer>
  <tokenizer class="solr.KeywordTokenizerFactory"/>
  <filter class="solr.LowerCaseFilterFactory"/>
 </analyzer>
</fieldType>
```

4. So now, if we would like to get all the categories that start with `boo`, along with the number of products in these categories, we can send the following query:

```
curl 'http://localhost:8983/solr/cookbook/select?q=*:*&rows=0&face
t=true&facet.field=category&facet.mincount=1&facet.limit=5&facet.
prefix=boo'
```

And the following response was returned by Solr:

```
<?xml version="1.0" encoding="UTF-8"?>
<response>
<lst name="responseHeader">
  <int name="status">0</int>
  <int name="QTime">42</int>
  <lst name="params">
    <str name="q">*:*</str>
    <str name="facet.limit">5</str>
    <str name="facet.field">category</str>
    <str name="facet.prefix">boo</str>
    <str name="facet.mincount">1</str>
    <str name="rows">0</str>
```

```
    <str name="facet">true</str>
  </lst>
</lst>
<result name="response" numFound="3" start="0">
</result>
<lst name="facet_counts">
  <lst name="facet_queries"/>
  <lst name="facet_fields">
    <lst name="category">
      <int name="books and tutorials">2</int>
      <int name="books">1</int>
    </lst>
  </lst>
  <lst name="facet_dates"/>
  <lst name="facet_ranges"/>
  <lst name="facet_intervals"/>
</lst>
</response>
```

As you can see, we have two categories each with a single product in them, so this is what matches our example data. Let's now see how it works.

How it works...

Our data is very simple; we have three fields for each of our documents—one for the identifier fields, one to hold the name of the document, and one for its category. We will use the `category` field to do the autocomplete functionality and we will use faceting for it.

If you take a look at the index structure, for the `category` field, we use a special type—the `text_lowercase` one. What it does is it stores the category as a single token in the index because of using `solr.KeywordTokenizerFactory`, but we also lowercase with the appropriate filter. This is because we want to send the lowercased queries when we use faceting.

The query is quite simple; we query for all the documents (the `q=*:*` parameter) and we don't want any results returned (the `rows=0` parameter). We will use faceting for autocomplete, so we turn it on (the `facet=true` parameter), and we will specify the `category` field to calculate the faceting on (`facet.field=category`). We are also only interested in faceting calculation for the values that have at least one document in it (`facet.mincount=1`) and we want the top five results (`facet.limit=5`). One of the most important parameters in the query is the `facet.prefix` one—with the use of this parameter, we will return on those results in faceting that start with the prefix defined by the mentioned parameter, which can be seen in the results. And of course remember that faceting results are by default sorted by their numerousness.

Handling time-sliced data using aliases

There are situations in which time-sliced data is the only logical solution to go for. For example, if you are indexing logs to your SolrCloud cluster, you probably want to divide the data in time slices depending on how much data you have—if you only have index logs with error level, then you can probably live with monthly collections. If you are indexing all logs from all your applications, daily collections will probably be the way to go. With the time-sliced collections, there are a few things that the application needs to handle; for example, knowing to which collection it should currently send data to and which collection or collections should be used for querying. To simplify this, Solr allows you to use aliases and this recipe will show you how to handle that.

Getting ready

We assume that we already have our configuration stored in ZooKeeper and we have created a SolrCloud cluster. If you don't know how to do this, refer to the *Creating a new SolrCloud cluster* recipe in *Chapter 7, In the Cloud*.

How to do it...

Let's assume that we want to create daily indices, because we use our SolrCloud cluster to store logs coming from different applications in our environment. I also assume that we only want to search in day or week intervals:

1. We will start by creating an initial collection that will hold our data. To do this, we run a command similar to the following one:

```
curl 'localhost:8983/solr/admin/collections?action=CREATE&nam
e=logs_2014-11-10&numShards=1&replicationFactor=1&collection.
configName=logs'
```

2. Now to simplify indexing, we will create an alias called `logs_index` so that our indexing application always uses the same collection name. We do this by running the following command:

```
curl 'localhost:8983/solr/admin/collections?action=CREATEALIAS&nam
e=logs_index&collections=logs_2014-11-10'
```

3. We also said that we want to simplify querying so that our UI doesn't need to worry about collections and their names. We need to create two aliases—we do this by running the following commands:

```
curl 'localhost:8983/solr/admin/collections?action=CREATEALIAS&nam
e=logs_search_day&collections=logs_2014-11-10'
```

```
curl 'localhost:8983/solr/admin/collections?action=CREATEALIAS&nam
e=logs_search_week&collections=logs_2014-11-10'
```

4. Now, let's create a new daily collection using the following command:

```
curl 'localhost:8983/solr/admin/collections?action=CREATE&nam
e=logs_2014-11-11&numShards=1&replicationFactor=1&collection.
configName=logs'
```

5. After this has been done and the day ended, we need to run a command to alter our aliases. First, we need to alter our `logs_index` alias to point to a new, empty collection. We do this by running the following command:

```
curl 'localhost:8983/solr/admin/collections?action=CREATEALIAS&nam
e=logs_index&collections=logs_2014-11-11'
```

6. Now we need to update aliases used for searching. We can do this by running the following commands:

```
curl 'localhost:8983/solr/admin/collections?action=CREATEALIAS&nam
e=logs_search_day&collections=logs_2014-11-11'
curl 'localhost:8983/solr/admin/collections?action=CREATEALIAS&nam
e=logs_search_week&collections=logs_2014-11-10,logs_2014-11-11'
```

Unfortunately, this is the only thing that we will have to automate ourselves—switching aliases. The rest will be handled by Solr. Now let's see how all this works.

How it works...

We started by creating a new collection. The collection is called `logs_2014-11-10` and it will be used to store logs from November 10, 2014. However, we don't want our application to know the logic behind the naming of the collections. It might happen that we will change the naming and we don't want to force the application to be changed during the same time. Because of this, we created two aliases for searching and one for indexing. We will always use a single alias pointing to only a single collection for indexing. Actually, Solr won't index data if an alias points to more than one collection. Of course, the `logs_search_day` alias will also point to a single collection—the most recent one and the `logs_search_week` alias will cover the whole week (in our case, we start with a single collection, that's why it covers only a single collection initially).

Alias creation is very simple. We run a command to the same REST API that we used during the collection creation—to `/admin/collections`. We specify the `action=CREATEALIAS` command. We need to provide two things—first, the name of the alias we want to use (we do this by providing the `name` parameter) and the list of comma-separated collections that should be grouped with that alias (using the `collections` parameter).

After adding a new collection and when a new day comes, we need to switch our aliases. We again run the same command that we used to create the `logs_index` alias, but instead of pointing it to the `logs_2014-11-10` collection, we point it to the newest collection, which is `logs_2014-11-11`. Solr will just overwrite the old alias definition. A similar thing is done for the aliases used for searching. We point the `logs_search_day` alias to the newest collection, which is `logs_2014-11-11`, and now we point the `logs_search_week` alias to two collections (we will point it to three collections on the next day and so on).

The only thing we need to worry about is making automation work to create new collections and switching the aliases, because Solr doesn't do that for us.

There's more...

There is one more thing I would like to describe when it comes to handling aliases.

Deleting an alias

In addition to creating aliases, Solr allows you to delete them as well. For example, if we would like to delete an alias called `logs_search_day`, we will run the following command:

```
curl 'localhost:8983/solr/admin/collections?action=DELETEALIAS&name=lo
gs_search_day'
```

As you can see, the only thing that we need to provide is the `action=DELETEALIAS` parameter and the name of the alias we want to delete using the `name` request parameter.

Boosting words closer to each other

One of the most common problems that users are struggling with is how to improve the relevancy of their results while using Apache Solr. Of course, the relevancy tuning is in most cases connected to your business needs, but one of the common requirements is to have documents that have all the query words in their fields on top of the results list. You can imagine a situation where you search for all the documents that match at least a single query word, but you would like to show the ones with the entire query words set first. This recipe will show you how to achieve that.

How to do it...

1. Let's start with the following index structure (add the following definition to your `schema.xml` file):

```
<field name="id" type="string" indexed="true" stored="true"
required="true" />
<field name="name" type="text_general" indexed="true"
stored="true" />
<field name="description" type="text_general" indexed="true"
stored="true" />
```

2. The second step is to index the following sample data:

```
<add>
 <doc>
  <field name="id">1</field>
  <field name="name">Solr and all the others</field>
  <field name="description">This is about Solr</field>
 </doc>
 <doc>
  <field name="id">2</field>
  <field name="name">Lucene and all the others</field>
  <field name="description">This is a book about Solr and Lucene</
field>
 </doc>
</add>
```

3. Let's assume that our usual queries look as follows:

```
http://localhost:8983/solr/cookbook/select?q=solr book&defType=edi
smax&mm=1&qf=name^10000+description
```

Nothing complicated, however, the results of such a query doesn't satisfy us, because they look similar to this:

```
<?xml version="1.0" encoding="UTF-8"?>
<response>
<lst name="responseHeader">
  <int name="status">0</int>
  <int name="QTime">2</int>
  <lst name="params">
    <str name="mm">1</str>
    <str name="q">solr book</str>
```

```
      <str name="defType">edismax</str>
      <str name="qf">name^10000 description</str>
    </lst>
  </lst>
  <result name="response" numFound="2" start="0">
    <doc>
      <str name="id">1</str>
      <str name="name">Solr and all the others</str>
      <str name="description">This is about Solr</str>
      <long name="_version_">1483649935327887360</long></doc>
    <doc>
      <str name="id">2</str>
      <str name="name">Lucene and all the others</str>
      <str name="description">This is a book about Solr and Lucene</
str>
      <long name="_version_">1483649935408627712</long></doc>
  </result>
  </response>
```

4. In order to change this, let's introduce a new handler in our `solrconfig.xml` file:

```
<requestHandler name="/better" class="solr.SearchHandler">
 <lst name="defaults">
  <str name="q">_query_:"{!edismax qf=$qfQuery
mm=$mmQuerypf=$pfQuery bq=$boostQuery v=$mainQuery}"</str>
  <str name="qfQuery">name^100000 description</str>
  <str name="mmQuery">1</str>
  <str name="pfQuery">name description</str>
  <str name="boostQuery">_query_:"{!edismax qf=$boostQueryQf
mm=100% v=$mainQuery}"^100000</str>
  <str name="boostQueryQf">name description</str>
 </lst>
</requestHandler>
```

5. So, let's send a query to our new handler by running the following query against Solr:

```
http://localhost:8983/solr/cookbook/better?mainQuery=solr book
```

We get the following results:

```
<?xml version="1.0" encoding="UTF-8"?>
<response>
<lst name="responseHeader">
  <int name="status">0</int>
  <int name="QTime">328</int>
</lst>
<result name="response" numFound="2" start="0">
  <doc>
    <str name="id">2</str>
    <str name="name">Lucene and all the others</str>
    <str name="description">This is a book about Solr and Lucene</
str>
    <long name="_version_">1483649935408627712</long></doc>
  <doc>
    <str name="id">1</str>
    <str name="name">Solr and all the others</str>
    <str name="description">This is about Solr</str>
    <long name="_version_">1483649935327887360</long></doc>
</result>
</response>
```

As you can see it works, so let's discuss how.

How it works...

For the purpose of this recipe, we used a simple index structure that consists of a document identifier, document name, and description. Our data is very simple as well; it just contains two documents, so let's just skip discussing it.

During the first query, the document with the identifier of `1` is placed on top of the query results. This is because our `name` field is highly boosted. However, what we would like to achieve is to be able to boost the name. In addition to this, we would like to have the documents with words from the query close to each other on top of the results.

In order to do this, we define a new request handler named `/better`, which will leverage the local params. The first thing is the defined `q` parameter, which is the standard query. It uses the extended `dismax` parser (the `{!edismax` part of the query) and defines several additional parameters:

- `qf`: This is the field that `edismax` should send the query against. We tell Solr that we will provide the fields by specifying the `qfQuery` parameter using the `$qfQuery` value.
- `mm`: This is the minimum that should match a parameter that tells `edismax` how many words from the query should be found in a document for the document to be considered a match. We tell Solr that we will provide the fields by specifying the `mmQuery` parameter using the `$mmQuery` value.

- `pf`: This is the phrase fields definition that specifies the fields on which Solr should generate the phrase queries automatically. Similar to the previous parameters we specified, we will provide the fields by specifying the `pfQuery` parameter using the `$pfQuery` value.
- `bq`: This is the boost query that will be used to boost the documents. Again, we use the parameter dereferencing functionality and we tell Solr that we will provide the value in the `bqQuery` parameter using the `$bqQuery` value.
- `v`: This is the final parameter that specifies the content of the query; in our case, the user query will be specified in the `mainQuery` parameter.

Basically, the preceding query says that we will use the `edismax` query parser, phrase, and boost queries. Now let's discuss the values of the parameters.

The first thing is the `qfQuery` parameter, which is exactly the same as the `qf` parameter in the first query we sent to Solr. With the use of this parameter, we just specify the fields that we want to be searched for and their boosts. Next, we have the `mmQuery` parameter set to `1`, which will be used as `mm` in `edismax`, which means that a document will be considered a match when a single word from the query will be found in it. As you remember, the `pfQuery` parameter value will be passed to the `pf` parameter and thus the phrase query will be automatically created on the fields defined in those fields.

And now the last and probably the most important part of the query—the `boostQuery` parameter whose value will be passed to the `bq` parameter. Our boost query is very similar to our main query; however, we can say that the query should only match the documents that have all the words from the query (the `mm=100%` parameter). We also specify that the documents that match that query should be boosted by adding the `^100000` part at the end of it.

To sum up all the parameters of our query, they will promote the documents with all the words from the query present in the fields we want to search for. In addition to this, we will promote the documents that have phrases matched. So finally, let's take a look at how the newly created handler works—as you can see, when providing our query to it with the `mainQuery` parameter, the previously second document is now placed as the first one, so we achieved what we wanted.

Using the Solr spellchecking functionality

Most modern search sites have some kind of user spelling mistakes correction functionality. Some of these sites have a sophisticated mechanism, while others just has a basic one. But that doesn't actually matter. If all the search engines have it, then there is a big probability that your client or boss will want one too. Is there a way to integrate such functionality into Solr? Yes, there is and this recipe will show you how to do it.

Getting ready

The spellchecker component configuration is something we discussed in the *Configuring the Solr spellchecker* recipe in *Chapter 1, Apache Solr Configuration*. So again, I'll only discuss the most important fragments.

How to do it...

1. Let's begin with the index structure (just add this to your `schema.xml` file):

```
<field name="id" type="string" indexed="true" stored="true"
required="true" />
<field name="name" type="text_general" indexed="true"
stored="true" />
```

2. The data that we are going to index looks as follows:

```
<add>
 <doc>
  <field name="id">1</field>
  <field name="name">Solr cookbook</field>
 </doc>
 <doc>
  <field name="id">2</field>
  <field name="name">Mechanics cookbook</field>
 </doc>
 <doc>
  <field name="id">3</field>
  <field name="name">Other book</field>
 </doc>
</add>
```

3. Our spellchecking mechanism will work on the basis of the `name` field. Now, let's add the appropriate search component to the `solrconfig.xml` file:

```
<searchComponent name="spellcheck" class="solr.
SpellCheckComponent">
 <str name="queryAnalyzerFieldType">name</str>
 <lst name="spellchecker">
  <str name="name">direct</str>
  <str name="field">name</str>
  <str name="classname">solr.DirectSolrSpellChecker</str>
  <str name="buildOnCommit">true</str>
 </lst>
</searchComponent>
```

4. In addition to this, we would like to have it integrated into our search handler, so we make the default search handler definition as follows (add this to your `solrconfig.xml` file):

```
<requestHandler name="/spell" class="solr.SearchHandler">
 <lst name="defaults">
  <str name="df">name</str>
  <str name="spellcheck.dictionary">direct</str>
  <str name="spellcheck">on</str>
  <str name="spellcheck.collate">true</str>
 </lst>
 <arr name="last-components">
  <str>spellcheck</str>
 </arr>
</requestHandler>
```

5. Now, let's check how it works. To do this, we will send a query that contains a spelling mistake—we will send the words `othar boak` instead of `other book`. The query doing this will look as follows:

```
http://localhost:8983/solr/cookbook/spell?q=name:(othar boak)
```

The Solr response for this query looks as follows:

```
<?xml version="1.0" encoding="UTF-8"?>
<response>
<lst name="responseHeader">
  <int name="status">0</int>
  <int name="QTime">11</int>
</lst>
<result name="response" numFound="0" start="0">
</result>
<lst name="spellcheck">
  <lst name="suggestions">
    <lst name="othar">
      <int name="numFound">1</int>
      <int name="startOffset">6</int>
      <int name="endOffset">11</int>
      <arr name="suggestion">
        <str>other</str>
      </arr>
    </lst>
    <lst name="boak">
      <int name="numFound">1</int>
```

```
            <int name="startOffset">12</int>
            <int name="endOffset">16</int>
            <arr name="suggestion">
              <str>book</str>
            </arr>
          </lst>
          <str name="collation">name:(other book)</str>
        </lst>
      </lst>
      </response>
```

As you can see from the response, Solr corrected the spelling mistake we made. Now let's see how it works.

How it works...

The index structure is pretty straightforward. It contains two fields—one to hold the unique identifier (the `id` field) and the other to hold the name (the `name` field). The file that contains the example data is simple too, so I'll skip discussing it.

As already mentioned at the beginning of the recipe, the spellchecker component configuration is something that I already covered in the *Configuring the Solr spellchecker* recipe in *Chapter 1, Apache Solr Configuration*. So again, I'll discuss only the most important fragments.

As you can see in the configuration, we defined a spellchecker component that will use Solr's `solr.DirectSolrSpellChecker` class in order not to store its index on the hard disk drive. In addition to this, we configured it to use the `name` field for spellchecking and also to use that field analyzer to process queries. Our `/spell` handler is configured to automatically include spellchecking results (`<str name="spellcheck">on</str>`) to create collation (`<str name="spellcheck.collate">true</str>`) and to use direct dictionary (`<str name="spellcheck.dictionary">direct</str>`). All these properties were discussed in the previously mentioned recipe.

Now let's take a look at the query. We send the `boak` and `othar` words in the query parameter (`q`). The spellchecker component will be activated automatically because of the configuration of our `/spell` handler. And that's actually all when it comes to the query.

Finally, we come to the results returned by Solr. As you can see, there were no documents found for the word `boak` and the word `other`; that's what we were actually expecting. However, as you can see, there is a spellchecker component section added to the results list (the `<lst name="spellcheck">` tag). For each word, there is a suggestion returned by Solr (the `<lst name="boak">` tag is the suggestion for the `boak` word). As you can see, the spellchecker component informed us about the number of suggestions found (the `<int name="numFound">` tag), about the start and end offset of the suggestion (`<int name="startOffset">` and `<int name="endOffset">`), and about the actual suggestions (the `<arr name="suggestion">` array).

The only suggestion that Solr returned was the `book` word (`<str>book</str>` under the suggestion array). The same goes for the second word.

There is an additional section in the spellchecker component results generated by the `spellcheck.collate=true` parameter—`<str name="collation">name:(other book)</str>`. It tells us what query Solr suggested to us. We can either show the query to the user or send it automatically to Solr and show our user the corrected results list—this one is up to you.

Using the Solr administration panel for monitoring

Monitoring is crucial for a production environment. We want to be able to see all the needed metrics that can show us whether our Solr cluster is healthy. We want to be able to see the operating system and Java Virtual Machine metrics, such as network statistics, garbage collector work, and so on. By default, Solr comes with the administration panel that allows you to see the basic statistics regarding it and the JMX connectivity so that we can integrate it with monitoring systems such as Ganglia. This recipe will show you what information you can get by looking at the Solr administration panel.

How to do it...

1. When opening the Solr administration panel in our browser (`http://localhost:8983/solr/#/`), we will see a view similar to the following one:

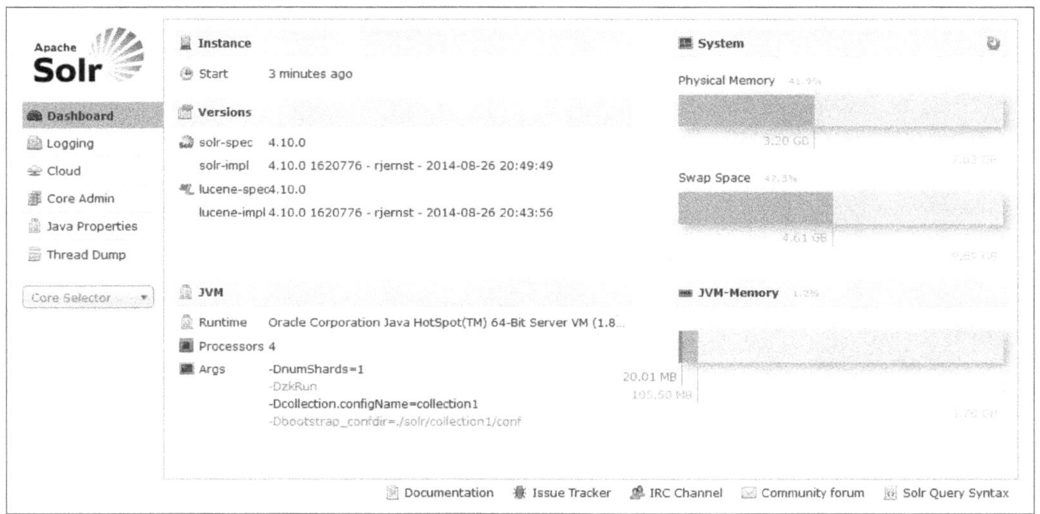

2. Next, let's take a look at the cluster state view. We can do this by pointing our web browser to `http://localhost:8983/solr/#/~cloud`. We will see a view similar to the following one:

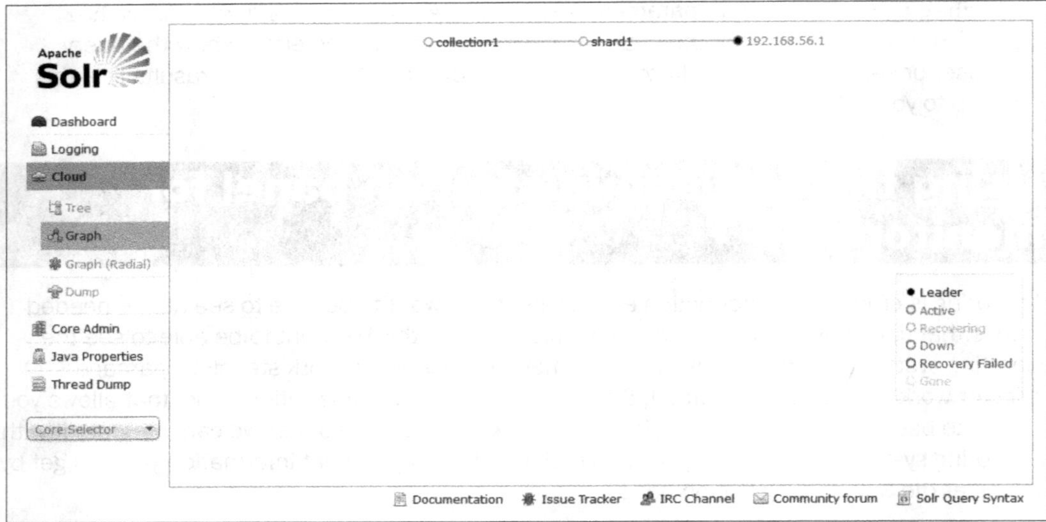

3. Of course, the cloud view is not the only thing. When choosing our collection from the left-hand side of the administration panel or going to `http://localhost:8983/solr/#/collection1`, we can see an overview of the collection as follows:

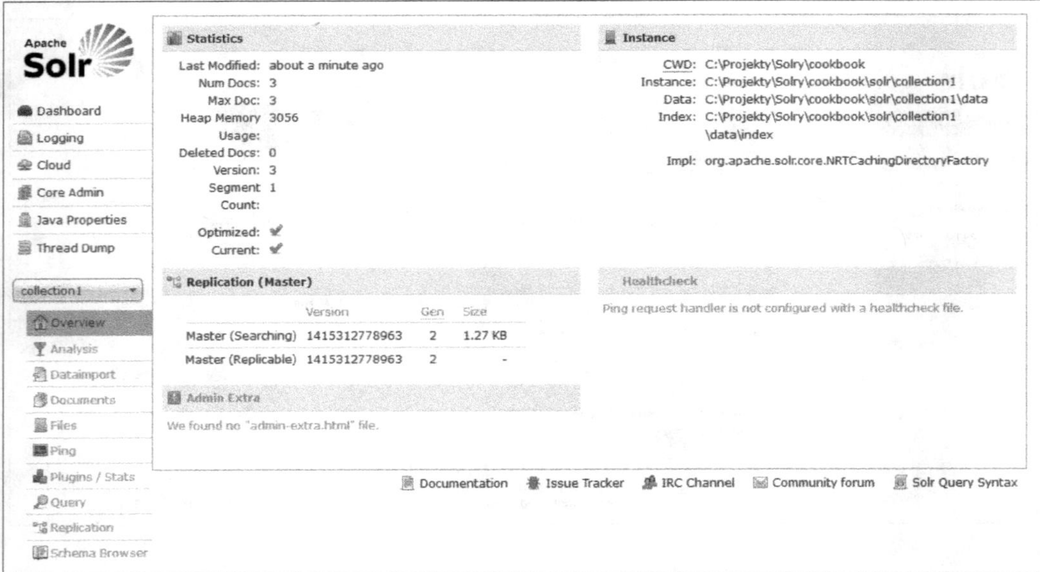

4. We can go even further and look at the statistics provided by each of Solr components. For example, when we take a look at the query result cache statistics, we will see a view similar to the following one:

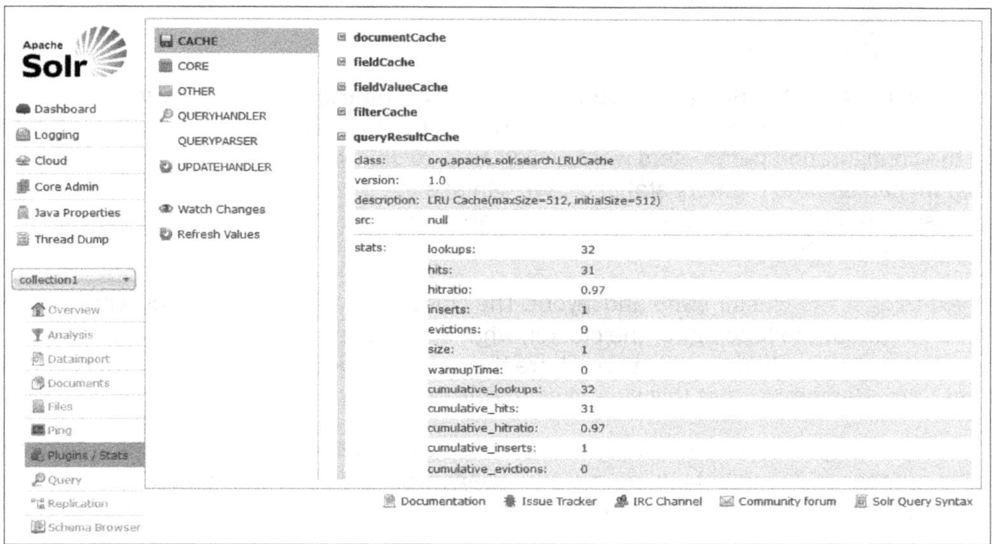

5. We can also see extended statistics for each of the handlers and components, both when it comes to searching and indexing. For example, if we take a look at the /`select` handler statistics after running a few queries, we will see the following:

We can, of course, continue the discussion and show more screenshots from the Solr administration panel, but I would just advise you to run Solr and just click through the functionality. Let's now take a look at what all this functionality provides.

How it works...

On the main page of the Solr administration panel (**Dashboard**), we can see various metrics related to Solr. We can see the version of Solr we are running, when the instance was started, what the configuration parameters were, which Java version was used, and so on. In addition to this, we can see the memory statistics. We can see the physical memory and how much of it is used, we can see the swap memory available, and finally, we can see the JVM memory—the one that Solr uses.

The next thing is the cluster state and layout. The cluster state view provides us with information about the topology of the cluster, what collections are deployed on our cluster, what are the shards of each collection, where they are deployed, and what their roles and statuses are. Remember that this view is only available when running Solr in SolrCloud view.

The **Overview** page for a collection gives you basic statistics about the core of the collection such as number of documents, heap memory usage, version of the index, number of segments, and so on. We can also see the directories and directory implementation used.

Finally, we looked at the statistics of different Solr components—the query result cache and the search handler registered under the `/select` name. As we can see, Solr provides different metrics depending on the component we are looking at. For example, the query result cache provides information on the size, number of hits, hit ratio, number of inserts and evictions, and so on. The search handler on the other hand provides information about a number of requests and errors, total time requests that were running, time-based statistics, and percentiles.

[Note that the metrics we just discussed can be also read using JMX, as Solr supports this.]

Of course, the Solr administration panel gives you a pretty good view on what is currently happening with Solr, but it doesn't allow you to compare metrics, see them graphed for ease of viewing, and so on. And the one main thing that really makes us look for a proper type of production monitoring software is that it doesn't store all the metrics. If something happens or is restarted, we lose the metrics.

There's more...

There is one more thing when it comes to Solr monitoring that I want to mention.

SPM Performance Monitoring & Alerting

Of course, working with the Solr administration panel or JMX is good, but when it comes to monitoring and performance analysis, you usually want to have a good view of what happened in the past, you want to be able to compare different periods, and have alerting functionality so that you are on top of things when something goes wrong. Such functionalities are not a part of Solr, but there are solutions out there that provide all the required pieces of a good monitoring platform. One of these solutions is SPM Performance Monitoring & Alerting (`http://sematext.com/spm/index.html`) provided as SaaS and on premises software by Sematext Group (`http://sematext.com`). There are also open source tools, such as Ganglia (`http://ganglia.sourceforge.net/`) with jmxtrans (`http://www.jmxtrans.org/`). For example, this is how the default SPM dashboard looks like, showing you the most interesting information related to Solr on one page:

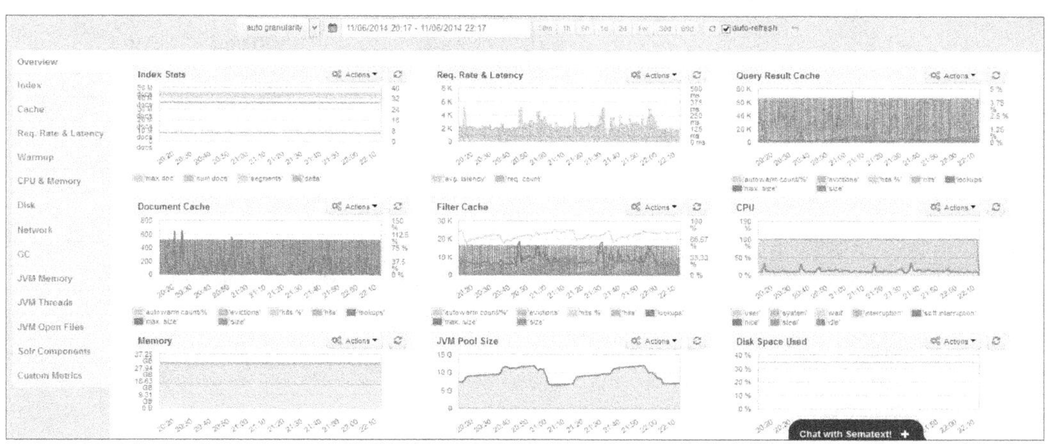

The default SPM dashboard

In addition to providing all the relevant and needed Solr metrics, SPM gives you an insight on JVM and operating system related metrics. Apart from this, it provides you with alerting capabilities and algorithmic anomaly detection that can help you foresee problems that are not yet present. Even though SPM is a commercial product, it has a free version that allows you to keep the last 30 minutes of your metrics for free and doesn't care about the maintenance of additional software inside your organization.

Automatically expiring Solr documents

There are use cases that require expiration of documents after a certain amount of time—they should either be deleted or marked as inactive after a given time or period. For example, let's assume that we have a web application that works as a link shortening service. One can paste a long link and get the short version of it. However, we would like the links to be expired after one hour from their creation. Of course, we can develop a periodic job on our application-side and make this happen, but we can also use Solr for this. This recipe will show you how to achieve such functionality with Solr.

How to do it...

For the purpose of this recipe, let's assume that we want our documents to expire 5 minutes after they were sent to indexation.

1. We will start with the structure of the index, which looks as follows (we add it to our `schema.xml` file):

```
<field name="id" type="string" indexed="true" stored="true"
required="true" />
<field name="url" type="string" indexed="false" stored="true" />
<field name="short" type="string" indexed="false" stored="true" />
<field name="user" type="string" indexed="false" stored="true" />
<field name="expiration_time" type="date" indexed="true"
stored="true" />
```

2. The second step is to define a new update request processor chain, which looks as follows (we put it in the `solrconfig.xml` file):

```
<updateRequestProcessorChain default="true">
  <processor class="solr.processor.
DocExpirationUpdateProcessorFactory">
    <int name="autoDeletePeriodSeconds">10</int>
    <str name="expirationFieldName">expiration_time</str>
  </processor>
  <processor class="solr.LogUpdateProcessorFactory" />
  <processor class="solr.RunUpdateProcessorFactory" />
</updateRequestProcessorChain>
```

3. Now, we can index the first document using the following command:

```
curl 'http://localhost:8983/solr/cookbook/update?_
ttl_=%2B5MINUTES' -H 'Content-type:application/xml' --data-binary
'<add>
 <doc>
```

```
    <field name="id">1</field>
    <field name="url">http://solr.pl/en/2014/10/31/lucene-
solr-4-10-2/</field>
    <field name="short">http://solr.pl/short/1</field>
    <field name="user">gr0</field>
  </doc>
</add>'
```

4. A minute later, we index the following document:

```
curl 'http://localhost:8983/solr/cookbook/update?_
ttl_=%2B5MINUTES' -H 'Content-type:application/xml' --data-binary
'<add>
  <doc>
    <field name="id">2</field>
    <field name="url">http://solr.pl/en/2014/09/04/apache-lucene-
and-solr-4-10/</field>
    <field name="short">http://solr.pl/short/2</field>
    <field name="user">gr0</field>
  </doc>
</add>'
```

5. Now, let's commit these documents by running the following command:

```
curl 'http://localhost:8983/solr/cookbook/update' -H 'Content-
type:application/xml' --data-binary '<commit/>'
```

6. After indexing them, we try running the following query:

   `http://localhost:8983/solr/cookbook/select?q=*:*`

   The response will be as follows:

```
<?xml version="1.0" encoding="UTF-8"?>
<response>
<lst name="responseHeader">
  <int name="status">0</int>
  <int name="QTime">0</int>
  <lst name="params">
    <str name="q">*:*</str>
  </lst>
</lst>
<result name="response" numFound="2" start="0">
  <doc>
    <str name="id">1</str>
    <str name="url">http://solr.pl/en/2014/10/31/lucene-
solr-4-10-2/</str>
    <str name="short">http://solr.pl/short/1</str>
```

```
    <str name="user">gr0</str>
    <date name="expiration_time">2014-11-03T12:09:15.002Z</date>
    <long name="_version_">1483752084606025728</long></doc>
  <doc>
    <str name="id">2</str>
    <str name="url">http://solr.pl/en/2014/09/04/apache-lucene-
and-solr-4-10/</str>
    <str name="short">http://solr.pl/short/2</str>
    <str name="user">gr0</str>
    <date name="expiration_time">2014-11-03T12:09:55.963Z</date>
    <long name="_version_">1483752127556747264</long></doc>
</result>
</response>
```

7. Now we should wait for 5 minutes and again run the same query, which looks as follows:

```
http://localhost:8983/solr/cookbook/select?q=*:*
```

Now, the response is different:

```
<?xml version="1.0" encoding="UTF-8"?>
<response>
<lst name="responseHeader">
  <int name="status">0</int>
  <int name="QTime">0</int>
  <lst name="params">
    <str name="q">*:*</str>
  </lst>
</lst>
<result name="response" numFound="1" start="0">
  <doc>
    <str name="id">2</str>
    <str name="url">http://solr.pl/en/2014/09/04/apache-lucene-
and-solr-4-10/</str>
    <str name="short">http://solr.pl/short/2</str>
    <str name="user">gr0</str>
    <date name="expiration_time">2014-11-03T12:09:55.963Z</date>
    <long name="_version_">1483752127556747264</long></doc>
</result>
</response>
```

Also, we can see the following message in the Solr's logs:

```
213361 [autoExpireDocs-10-thread-1] INFO  org.apache.
solr.update.processor.LogUpdateProcessor  – [collection1]
{deleteByQuery={!cache=false}expiration_time:[* TO
2014-11-03T12:05:25.794Z] (-1483752158835769344),commit=} 0 4
213361 [autoExpireDocs-10-thread-1] INFO  org.apache.solr.update.
processor.DocExpirationUpdateProcessorFactory  – Finished periodic
deletion of expired docs
```

This means that everything is working as it should be and Solr deleted the first document. If we would wait longer, we would see that the second document was deleted as well. Now, let's see how it works.

How it works...

As usual, we are starting with the structure of the index we are going to use. We need the identifier of the document, which is represented by the `id` field, the long URL address (the `url` field), the shortened URL (the `short` field), and the user who registered the URL address—the `user` field. Finally, the last field—`expiration_time` is the field that Solr will use to check whether the document should be deleted or not. This field should be based on the date and time types, which in our case is the `date` type.

The next thing we do is define a custom update request processor chain that we set to be the default one (`default="true"`). Next, we have an update processor class that is responsible for document deletion—`solr.processor.DocExpirationUpdateProcessorFactory`. We used properties to define the processor behavior. The first is `autoDeletePeriodSeconds` that tells Solr how often Solr should look for deleted documents. In our case, it will be every 10 seconds. What Solr does is runs a `delete by` query on the collection and will delete all the documents in the current time. The `autoDeletePeriodSeconds` property tells Solr how often such a query should be run. The second property—`expirationFieldName` tells Solr which the `delete by` query should use as the field to hold the expiration date of the document. In our case, it is our `expiration_time` field. The two additional processors are common—one is about logging the update process (`solr.LogUpdateProcessorFactory`) and the second one is about running the update itself (`solr.RunUpdateProcessorFactory`).

The next interesting thing is how we index our documents. As you can see, in addition to the document itself, we also provide an additional request parameter—`_ttl_`. It stands for time to live and specifies when the documents in the update request should be deleted. The value of the property can use the whole date math syntax that Solr allows you to use (which is described in `https://cwiki.apache.org/confluence/display/solr/Working+with+Dates`). We set it to `%2B5MINUTES` (which is `+5MINUTES` decoded). This means that Solr will take the current date and time, will add 5 minutes to it, and will write that information into the field defined in the update processor using the `expirationFieldName` field name.

As we can see, after waiting for some time Solr deleted and automatically refreshed the collection using a soft commit operation with the `openSearcher=true` property.

There's more...

There is one more thing that I would like to mention when it comes to automatic document expiration.

Changing the time to live parameter name

If we want, we can also change the name of the parameter that is used to provide time to live information for documents. To do this, we should use the `ttlFieldName` property and add it to the `solr.processor.DocExpirationUpdateProcessorFactory` parameter in our `solrconfig.xml` file. For example, if we would like to use the `expireAfter` property instead of `_ttl_`, we should configure our update request chain as follows:

```
<updateRequestProcessorChain default="true">
  <processor class="solr.processor.
DocExpirationUpdateProcessorFactory">
    <int name="autoDeletePeriodSeconds">10</int>
    <str name="ttlFieldName">expireAfter</str>
    <str name="expirationFieldName">expiration_time</str>
  </processor>
  <processor class="solr.LogUpdateProcessorFactory" />
  <processor class="solr.RunUpdateProcessorFactory" />
</updateRequestProcessorChain>
```

Exporting whole query results

One of the features of search engines such as Solr that users frequently ask about is the ability to pull the data from the search engine in some form. I'm not talking about a few hundred results returned by a query, but about all the documents that are indexed in a particular core or collection. With the new releases of Solr, we have the ability to scroll through the results and with some effort, we will be able to export all the results. However, with the release of Solr 4.10, we were also given a possibility of exporting fully sorted query results at once. This recipe will show you how to do that.

How to do it...

Let's assume that we have an index that contains book names and the number of votes users have given to those books and that our hypothetical index is large. What we would like to do is export all the books matching a particular query along with the number of votes they have to a separate file. The results of such a query can be massive:

1. We start with our index structure that contains the following fields (we just put the following entries into the `schema.xml` file):

```
<field name="id" type="int" indexed="true" stored="true"
required="true" />
<field name="name" type="text_general" indexed="true"
stored="true" />
<field name="votes" type="int" indexed="false" stored="false"
docValues="true" />
<field name="name_export" type="string" indexed="false"
stored="false" docValues="true" />
```

2. We also need to define a copy field that we also put into the `schema.xml` file:

```
<copyField source="name" dest="name_export" />
```

3. The example data we will use is small and looks as follows (this will only serve the purpose of showing the export functionality):

```
<add>
 <doc>
  <field name="id">1</field>
  <field name="name">Solr cookbook</field>
  <field name="votes">5</field>
 </doc>
 <doc>
  <field name="id">2</field>
  <field name="name">Mechanics cookbook</field>
  <field name="votes">12</field>
 </doc>
 <doc>
  <field name="id">3</field>
  <field name="name">Other cookbook</field>
  <field name="votes">1</field>
 </doc>
 <doc>
  <field name="id">4</field>
  <field name="name">Yet another cookbook</field>
  <field name="votes">0</field>
 </doc>
</add>
```

4. Now, let's take a look at the configuration of Solr. First, we need to add the following request handler definition to our `solrconfig.xml` file:

```
<requestHandler name="/export" class="solr.SearchHandler">
  <lst name="invariants">
    <str name="rq">{!xport}</str>
    <str name="wt">xsort</str>
    <str name="distrib">false</str>
  </lst>
  <lst name="defaults">
    <str name="df">name</str>
  </lst>
</requestHandler>
```

5. Finally, we need to disable lazy fields loading by putting the following entry into our `solrconfig.xml` file (or modifying the existing configuration):

```
<enableLazyFieldLoading>false</enableLazyFieldLoading>
```

Now, we can export our data by running the following command:

```
curl 'localhost:8983/solr/cookbook/export_books?q=cookbook&sort=vo
tes+asc&fl=name_export,votes'
```

The result returned by Solr for our example is as follows:

```
{"numFound":4, "docs":[{"name_export":"Yet
another cookbook","votes":0},{"name_export":"Other
cookbook","votes":1},{"name_export":"Solr
cookbook","votes":5},{"name_export":"Mechanics
cookbook","votes":12}]}
```

As we can see, our data was exported. Let's take a look at how it works now.

How it works...

Before we start, remember that the feature you are reading about was introduced in Solr 4.10 and is in a very simple form. For example, in Solr 4.10, it required that fields used for sorting and displaying during export were using `doc` values. It uses a stream sorting technique that enables you to send results within milliseconds after the request was made. This can change in the future, so keep an eye on Solr release notes and sites such as `http://solr.pl` for more information about this.

We start with the index structure, which is similar to most of the recipes is pretty simple. It contains four fields—one to hold the unique identifier of the document (the `id` field), one to hold the name of the book (the `name` field), the third one to hold the number of votes the book was given (the `votes` field), and finally, the last field, `name_export`, we will use for exporting. Solr export functionality allows you to export and sort only on those fields that have `doc` values enabled. Because of this, we need to set the `docValues` property to `true` for the `votes` field and create a new field called `name_export`, because `doc` values can't be turned on for analyzed fields. We also introduced a copy field section to tell Solr to automatically copy the contents of the `name` field into the `name_export` field, so we don't have to worry about that.

Now, let's get to our `/export_books` request handler definition. As you can see, it is based on the standard `solr.SearchHandler` handler, but it contains some additional properties that we didn't see till now. To use Solr export functionality, we need to provide three properties. First, we specify the `rq` parameter to `{!xport}`. The `rq` stands for re-ranking query and to use Solr export functionality, we need to set it to `{!xport}`; otherwise, it won't work. The second parameter—the `wt` one—specifies the response writer and for export functionality, it needs to be set to `xsort`. Finally, we need to set the `distrib` parameter to `false` so that the request is not propagated to other shards and is only executed locally.

Note that initially, Solr export functionality didn't support distributed operations. Exporting data for collections that are built of more than a single primary shard needs to be done manually, shard by shard. This is going to change in future Solr releases.

As you can see, the three mentioned parameters were placed into the `invariants` section of the request handler definition so that the user can't overwrite them by providing the same parameter during a query. We also defined the default search field using the `df` property.

One more thing that we did is setting the `enableLazyFieldLoading` property in `solrconfig.xml` to `false`. This is needed because the initial implementation of Solr export functionality contains a bug that will result in query failures when the `enableLazyFieldLoading` property is set to `true`.

After this, we are ready to export our results. In the example, we exported all the documents matching the `cookbook` query (sent against the default search field, which is `name` in our case). The export functionality in Solr allows you to provide two properties in addition to the query—the `sort` property and the `fl` property. The `sort` property can hold up to four fields and defines how the documents in the export should be sorted. In our case, we want the documents to be sorted in an ascending order based on the number of votes. The `fl` property defines which fields should be exported for each document—in our case, it is `name_export` and `votes`. Remember that each field used in the `sort` property or the `fl` property has to use `doc` values—this is a requirement for now.

As you can see, the exported data is what we actually wanted and was exported in JSON. This is the only format supported for now. The good thing about this functionality is that we can export even massive datasets without putting too much pressure on Solr, so you can use it whenever you need to export large amounts of data.

Index

Symbol

A

B

C

T

U

V

W

X

Z

Thank you for buying
Solr Cookbook
Third Edition

About Packt Publishing

Packt, pronounced 'packed', published its first book, *Mastering phpMyAdmin for Effective MySQL Management*, in April 2004, and subsequently continued to specialize in publishing highly focused books on specific technologies and solutions.

Our books and publications share the experiences of your fellow IT professionals in adapting and customizing today's systems, applications, and frameworks. Our solution-based books give you the knowledge and power to customize the software and technologies you're using to get the job done. Packt books are more specific and less general than the IT books you have seen in the past. Our unique business model allows us to bring you more focused information, giving you more of what you need to know, and less of what you don't.

Packt is a modern yet unique publishing company that focuses on producing quality, cutting-edge books for communities of developers, administrators, and newbies alike. For more information, please visit our website at `www.packtpub.com`.

About Packt Open Source

In 2010, Packt launched two new brands, Packt Open Source and Packt Enterprise, in order to continue its focus on specialization. This book is part of the Packt open source brand, home to books published on software built around open source licenses, and offering information to anybody from advanced developers to budding web designers. The Open Source brand also runs Packt's open source Royalty Scheme, by which Packt gives a royalty to each open source project about whose software a book is sold.

Writing for Packt

We welcome all inquiries from people who are interested in authoring. Book proposals should be sent to `author@packtpub.com`. If your book idea is still at an early stage and you would like to discuss it first before writing a formal book proposal, then please contact us; one of our commissioning editors will get in touch with you.

We're not just looking for published authors; if you have strong technical skills but no writing experience, our experienced editors can help you develop a writing career, or simply get some additional reward for your expertise.

Apache Solr 4 Cookbook

ISBN: 978-1-78216-132-5 Paperback: 328 pages

Over 100 recipes to make Apache Solr faster, more reliable, and return better results

1. Learn how to make Apache Solr search faster, more complete, and comprehensively scalable.
2. Solve performance, setup, configuration, analysis, and query problems in no time.
3. Get to grips with, and master, the new exciting features of Apache Solr 4.

Scaling Apache Solr

ISBN: 978-1-78398-174-8 Paperback: 298 pages

Optimize your searches using high-performance enterprise search repositories with Apache Solr

1. Get an introduction to the basics of Apache Solr in a step-by-step manner with lots of examples.
2. Develop and understand the workings of enterprise search solution using various techniques and real-life use cases.
3. Gain a practical insight into the advanced ways of optimizing and making an enterprise search solution cloud ready.

Please check **www.PacktPub.com** for information on our titles

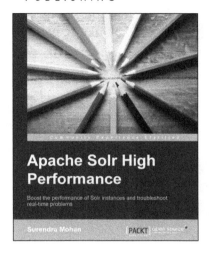

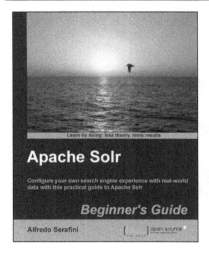

www.ingramcontent.com/pod-product-compliance
Lightning Source LLC
Chambersburg PA
CBHW062054050326
40690CB00016B/3090